It's Our Day

CultureAmerica

Karal Ann Marling
Erika Doss
SERIES EDITORS

It's Our Day

AMERICA'S LOVE AFFAIR WITH
THE WHITE WEDDING, 1945–2005

Katherine Jellison

UNIVERSITY PRESS OF KANSAS

© 2008 by the University Press of Kansas
All rights reserved

Published by the University Press of Kansas (Lawrence, Kansas 66045),
which was organized by the Kansas Board of Regents and is operated and
funded by Emporia State University, Fort Hays State University, Kansas
State University, Pittsburg State University, the University of Kansas, and
Wichita State University

Library of Congress Cataloging-in-Publication Data
Jellison, Katherine.
It's our day : America's love affair with the white wedding, 1945–2005 /
Katherine Jellison.
p. cm. — (CultureAmerica)
Includes bibliographical references and index.
ISBN 978-0-7006-1559-9 (cloth : alk. paper)
1. Marriage customs and rites—United States. 2. United States—Social life and
customs—1945–1970. 3. United States—Social life and customs—1971– I. Title.
GT2703.J45 2008
392.50973—dc22   2007035444

British Library Cataloguing-in-Publication Data is available.

Printed in the United States of America

10 9 8 7 6 5 4 3 2 1

The paper used in this publication is recycled and contains 50 percent
postconsumer waste. It is acid free and meets the minimum
requirements of the American National Standard for Permanence of Paper
for Printed Library Materials z39.48-1992.

FRONTISPIECE. *Bride and groom, 1949. (Author's collection)*

To my father
and in memory of
my mother

Contents

Acknowledgments *ix*

Introduction *1*

Chapter *1*

The Best of Everything: The White Wedding
in American Culture, 1945–2005 7

Chapter *2*

Look Like a Princess: The Wedding Gown *63*

Chapter *3*

Like a Royal Wedding: The Celebrity Wedding *112*

Chapter *4*

Watching *Cinderella* on Video: The Movie Wedding *148*

Chapter *5*

Addicted to the Show: The Reality Wedding *181*

Epilogue *231*

Notes *237*

Bibliography *271*

Index *291*

Acknowledgments

I owe a debt of gratitude to numerous institutions and individuals who helped make this book possible.

I began this project many years ago while on the faculty at Memphis State University (now the University of Memphis). I remain grateful to the Center for Research on Women, which in my last semester at Memphis State funded a course reduction that enabled me to launch the research for this book. My chairperson at the time, Jack Hurley, also deserves gratitude for readily agreeing to the arrangement. The person who hired me away from Memphis State, Bruce Steiner, was an equally supportive champion of the project. As chair of the Ohio University History Department, he convinced the College of Arts and Sciences to fund several of my preliminary research trips. The Iowa Sesquicentennial Commission and the State Historical Society of Iowa also provided early financial support.

In the project's closing months, the Ohio University College of Arts and Sciences again provided invaluable assistance by releasing me from teaching duties in fall 2006. I wish to thank former History Department chair Steve Miner for negotiating this arrangement. More important, I want to thank Steve, in his current role as director of Ohio University's Contemporary History Institute, for providing me with a quiet place to finish my writing. Virginia Woolf was right; a room of one's own makes all the difference. And a room with a view is nice too. As I write these lines while gazing out my window at the Contemporary History Institute, I remember one of the reasons I relocated to Ohio University. The day of my job interview was one much like this—crystal blue skies and a blanket of new snow on this beautiful old campus.

In the closing weeks of my work on this book, the Ohio University Research Committee, the Department of History, the Contemporary History Institute, and the Office of Research and Sponsored Programs generously granted funds to acquire many of the illustrations for this book. I want to thank History Department chairperson Norm Goda, department administrator Sherry Gillogly, and Contemporary History Institute director Steve Miner for helping me secure these funds. And a heartfelt thank-you goes to another talented denizen of Ohio University, photographer Michael DiBari Jr.

In addition to acknowledging those who provided time, space, and funds for the creation of this book, I must also thank the archivists and librarians who assisted with research for the study. I am particularly grateful to Sam Rushay of the National Archives's Nixon Presidential Materials staff and to the staffs of the Hagley Museum and Library, the Conde Nast library, and New York's Museum of Television and Radio. I owe a special debt to those brides, grooms, and members of the wedding industry who shared their stories with me.

Many colleagues have read portions of the manuscript and offered their invaluable insights. Among those who read substantive portions and provided extensive counsel were Linda Kerber, Benita Blessing, Kevin Mattson, Steve Rubenstein, Steve Miner, and, the most ruthless critic of them all, Jackie Wolf. Without a doubt, Jackie's keen eyes made this a much stronger piece of scholarship. Cele Otnes provided me a copy of her own book manuscript several months before it was published, and she and her coauthor Elizabeth Pleck were among the many scholars who made helpful suggestions about my work when I presented it on the conference circuit. I must also thank the coeditors of the CultureAmerica series, Erika Doss and Karal Ann Marling, for their excellent advice. I have thanked many of these scholars, as well as several others, for more specific contributions in the appropriate endnotes.

I have been very privileged over the years to work with some talented and generous graduate students who also contributed significantly to this study. I particularly wish to thank the following former students: Jamie Fries and Matt Daiker for their research assistance; Kim Little, Bonnie Hagerman, and Kathy Keltner for research materials and their boundless enthusiasm; and Carolyn Herbst Lewis and Carrie Pitzulo for organizing a 2005 Berkshire conference panel that infused this study with new energy. Thanks also to current student Sherry Hill.

For their moral support and continued interest in my scholarship, I thank the following present and former Ohio University colleagues: Sholeh Quinn, Mary Anne Reeves, Marvin Fletcher, Dean Kotlowski,

Lon Hamby, Misty Milstead—and once again, Jackie Wolf, Steve Miner, and Sherry Gillogly. Among members of the larger History Department family, Florence McGeoch, Joyce Hamby, and the late Hilary Fletcher contributed research materials and enthusiasm to the endeavor. At the Contemporary History Institute, Kara Dunfee provided invaluable administrative assistance. I also greatly appreciate the sustained interest and support of dear friends and colleagues from my University of Iowa days, including Sharon Wood, Terri Snyder, and—once again—Linda Kerber.

I have enjoyed an ideal working relationship with the University Press of Kansas, and I particularly wish to thank Fred Woodward, Susan Schott, Susan McRory, and—above all—Kalyani Fernando. And thanks to Lon Hamby for advising me to publish this book with UPK.

Finally, I owe a large debt to members of my family. My husband, David Winkelmann, came up with the idea for this book in the first place, and he also suggested the title. My sister, Sandra Jellison-Knock, took on more than her fair share of family obligations, and her sacrifices made this book possible. Whenever my responsibilities as a teacher, scholar, and administrator got me down, my nephew Keenan Jellison-Knock made me laugh. And my brother-in-law, Randy Jellison-Knock, patiently endured it all. My parents, Bill Jellison and Margaret Brown Jellison, were interested in this project from the beginning and encouraged me through the many years of its development, even as they themselves faced disability and illness. In 1949 they launched their marriage with a white wedding, and the relationship lasted until my mother's death nearly fifty-three years later. I thank them for their courage and example.

Athens, Ohio
February 2007

Introduction

In June/July 2000, the editors of *Ms.* published a special issue investigating—and to a great extent celebrating—American marriage. For long-time readers of the nearly thirty-year-old publication, this was unlikely subject matter. As the editors themselves noted, "Once upon a time, marriage and feminism seemed like a match made in hell." But times had changed. The editors explained that marriage was now being "reinvented by feminist women and men every day of their lives," and "same-sex marriage [was] on the table with an energy and insistence . . . never seen before." Illustrating this analysis were numerous photographs of smiling same-sex and heterosexual couples, the majority of them in formal wedding attire. Regardless of race, age, political persuasion, or sexual orientation, most of the men sported tuxedos and boutonnieres, and most of the women wore white gowns and clutched elaborate bouquets.[1]

The positive images of marriage, weddings, and wedding industry products that *Ms.* presented in 2000 contrasted sharply with earlier feminist interpretations of these institutions. Feminists of the 1960s and 1970s characterized traditional marriage as harmful to women and routinely criticized formal weddings as symbolic of everything wrong with role-based heterosexual unions. Rituals in which fathers gave away white-gowned brides to waiting grooms idealized patriarchy and bridal virginity, perpetuated society's obsession with female beauty, emphasized socially constructed differences between men and women, and glorified the unrealistic notion of all-consuming romantic love. To make their point, some of the era's radical feminists performed acts of guerrilla theater at bridal industry product fairs. Most notoriously, as brides-to-be perused displays at a 1969 Madison Square Garden event, members of the New York–based Women's International Terrorist Conspiracy from Hell (WITCH) and women affiliated with the Brooklyn branch of Students for a Democratic Society (SDS) released a batch of white mice into the startled crowd. Proclaiming that marriage "oppress[ed] everyone, and particularly women," protesters wore black veils, carried placards that read "Always a Bride, Never a Person," and sang "Here Comes the Slave, Off to Her Grave."[2]

As the *Ms.* cover story indicated, these acts of civil disobedience did little to undermine marriage and weddings, despite all the other cultural and social changes of the era. Both institutions remained highly valued and were even gaining new adherents. Lesbians and gays now strongly agitated for inclusion, and *Ms.* founder Gloria Steinem set aside her aversion to matrimony in 2000 to wed activist David Bale in a traditional Cherokee ceremony. The sixty-six-year-old first-time bride wore jeans for the occasion, but the overwhelming majority of Americans still opted to marry in formal fashion, regardless of their gender politics. As feminist journalist Susan Weidman Schneider observed, "Even staunch advocates of women's equality seem comfortable, at least for a few hours, enacting what appears to be a classic sexist drama—bride in virginal white, 'given away' or handed off from her family of origin to her husband."[3]

The formal wedding's resilience in the face of enormous cultural change was the product of complex interactions between the wedding industry and its predominantly female clientele. In a seminal essay published at the time of fervent feminist criticism of weddings in the 1970s, historian Carroll Smith-Rosenberg examined women's homosocial activities in the nineteenth century and correctly noted that weddings were "one of the last female rituals remaining in twentieth-century America." And for the most part, weddings continued to be female-centered celebrations in the early twenty-first century. A growing number of gay men participated in commitment ceremonies that incorporated aspects of the formal wedding—even though most jurisdictions did not recognize same-sex unions as legal marriages. And the popular press noted an increase in "metrosexual" grooms: straight men with supposedly gay consumer tastes who enthusiastically joined their brides in pursuit of the perfect wedding. But most twenty-first-century weddings remained firmly embedded in what Smith-Rosenberg called the "Female World of Love and Ritual." Brides and their mothers, sisters, and other female relatives and friends remained the wedding's chief planners, consumers, and participants. And on the other side of the counter frequently stood female wedding coordinators, cake makers, clothing merchants, and other businesswomen who made their living in this hospitable, female-oriented sector of American enterprise.[4]

Rhetoric justifying this sale and purchase of lavish weddings suggested that a white-gowned bride, multitiered cake, and exchange of shiny rings represented American tradition. Clearly, even nontraditionalists—such as feminists and same-sex couples—could not resist the lure of these allegedly longstanding customs. In reality, however, the notion that a wedding necessarily required elaborate props and a bride all dressed in white was a relatively recent concept. Queen Victoria made these elements of the so-called white wedding fashionable among elite Britons and Americans with her 1840 marriage to Prince Albert. And in the second half of the nineteenth century and the early decades of the twentieth century, a significant number of urban middle-class brides and grooms joined the ranks of white-wedding participants. The consumer base for this style of celebration further expanded after World War II, when rising incomes and mass-produced synthetic-fabric wedding gowns made the formal wedding affordable for the greater population. The network of clothiers, caterers, jewelers, florists, printers, photographers, and others who for a hundred years had provided white weddings for the nation's elite and urban middle class now extended their goods and services to the working class and to middle-class Americans who lived beyond the nation's cities and suburbs. By 1970 white-wedding ceremonies launched approximately 80 percent of all first-time marriages.[5]

In taking the white wedding to the masses, the wedding industry capitalized on dominant postwar gender prescriptions that urged grooms to be financial providers and brides to be housewife-consumers who kicked off a lifetime of domestic spending with the purchase of a formal wedding gown. And in the first quarter century following World War II, wedding industry customers conformed to this prevailing ideology, accepting the premise that a "woman walked up the aisle a bride and back down it a housewife, whether or not she continued to work or study." In actuality, the husband-provider/wife-consumer model applied almost exclusively to middle-income Caucasian marriages. But at a time when the middle class was growing dramatically and popular culture—particularly television—projected white middle-class life as the aspirational standard, the wedding industry successfully convinced most couples to adopt the formal wedding and all it popularly symbolized. Brides and their shopping companions thus enthusiastically responded to retailers who characterized the white wedding as a celebration of all women's domestic role. The shopping experience itself frequently served as a training exercise in domestic consumption. Mothers helped daughters choose wedding clothes, decorations, and menu items as a sort of dress rehearsal for the tasks a bride would soon undertake in her own home. Other female relatives and friends offered opinions on the bride's purchases and on the china, silverware, and other domestic paraphernalia she registered for as gifts. And when department store personnel directed a customer to the bridal salon, they often deliberately walked her through the housewares department, the infant wear section, and other parts of the store she would later patronize as a young wife.[6]

But even as the white wedding achieved widespread acceptance, the potential for its demise loomed ominously. By 1970 the counterculture, the civil rights movement, organized feminism, and increased non-Western immigration all challenged the standards on which the postwar wedding and wedding industry were based. Journalists, social commentators, and even some members of the wedding industry predicted the wedding's extinction as more Americans now questioned the gender and consumer values of the white middle class. The decline of department stores that enabled one-stop shopping for domestic goods also seemed to threaten the future of wedding consumption.

Rumors of the white wedding's imminent demise, however, were greatly exaggerated. The ritual had become the American way to wed, supporting a multi-billion-dollar industry. And planning, purchasing, and enacting the formal wedding provided memorable ways for female friends and relatives to interact and sustain their relationships. Wedding producers and consumers did bow to social and demographic change and recast the purposes of a formal wedding. Customers and tradespeople no longer bought and sold the white wedding primarily as a celebration of female domesticity. Instead, they worked to reshape the ritual's meaning in ways that comfortably accommodated more nonwhites, divorcees, older and career-minded women, and persons in same-sex relationships. As it had for earlier participants, the white wedding enabled these newcomers to experience and project a sense of personal stability, material success, and involvement in the national culture.[7]

As the twentieth century came to a close, the white wedding was more popular than ever, resulting in widespread spending. At the turn of the twenty-first century, annual wedding-related purchases totaled an estimated $50 billion. Estimates in 2005 placed that figure at $70 billion and the average price of an American wedding at nearly $30,000—or roughly two-thirds of the annual mean family income. For most people, the capital-intensive formal wedding remained the only acceptable way to marry. One study found that 20 percent of cohabiting couples did not marry simply because they could not afford a "real wedding." As the study's primary investigator noted, "The perceived cost of the wedding—what we as a culture have now decided is the standard for a wedding—is very powerful."[8]

This book examines the development of America's precise—and expensive—standards for celebrating weddings. In doing so, it necessarily focuses on the period following World War II, when "consumer culture had begun to crowd out all other cultural possibilities." But it goes beyond discussion of the rise of the democratized white wedding in the years of postwar prosperity. This study also considers how the ritual maintained its staying power over the course of the next six decades in the face of extraordinary social, cultural, political, and economic change. Most centrally, then, this book examines how Americans guaranteed the survival of the white wedding into the twenty-first century by amending the ideology that supported it and reinterpreting the functions the rite served. While previous studies have examined the establishment, growth, and marketing strategies of a national wedding industry, none has yet approached the topic squarely within the context of cultural change since World War II, systematically analyzing the cultural mechanisms that disseminated, updated, and sustained the notion that a white wedding was the American way to marry.[9]

This study begins by discussing how major political, economic, and demographic changes between 1945 and 2005 altered ideas communicated by the white wedding about gender, race, and class. It then goes on to assess how Americans learned about the ritual and its shifting meanings. A variety of institutions familiarized Americans with the white-wedding ideal and its changing purposes, but four sources were particularly effective in spreading the message. The bridal-wear business, celebrity weddings, movie weddings, and media coverage of "the wedding next door"—non-celebrity events that nevertheless achieved national exposure in magazines, on television, or on the Internet—all communicated the continuing but amended significance of the white wedding. And each of these conduits of information receives chapter-length treatment here, beginning with the buying and selling of wedding dresses.

The democratized formal wedding weathered and adapted to higher divorce rates; older age at first marriage; and changing gender roles, sexual attitudes, and retailing trends. In the process, its meaning evolved. In a period that prized bridal virginity and youthful marriage, idealized family life, and celebrated economic prosperity, the woman who wore a white gown in 1945 communicated that she was a virginal Cinderella marrying her one true love, from a family prosperous enough to afford a white wedding, and entering a life-long relationship that would ideally produce children. Six decades later, when a woman donned a white wedding gown, she did not necessarily communicate any of these ideas. In a society that now encouraged most women to wear white dresses when they married—regardless of age, sexual experience, marital history, class background, or desire to have children—the gown primarily signified that she was a bride. At a time when Americans increasingly viewed weddings as professionally orchestrated public performances, the white gown was the standard costume. The wedding consumer of 2005 had possibly never seen a woman marry in any other kind of clothing. And although a rare occurrence, she might have even viewed a same-sex ceremony that featured men dressed in white gowns. The wedding dress was no longer a luxury that represented conformity to prized middle-class values but was instead the nearly universal emblem of an American wedding celebration, regardless of the participants' background and values. The white gown still had the power to bestow on its wearer an aura of belonging to upwardly mobile American society, but a much broader group of consumers could now lay claim to that sense of satisfaction in the more tolerant and inclusive America of the twenty-first century.[10]

THE BEST OF EVERYTHING

The White Wedding in American Culture, 1945-2005

In 2003, Molly Jong-Fast squeezed her seven-months-pregnant figure into a white wedding gown, took the arms of both her father and stepfather, and strode down the aisle to be married in "the sort of mega-wedding Jewish princesses dream about." Beaming from her place among the 400 wedding guests, the mother of the bride took satisfaction knowing that she had made the event possible. She had encouraged her daughter's dreams. She had written the checks to the wedding planner. And thirty years earlier, she had written *Fear of Flying*—the classic novel of female sexual liberation. Although initially dismayed by her daughter's decision to marry under a hand-painted chuppah with nine bridesmaids, Erica Jong soon realized that the young bride was not rejecting her feminist heritage. Instead, Molly Jong-Fast was embracing an updated version of marriage—and of weddings—that her mother's generation had helped create. For her, marriage was not a compulsory relationship "in which women were unable to express their needs" but was instead a freely chosen "alliance of equals." As Jong wrote a week after the ceremony, "My daughter wants all the things I rebelled against: early motherhood, the engagement ring, a white wedding, bonding, nesting, Tiffany china. But she also wants the things I fought for: an egalitarian marriage, her own name, her own profession. She expects to have it all." Speaking for herself and other second-wave feminists, Jong concluded, "Perhaps our daughters don't have to rebel against tradition because we have changed that tradition."[1]

Jong's use of the term "changed tradition" probably struck many of her readers as an oxymoron. According to popular definition, a tradition is an unchanged practice handed down from generation to generation. By that definition, however, the white wedding does not qualify as a tradition—at least not in most American families. Jong's own family history is illustrative. Her parents wed in a Depression-era ceremony at city hall. Jong herself married four times with little fuss, the last time "in a red dress by a pond in the Vermont woods." The white wedding "tradition" in Jong's family thus only began in the twenty-first century with her daughter Molly's elaborate ceremony.[2]

Whether they were native-born or—like Jong's family—from an immigrant background, most Americans did not purchase all the trappings of a white wedding until relatively recent times. Prior to World War II, they either married informally or staged weddings that were a patchwork of home-produced and purchased goods and services (see Figure 1.1). When Jong's parents married in 1933, only upper-class and upper-middle-class urbanites could purchase all the elements of a lavish formal wedding. But even though they did not yet enjoy such celebrations themselves, most consumers already knew something about professionally produced white weddings. Print ads for department store bridal salons, radio commercials for wedding products, and wedding scenes in Hollywood movies familiarized average Americans with the expensive white wedding. More important, etiquette books and women's magazines recommended elaborate white weddings as the most appropriate way to marry. According to these sources, an elegant white gown was preferred bridal attire. But this garment—like other luxury goods—remained out of reach for many consumers. Emily Post advised in her 1937 etiquette guide that it was "always proper for a bride to wear a white dress and veil," but she bowed to reality by noting that a bride might instead choose "to be married in a traveling dress."[3]

Americans knew about the lavish white wedding before World War II, but the war caused more of them to consider it seriously for themselves. Higher wartime incomes, advertising that associated marriage and weddings with American war aims, and the rush to marry before young men

FIGURE 1.1. *Typical of the times, this couple's 1930 wedding featured both purchased and home-produced items. The bride and her mother bought the flapper-style gown in a local dress shop, but the bride's mother and sister cooked the wedding dinner themselves and served it in their home. (Author's collection)*

left for distant military service all contributed to the popularity of marriage and formal weddings. In total, the number of marriages begun between 1940 and 1943 exceeded prewar predictions by more than one million. The war's potential to suspend romantic relationships and other pleasures for the foreseeable future caused couples to hasten their marriage plans and often strengthened their desire to wed—if possible—in a ceremony with all the trimmings. Only four days after the attack on Pearl Harbor, Atlanta secretary Barbara Wooddall expressed a typical sentiment when she wrote her boyfriend Charles Taylor: "There is no doubt in my mind as to who shall win the war, but how long will it take us? It makes you feel like getting the best of everything before it's all gone." But four months later, rather than celebrate a wedding that was "the best of everything," the couple eloped during Private Taylor's Easter furlough. An Oakland, California, woman spoke for many of her generation when she noted that wartime concerns pushed her into marriage: "Maybe we wouldn't have gotten married, if it hadn't been for the necessity of hurrying to make up our minds." The lyrics of a big band song echoed these concerns when it asked whether love or "conscription" prompted the nation's marriage boom. First Lady Eleanor Roosevelt even used one of her frequent radio broadcasts to warn Americans that too many "eligible young women" were being pushed into "hasty marriages" by "patriotic fervor." In 1942, the first full year of American involvement in the war, the stampede to the altar boosted the marriage rate from a peacetime 11.9 marriages per 1,000 population to a record 13.2 per 1,000. And the results of a 1942 survey showed that 80 percent of women about to marry wanted a formal wedding.[4]

Wartime propaganda encouraged this enthusiasm for marriage and weddings. A youthful male voice informed listeners to a government-sponsored 1942 radio broadcast that the war was "[a]bout love and gettin' hitched, and havin' a home and some kids, and breathin' fresh air out in the suburbs . . . about livin' and workin' *decent*, like free people." Under the auspices of the War Advertising Council, the manufacturers of a variety of consumer goods joined the government in making an explicit connection between war goals and the ideal American marriage and family. An insurance company ad characterized the war as a "fight to keep our country a safe place for the wives we love, a place where our children can grow up free and unafraid." Several companies advertised their products with the image of a white-clad bride, often standing beside a groom in formal military uniform. These were frequent advertising characters, even though marriage in a formal ceremony was an infrequent experience in wartime America. More Americans said they wanted a white wedding, but rationing restrictions, the belief that luxurious celebrations during war were unpatriotic, and rushed wartime ceremonies contributed to the ritual's relative scarcity. War-era advertising, however, promised better times to come by heavily relying on the image of the formal wedding and the idealization of marriage and family that it represented. The ubiquitous Woodbury soap campaign featured real-life, well-to-do brides ("Woodbury Debs") wearing full white wedding regalia, cutting into huge wedding cakes, carrying ornate bouquets, or posing with their exquisitely dressed bridesmaids (Figure 1.2). These sumptuously attired brides were clearly shorthand symbols of marriage. And happy marriages would be the foundation of a prosperous and secure postwar society free from the worries of economic depression and armed conflict and ready for the full realization of the American dream.[5]

This upbeat image of postwar marriage and family life prescribed starkly different roles for women and men. Pundits warned the 6.5 million women who joined the home-front workforce that wives who remained employed would "bankrupt" American marriage and create a postwar nation of neglected husbands and unsupervised juvenile delinquents. The Eureka vacuum cleaner company reminded women war workers that they toiled "for freedom" and the opportunity to return to full-time homemaking after the war: "You're fighting for a little house of your own, and a husband to meet every night at the door . . . for the right to bring up your children without the shadow of fear." Wartime publicity thus promoted a vision of postwar America in which wage-earning husbands provided sturdy single-family dwellings and stay-at-home wives turned them into happy havens. The January 1945 cover of *House Beautiful*, with its picture of a soldier returning to a well-maintained residence, drove the point home by asking the female reader: "Will You Be Ready When Johnny Comes Marching Home?"[6]

Americans responded positively to these prescriptions for postwar life. In 1946 the nation's marriage rate surpassed even its wartime heights

FIGURE 1.2. *During World War II and the early postwar period, the makers of Woodbury facial soap advertised their product with photographs of exquisitely gowned debutantes marrying uniformed officers.* (Life, 5 June 1950, p. 61)

and was now double that of any prewar year. Americans focused on marriage and family life as never before. As one young war bride noted, "The idea was to live through the war years, get back with our husbands, have kids and raise a family." And although 25 percent of married women remained in the postwar workforce, they largely shifted to part-time jobs or lower paying full-time work that accommodated their household duties and did not challenge the primacy of the male breadwinner. Men also rushed to the comfort of postwar domesticity, heeding advisors who told the returning serviceman that he had "fought for the right to found a family, the privilege of building an enduring home under the folds of freedom's flag." Many viewed marriage as the doorway to middle-class success; once it was achieved, the rest of the American dream would fall into place. Staff Sergeant Sam Goldenberg, who in 1942 had eloped with a woman he met on a weekend furlough, returned from Germany to face 1946 with a wife he barely knew and a daughter he had never seen, but like millions of other veterans he was determined to enjoy a happy home life because "a normal family" was the only "thing he wanted from the rest of his life." For Goldenberg, as for many returning veterans, a "normal" family life meant one that more nearly approximated that of the native-born middle class. And indeed, a few years after returning from the war, Goldenberg Anglicized his family's Jewish surname to Gordon and moved them from the Bronx to the suburbs.[7]

While wartime advertising and the era's emerging domestic ideal whetted Americans' appetite for marriage and weddings, the postwar economy provided consumers with the financial resources to satisfy their hunger. A 1946 Gallup poll indicated that after nearly two decades of economic depression, rationing, and shortages, Americans were in a mood to spend their extra income rather than save it. With Social Security easing their fears of poverty in old age and veterans' mortgages facilitating home ownership, for the first time many Americans could afford to buy the extras that enhanced a family's comfort and social status. And this family-oriented spending would continue for another decade and a half.[8]

Reflecting the dramatic increase in the nation's marriage rate, acknowledging the nation's growing interest in family-oriented consumer spending, and recognizing Middle America's already existing familiarity with the white-wedding concept, business persons increasingly turned their attention to selling wedding goods and services in the years following World War II. Existing businesses began providing or explicitly promoting wedding-related services. In 1946, for instance, the A&P grocery chain began mass-producing wedding cakes to sell in its supermarkets throughout the country. Family restaurants, such as Palumbo's in Philadelphia, began specializing in wedding receptions that featured huge cakes, four-course meals, and an automatic rice-throwing machine. A greater number of department stores with a predominantly middle-class clientele, such as the Philadelphia-based Strawbridge and Clothier store, followed the lead of more upscale emporiums and began to establish bridal service sections, which sold wedding and trousseau clothing and aided brides-to-be in their selection of wedding invitations and china, silver, glass, and linen patterns.[9]

The woman-centered nature of the marriage ritual ensured that the expanding postwar wedding industry would particularly attract female entrepreneurs. At a time when many barriers to success existed for women elsewhere in the business world, the wedding trade was one place where ambitious and talented women could find a home. After the war, former department store buyer Priscilla Kidder launched her own wedding gown design firm, and her Priscilla of Boston company ultimately became one of the leading enterprises in the industry. In the postwar years, Wilmington, Delaware, caterer Edith McConnell expanded her existing business and began advertising it with the slogan, "Wedding cakes of beautiful design, our specialty" (Figure 1.3). Around the nation, other women opened or expanded wedding-oriented businesses in response to America's promarriage climate.[10]

The growing postwar wedding industry was, in the words of one of its pioneers, "a marketing business" from the beginning. Leading the way in publicizing the industry's wares was *Bride's* magazine and its major postwar competitor, *Modern Bride*. Both periodicals advertised the bridal wear, trousseau, and home-furnishing items available at the nation's department stores. *Bride's* had begun publication in 1934 as a wedding guide for women whose engagement announcements appeared in the East Coast society pages. Typical early articles advised the bride-to-be how to "capture" and "train" a housemaid for her honeymoon

*Our Exclusive Catering Service
Is at Your Disposal*

Wedding cakes of beautiful
design, our specialty

We are now making Birthday and Wedding Cakes for the
fifth generation of Delawareans

E. N. McCONNELL
CATERER   CONFECTIONER
213 WEST NINTH STREET   WILMINGTON, DELAWARE
PHONE 5015

FIGURE 1.3. *In the postwar period, Wilmington, Delaware, caterer Edith
McConnell advertised her business as specializing in elaborate wedding cakes.
(Hagley Museum and Library)*

nest and pictured extravagant wedding receptions at exclusive New York clubs. As portrayed in these early issues, the American bride possessed unlimited resources and imagination. A bridal character quoted in the Autumn 1940 edition exhibited a strong consumer ethos when she noted, "Since this is my day, my hour, my moment and I have the world of wedding finery at my feet, I can and will indulge myself with any fanciful ideas that may snare my imagination." In the pages of *Bride's*, every wife-to-be pursued a romantic consumer fantasy.[11]

Following World War II, *Bride's* expanded its promise of fairytale weddings beyond its well-to-do East Coast audience to brides who shopped at middle-class department stores in Kansas City, Denver, Seattle, and other far-flung locations. One 1946 *Bride's* article demonstrated the range of pocketbooks that the periodical now targeted by presenting advice on how to execute a variety of weddings, from a formal cathedral ceremony and private club reception for $1,830 ($18,994 in today's currency) to an "informal, intimate" wedding for $195 ($2,024 in current dollars). Eventually available at newsstands, supermarkets, and libraries throughout the country, the publication's readership had obviously moved beyond the debutante set. The periodical's prewar philosophy, however, remained intact: a bride should exploit her available resources to the fullest in order to make her wedding day the fulfillment of a romantic fantasy.[12]

The postwar wedding industry's use of fairytale images reflected the endurance of the Cinderella myth, with its message that marriage was the most acceptable means for a woman to escape an inferior social position. One woman who wed during this period remembered that her mother was "obsessively anxious" for her to "marry well." She herself could see no alternative: "My future was a blank. It had never occurred to me that I could take care of myself—either I stayed with my dad or I got married." Like others of her generation, this woman doubted her ability to achieve middle-class security on her own and instead believed that the only way to maintain or improve her class status was by attaching herself to a successful man. And in contrast to so many young women's daily grinds in low-paying "women's jobs," the image of a glamorous wedding was enticing. For one day, a woman could be a real-life Cinderella, an ordinary person transformed into the belle of the ball. A parent viewing these advertising images might come away with a different but related message. Hosting a fabulous wedding demonstrated that the bride's family had achieved a certain level of material success. As in the original Cinderella story, marriage in the appropriate setting—and to the appropriate man—announced to the world that a young woman and her family were assuming their rightful place in the American class structure. In the fairy tale, Cinderella was an orphaned rich girl forced to live like a servant until the right paraphernalia (provided by a fairy godmother) and the right marriage (to a prince) restored her to her rightful class. In real life, a daughter's marriage surrounded by the right accouterments (provided by the wedding industry) and to the right man (a good provider) declared to the world that a family with working- or lower–middle-class origins had moved up in the pecking order. Evidence indicates, in fact, that in an attempt to emulate the class status of the groom, families of brides who married "up" spent more elaborately on wedding celebrations than brides who married at or below their own class.[13]

Bridal magazines were only one cog in a vast postwar publicity machine that familiarized a broad cross-section of the nation with the goods and services of the wedding industry and normalized the concept of the capital-intensive white wedding. The major conduits of postwar popular culture—movies, magazines, and eventually television—all spread the word that Americans from diverse walks of life could aspire to the white wedding and take advantage of the goods and services of the wedding industry. A newsstand browser did not have to be a devotee of bridal magazines—and thus already a self-selected consumer of wedding industry propaganda—in order to be aware of the commercialized wedding ideal. In 1946 general audience magazines saw an explosion in the number of advertisements incorporating wedding images. For example, in *Life*, the nation's most popular magazine, images of brides in white gowns and veils sold wedding-related products such as De Beers diamonds, Artcarved and Keepsake rings, Community silverplate ware, and Lane hope chests, but they also sold mundane items like shaving cream, cigarettes, beer, whiskey, doorbells, mouthwash, laxatives, toothpaste, and toothbrushes. In comparison to the war years, ads appearing in 1946 exhibited more diversity in the types of brides and grooms pictured enjoying the elegant white wedding. In a De Beers ad, a clearly identified Jewish couple appeared for the first time in a promotional campaign, marrying in front of a rabbi and under a traditional chuppah. And, with the exception of the continuing Woodbury Debs ads and a handful of other campaigns, the advertising of this period did not explicitly tie the white wedding to the moneyed elite. To the contrary, some of these advertisements emphasized the more modest circumstances of the brides and grooms pictured in their layouts. Such advertising advanced the message that ordinary folks could—and should—patronize the appropriate commercial establishments to purchase the elements of a formal wedding.[14]

The advertising patterns established in 1946 continued in the pages of *Life* and other popular magazines for another seven years—a period that advertising historians have defined as the "catching up" years of postwar prosperity. During these years, Americans focused on purchasing merchandise that they had abstained from buying during the Depression and war years. Many of the products promoted in these ads were inexpensive, quickly consumed items such as toothpaste and mouthwash. From 1947 onward, however, the majority of products promoted using images of the white wedding were more expensive goods that had been difficult to afford or unavailable in preceding years. Brides continued to sell pricey wedding-related goods such as hope chests, silverware, and diamond rings (Figure 1.4). But they now promoted a variety of other big-ticket items as well: radios, vacuum cleaners, juke boxes, kitchen ranges, Swiss watches, automobile tires. Formally attired brides also showed up in life insurance ads. At a time when Americans could finally afford to buy costly goods that contributed to the comfort and security of family life, the white-clad bride was the recognized symbol of both domestic happiness and domestic spending.[15]

By 1950 the growing wedding industry was not only targeting families already ensconced in the middle class but was beginning to focus on families only recently arrived or aspiring to middle-class status. At this time, the number of American families classified as earning an annual middle-class income—$5,000 after taxes—was growing by more than one million households a year, a pace that would continue through the end of the decade. The booming economy of these years encouraged brides and grooms to establish their new households at very young ages. The era's glorification of married love and its sexual double standard,

FIGURE 1.4. *Two fantasy figures of postwar womanhood—Miss America and the American Bride—advertised Lane hope chests as "the practical love-gift" and "the gift that starts the Home." (Life, 5 June 1950, p. 18)*

which sanctioned sexual expression for women only within marriage, contributed to the formation of households by very young couples. In the words of one teenage bride of the era, "I got married in order to have a sex life. I thought that was why everyone got married." As a result of these economic and ideological factors, women's median age at first marriage, which was 21.5 years in 1940, fell to 20.3 years by 1950. For men during this same period, median first-marriage age dropped from 24.3 years to 22.7. In the fifteen years following Pearl Harbor, in fact, the percentage of men who married in their early twenties doubled. During this same period, economic prosperity and younger marriages also resulted in a doubling of the fertility rate for women in their early twenties. The postwar Baby Boom was underway.[16]

With the marriage rate double that of the prewar period, a 28 percent increase in the total number of families, and a skyrocketing birthrate, America was now predominantly a nation of young families. And most of these families identified themselves as middle-class at a time when the nation was enjoying a 60 percent rise in average income, experiencing 64 percent of its population growth in the suburbs, and increasing its spending on household furnishings and appliances by 240 percent. Automobiles, single-family dwellings, and formal weddings were particularly popular signifiers of middle-class status and stability. Consumers used these purchases not only to advertise their families' class status but also to enhance their families' emotional well being. At a time when psychologists, educators, social workers, clergy members, and the press promoted the notion of family "togetherness," family members exhibited their solidarity by gathering together around a new television set or backyard barbeque pit, piling into the station wagon for a family vacation, or standing next to one another smiling in the receiving line at an elegant wedding reception. New housing developments, shopping centers, car dealerships, and vacation resorts sold themselves by reflecting the ideals of the financially and emotionally stable middle class.[17]

Capitalizing on the continuing mania for marriage and family, businesses of the 1950s provided a variety of goods and services to clothe, house, feed, and celebrate the nuclear family. American enterprise focused particular attention on the inaugural event in the life of a happy family—the wedding celebration. At a time when Americans viewed marriage as the most desirable institution for refuge from the complex Cold War–era world, getting married remained essential. In the words of one lesbian who married and became an unhappy suburban housewife: "I do remember thinking always that the goal was marriage, always marriage, whatever else you felt." The burgeoning wedding industry, ably aided and abetted by the media, told Americans just how and with what the marriage ritual should be performed. Images of the elaborate white wedding were even more numerous in the 1950s than they had been in the late 1940s.[18]

By 1952 the increased publicity and acceptance of the white wedding resulted in $3 billion in wedding-related sales for the 1.5 million couples who married that year. Industry insiders estimated that consumers spent $375 million on clothing for brides, their mothers, and their bridesmaids; $225 million on trousseau lingerie; $650 million on other trousseau items; $850 million on wedding gifts; and a whopping $1 billion on receptions, honeymoons, and home furnishings. The *Bride's* magazine handbook for newlyweds encouraged this spending, telling readers, "You are helping to build greater security for the industries of this country. . . . What you buy and how you buy it is very vital in your new life—and to our whole American way of living."[19]

At this point in the industry's history, most of these sales occurred in the nation's department stores, where the rule of thumb was that every bride-customer should be exposed to a "threefold must-buy market." Salespeople encouraged each bride who walked into the doors of the department store to buy items for the wedding day itself, for her honeymoon trousseau, and for her new home. In order to ensure communication of the "threefold must-buy" message, department stores hired bridal consultants to coordinate customers' purchases and make sure that young women and their mothers visited not only a store's bridal-wear shop but its lingerie, ready-to-wear, gift, and home-furnishing departments as well. Consultants even encouraged the growing popularity of wedding showers and aided the bride's friends in organizing and acquiring the appropriate props and gifts for those occasions (Figure 1.5). By the early 1950s bridal consulting had become such an integral part of the

FIGURE 1.5. *Among the items that sales personnel urged customers to purchase for a 1950s bridal shower was this wedding-themed bingo game. (Author's collection)*

wedding industry—and such an attractive, well-paying type of employment for women involved in retail sales work—that institutions such as New York's Barmore School offered job training courses in the field.[20]

National advertising campaigns paralleled in-store marketing schemes and likewise promoted ideal marriage celebrations, family life, and domestic consumerism. By the mid-1950s Americans had finally satiated their pent-up demand for consumer goods harbored during the Depression and war years, and American businesses grew fearful that they would lose the customers they had so carefully cultivated since the war's end. So advertisers now raised the bar for achievement of the American dream. While in 1946 advertisers represented ownership of a car and a home as the ultimate middle-class goals, they now suggested that the good life included a second car and a television set. Along with their upscaling of the middle-class dream, advertisers of the mid-1950s also worked to make the white wedding synonymous with the basic well-being and survival of the American family. The increasing number of automobile and insurance company ads that included pictures of formally dressed brides and grooms stressed that the purchase of a car or life insurance policy guaranteed that a newly married couple would "start off right" and maintain their relationship on a "sound basis." Even an ad for the coffee substitute Postum pictured a bride modeling her gown for admiring family members and emphasized family survival and cohesion: "Wedding preparations bring the whole family closer to each other . . . and Postum is the drink the whole family can enjoy together"[21] (Figure 1.6).

Madison Avenue most frequently connected formal weddings and family values in advertisements for products directly related to the white wedding itself. In 1957 a series of International Sterling ads tied the concept of the white wedding—and expensive wedding gifts such as fine silverware—to the idea of family legacy. In one ad, a young bride told her mother that although she had once been a "modern, practical type" who did not want the "fuss and feathers" of a formal wedding, meeting Bob had changed her mind and made her realize that she "wanted a church wedding. And possessions that [were] real and lasting . . . 'family silver' that [she and Bob could] hand down to [their] grandchildren." In another ad, a teenage bridesmaid vowed to have everything that her sister Kate now enjoyed—including a catered wedding celebration and a set of International Sterling silverware. Advertising that tied buying elements of the wedding from strangers to tradition and family helped equate the accouterments of the white wedding with family stability. Similarly, ads that employed a wedding theme but did not promote products directly associated with weddings suggested that items such as cars and life insurance were among the new must-haves to establish a proper middle-class home.[22]

Constant exposure to the white wedding and other domestic images caused women to pursue marriage as an obligatory goal. A 1955 survey of young single women noted that participants eagerly sought to avoid permanent single status and the specter of becoming an "old maid"— "a person who had failed so seriously in her undertaking or execution of a woman's role that she hadn't even established the marriage prerequisite to having a home." To the survey respondents, women who remained

"Get under the veil, princess . . . I'll hold your Postum"

Wedding preparations bring the whole family closer to each other . . . and Postum is the drink the whole family can *enjoy* together.

You'll like the *different* flavor . . . grain-rich, slow-roasted . . . a wonderful change from every-day hot drinks . . . a treat at any time of the day.

And *everybody* can drink Postum . . . it's 100% caffein-free . . . 100% safe even for your children. Postum helps you round out your evenings with a good night's sleep.

For less than a penny a cup, start *your* family on the change to this different hot drink *today*.

Enjoy Postum, the hot drink with a __different__ flavor . . .

A Product of General Foods

FIGURE 1.6. *Emphasizing a number of popular advertising themes of the period, a 1957 Postum ad shows parents, siblings, and even the family dog uniting to focus their attention on a "princess bride." (*Life, *18 March 1957, p. 167)*

single throughout their adult lives "were not figures of horror so much, nor of abhorrence, as they were objects of somewhat condescending pity."[23]

Women of the era who neglected accepted wisdom and did not marry at an early age could find themselves unwittingly ending all hope of eventual marriage and social acceptance. One woman who did not follow the conventional wisdom of the 1950s remembered, "The expectation was clear: Get married and have children. It was absolutely taken for granted. There was no other way. It was perfectly obvious to me that after college, I'd work for a year or two, meet a nice man, have a nice loving husband and some nice loving children." Nevertheless, her pursuit of a Capitol Hill job and a series of temporary sexual relationships soon left the young college graduate out of the running to become a wife and mother. In failing to play by the gender rules of her generation, the woman ultimately faced society's disapproval and doubts about her own self-worth: "It just didn't occur to me that I could become a professional or get a PhD. I was too scared. Lack of confidence in my intelligence and ability tied in with being single—feeling different, alone." Under circumstances such as these, most young people chose the course of least resistance— marriage and parenthood.[24]

As the 1950s ended, the popularity of marriage and the penchant for family-oriented consumer spending continued unabated. At the close of the decade, 14 million seventeen-year-old girls across the nation were already engaged to be married. And Americans continued to celebrate the nuclear family by building homes and buying domestic-oriented goods. One-fourth of the single-family homes standing in 1960 had been built since 1950, and 62 percent of Americans now owned their own homes— up from 44 percent in 1940. White-collar workers now outnumbered blue-collar workers, and the nation's suburbs were booming. The author of a 1960 study on the psychology of consumerism noted that the impact of suburbia on consumer behavior could "hardly be overstated." In these crabgrass frontiers, people married at a young age, had several children in the early years of marriage, lived in attractive neighborhoods, and purchased cars, washing machines, refrigerators, television sets, and other appropriate appliances. To demonstrate that one's family was sharing in the era's prosperity, suburbanites no longer considered these purchases luxuries but necessities. At the same time, the era's mass media—particularly its commercially sponsored television sitcoms—busily projected middle-class suburban life as the national norm, convincing members of the white working class to aspire to suburban consumer practices.[25]

As the 1960s began, the white wedding was apparently among the nation's new consumer necessities—both in the suburbs and elsewhere. In 1960, when the median family income was $4,970 and an expensive new car cost $3,140, the average American wedding cost $3,300. The typical bride spent $243.29 for her trousseau, her groom spent $398.79 for an engagement ring, and their honeymoon cost $361. In addition to the expenses that the bride, the groom, and their families incurred, the cost of being a wedding guest also rose. The typical bride and groom received $1,003 worth of gifts in 1960. *U.S. News and World Report* estimated that newlyweds were now worth $23 billion a year to the nation's economy.[26]

Through the first half of the 1960s, the varied personnel involved in the wedding business designed imaginative and persistent schemes to ensure that customers purchased their products. Television commercials, celebrity endorsements, and department store seminars on organizing a proper wedding all attracted consumers to wedding products. These promotional stunts only worked, of course, if brides were already committed to the idea of a formal white wedding. And they were. According to one estimate, 85 percent of the nation's brides were indeed opting for elaborate, formal ceremonies. The white wedding's popularity lay in the continued prosperity and promarriage sentiments of this period but also resulted from some unique demographics. Most brides in the mid-1960s married between the ages of 18 and 24, which meant that they were born either during World War II or immediately thereafter. Parents of these war babies and Baby Boomers pushed them—and their male counterparts—to marry at such young ages because the older generation still strongly believed in the early marriage script they themselves had followed in the 1940s.[27]

Parents' concerns also dictated how marriage celebrations of the period were staged. As journalist Kitty Hanson reasoned in her investigation of the mid-1960s wedding business, the mothers of most brides had probably married during World War II, when "weddings were simple, hurried, often drab; set in the context of war, urgency, and short leaves." To compensate for the lack of luxury at their own weddings, mothers and fathers of the 1960s encouraged their daughters to marry in lavish fashion. Having spent their own youths amid the austerity of economic depression and war, male breadwinners of the period relished the opportunity to provide their families with all the appropriate middle-class status symbols—including the elaborate white wedding. As one psychologist of the era noted, "Any father who complains he is spending thousands for his daughter's wedding . . . isn't complaining. He's bragging." In order to play the coveted roles of consumer and provider, middle-class mothers and fathers of the 1960s encouraged their children to marry in white-wedding splendor.[28]

Another factor contributing to the popularity of the white wedding in the 1960s was that the first of the Baby Boomers were now reaching marriageable age. Members of this large cohort of consumers born between 1946 and 1964, whose entire life experience had occurred during postwar prosperity, were used to spending a significant amount of disposable family income. By the mid-1960s the average teenage girl was spending $489 per year, approximately one-tenth of her family's total income, on consumer items for herself. Teenagers were spending $3.6 million on clothes each year. They owned a million television sets, 10 million record players, and 20 million radios. Teenagers accounted for a full 20 percent of the nation's annual new and used car sales. By the mid-1960s teenage girls made up 12 percent of the country's female population but purchased 27 percent of all cosmetics and 50 percent of all phonograph records. For such consumer-minded young women, spending lavishly on a wedding was merely part of a larger pattern of behavior.[29]

Even the social and political upheavals of the latter years of the decade did not seriously threaten the wedding industry or traditional ideas about marriage. Angst over the military-industrial complex and U.S. involvement in the Vietnam War did not lead to rejection of the wedding-industrial complex as yet another capitalist conspiracy. Instead, according to wedding industry insiders, Vietnam-era draft policies that excluded married men were a real boon to business, thanks to the "rush of fellows trying to beat the draft by getting married." The counterculture of the late 1960s also failed to make a noticeable dent in the wedding business. Although the 1967 Central Park wedding of Anita Kushner and Abbie Hoffman—in which the bride and groom recited their vows in bare feet and then joined their guests to smoke marijuana—grabbed headlines, the commercialized white wedding had become such an ingrained feature of American life that few other couples followed their example. In fact, the wedding industry eventually co-opted elements of counterculture style. New York's exclusive Bergdorf Goodman store, for instance, offered its version of a "hippie wedding dress" for $500 (equivalent to $2,421 today). The emerging second-wave feminist movement and its criticism of patriarchal family life also failed to dampen Americans' enthusiasm for white weddings and the conventional marriages that they celebrated. If Betty Friedan's relatively staid critique of middle-class housewifery in *The Feminine Mystique* (1963) had not yet gained mainstream acceptance, then certainly radical feminist arguments about a "politics of housework" and men as the "agents of oppression" were not even a blip on the national radar screen.[30]

As the 1960s ended, marriage and formal weddings were still highly popular institutions. By 1970 the same percentage of the U.S. population traveled to the altar as it had in 1960, and over 84 percent of the women marrying did so in formal wedding gowns. The white wedding had survived the turbulent 1960s to thrive and prosper. In 1967, 73 percent of first-time American weddings were formal events featuring a religious ceremony, an elaborate bridal gown, and a wedding party. That statistic rose to 80 percent by 1971. The white wedding was obviously alive and well in the Age of Aquarius and continuing to attract new adherents.[31]

The bibles of the wedding industry, the nation's bridal magazines, played a role in bringing the white wedding to an expanding audience. *Bride's* magazine, for instance, attempted in the late 1960s to reach beyond its usual white Protestant upper-middle-class readership and now occasionally featured black models in African-inspired bridal fashions and provided diagrams for the proper positioning of bride, groom, and attendants at Orthodox Jewish ceremonies. By 1969 the periodical even dispensed advice for divorcees on how to plan a second wedding, a formerly taboo subject, and instructed working-class brides on how to decorate their mobile homes.[32]

Despite these occasional nods to bridal diversity, the wedding industry and media of the 1960s continued to promote weddings and marriage based largely on an upper-middle-class, Anglo American model. In 1969, when a well-paid American worker earned $8,000 a year, readers of *Bride's* magazine perused a sample wedding budget that totaled $9,951.36, including $650 for a wedding gown and $3,375 for a dinner reception. For many members of the middle and working classes, the only means of affording such prescribed luxury was to dip into savings accounts, buy on installment plans, or take out a second mortgage. Others took advantage of the new "universal" credit cards that could be used at numerous retail locations and charged a portion of their expenses to Diner's Club or American Express.[33]

As it had since the early postwar period, the wedding industry of the 1960s presented the American bride as queen for a day in a pageant of her own design. One bridal consultant of the 1960s succinctly summarized the Cinderella mentality that members of the industry exploited as they sold goods and services to the customer-bride: "This is her day, her show. She is the whole works: producer, director, and star." Once "her day" was over, however, the American bride of the 1960s relinquished her starring role. As the American housewife, she would continue the frenzy of domestic spending initiated by her wedding preparations, but she would do so as a supporting player to her breadwinner husband.[34]

Contrary to popular belief, the key decade for change in women's approach to weddings and marriage was not the 1960s but the 1970s, when the nation witnessed a frontal assault on the domestic ideology and national prosperity that had launched and initially sustained the postwar white wedding. High-profile challenges to the postwar domestic ideal emerged early in the decade. The year 1970 alone saw publication of such classic second-wave feminist texts as Kate Millett's *Sexual Politics*, Shulamith Firestone's *The Dialectic of Sex*, Germaine Greer's *The Female Eunuch*, and editor Robin Morgan's anthology of liberationist writings entitled *Sisterhood Is Powerful*. The authors of these works argued for an end to the sexual double-standard and conventional heterosexual marriage and discussed alternative ways for women to achieve sexual and emotional fulfillment and economic justice in a society transformed by radical feminism. The majority of Americans did not read any of these books, but the era's mass media nevertheless exposed the nation—often in sensationalistic fashion—to the major ideas contained in these works. In the early 1970s popular magazine cover stories and television news programs frequently profiled feminist authors and spokeswomen who asserted that only men really benefited from traditional heterosexual marriage. According to this argument, a wife provided her husband with sexual favors, children, and a lifetime of free maid service in exchange for the adequate economic support that she was denied direct access to by the sex-segregated labor market. With the husband holding all or most of the economic cards, the wife found herself with limited decision-making power and few viable alternatives for financial survival outside of the relationship.[35]

At the same time that Americans were becoming aware of the growing call for a feminist revolution, they were also experiencing a revolution in the nation's divorce laws. While World War II and the immediate postwar years had witnessed a substantial rise in the nation's marriage rate, the 1940s and early 1950s also saw a rise in the U.S. divorce rate. During this time, the divorce rate rose approximately 20 percent over the prewar era, in part because people ended hastily formed wartime marriages or terminated older unions that had succumbed to the stress of wartime conditions. Also, couples who had balked at the expense of a formal legal divorce during the Depression were now able to afford that option. But the major reason for rising divorce numbers was probably the heightened expectations that Americans now held for marriage. If a marriage did not match the romantic, sexual, and emotional needs that Americans now believed it should provide, they more readily ended it. The increased postwar desire for divorce, along with implementation of legal reforms, translated into nearly one in four marriages ending in divorce in the late 1940s and early 1950s. This rate reached a plateau during the height of the postwar domestic ideal, the 1955–1963 period, only to begin rising again in the mid-1960s. At this same time, in conformity with changing social standards, several states began to modernize existing divorce laws. Most significantly, in 1966, New York, then the nation's second most populous state, amended its notoriously restrictive statute to include reasons other than adultery as grounds for divorce. Then, on New Year's Day 1970, California became the first state in the union to allow divorce on nonadversarial grounds, ending the practice of one spouse assuming guilt or fault for the end of a marriage. Other states quickly followed suit, either implementing "irretrievable breakdown" of a marriage or incompatibility of the spouses as the only grounds for divorce or adding this no-fault option to existing grounds such as adultery, cruelty, or abandonment. By August 1977 only three states continued to practice an adversarial system of divorce in which one party always assumed guilt for the end of the union.[36]

At roughly the same time that no-fault laws were simplifying the pathway to legal divorce, the Roman Catholic Church was softening its historic antidivorce stance and becoming more generous in granting church annulments to marriages that had ended in civil divorce. As a result, a greater number of the nation's Catholics could now end unhappy marriages via divorce but still maintain the option of marrying a new spouse in a Catholic ceremony. Legal reforms in the 1970s, along with nearly simultaneous changes in Roman Catholic church policy, contributed to a skyrocketing divorce rate. By the early 1980s some estimates indicated that one in two marriages was ending in divorce.[37]

In addition to contributing to the nation's divorce rate, the no-fault revolution of the 1970s also helped dismantle the idea that marriage was a contract in which the husband automatically assumed economic support of the wife. When a marriage ended with neither spouse at fault, the law could no longer require a cruel, adulterous, or otherwise guilty husband to pay his ex-wife alimony. Additionally, the U.S. Supreme Court rendered the concept of alimony gender-neutral when it ruled in the late 1970s that women as well as men could be potentially liable for the financial support of an ex-spouse. In practice, however, evolving divorce laws of the 1970s led to a situation in which the typical ex-spouse— whether male or female—was expected to be self-supporting and also contribute to the economic support of any minor children that the marriage had produced. This new gender neutrality in the nation's divorce settlements not only helped dismantle the patriarchal notion of the male breadwinner but also contributed to the feminization of poverty at a time when women's earnings still lagged significantly behind men's. Support of one's self—and possibly also one's children—often proved difficult on a "woman's wage," and a woman's material quality of life usually suffered noticeably in the aftermath of a divorce.[38]

Divorced women were not the only Americans who faced strained economic circumstances in the 1970s. In the opening years of the decade, an 8 percent inflation rate, a growing national budget deficit, and the loss of domestic and export markets for American manufactured goods all conspired to reverse thirty years of U.S. economic progress. Then, in 1973 a powerful cartel of petroleum-exporting nations instituted an oil embargo that compounded American economic woes by adding to the inflation rate and highlighting the dangers of the country's reliance on foreign energy sources. Throughout the remainder of the decade, real income in the United States declined by 15 percent, inflation drove housing and new car prices steadily upward, and the median price of a new single-family dwelling doubled. The American standard of living, the wonder of the postwar world, now began to fall below that of several European countries. Economic realities were making it more and more difficult for the nation's families to realize the American dream of material security and abundance without a second income. The number of wage-earning wives thus grew significantly in the 1970s, with a particularly sharp rise in employment rates for women with minor children. By the middle of the decade, two in five married mothers of preschool-age children and over half of American wives with school-age children were in the paid labor force.[39]

The increase in women's paid employment in the 1970s further undermined postwar ideas and practices regarding marriage. Demographers primarily attributed a rise in female marriage age during the decade to women's increased workforce participation. For young women who were born in the early 1950s and beginning to marry in large numbers in the early 1970s, the median age at first marriage was 21 years, as opposed to the median age of 20.3 years two decades earlier. With workforce participation increasingly becoming a permanent feature of an adult woman's life, American women were taking extra time to train for and establish themselves in jobs before they entered marriage. Older brides generally translated into older grooms, as women continued the long-term trend of marrying up the prestige ladder by finding mates who exceeded them in age and income. The later start in marriage for women of the 1970s generally translated into a later and abbreviated period of reproduction for themselves and their partners. Whereas in 1957 only 29 percent of Americans in the 21–29 age range had been childless, by 1976, 50 percent of persons in that age range had no children. This delay in childbearing contributed further to the overall decline in the national birthrate that had begun in the mid-1960s. In addition to female employment having an effect on marriage age and birthrate, it had an impact on the nation's divorce rate. Demographers attributed the doubling of the nation's divorce rate between 1966 and 1976 in part to women's expanded presence in the workplace. Women who earned a wage of their own were simply less reluctant to end unhappy marriages.[40]

In contrast to the anomalous twenty years that preceded it, the 1966 to 1976 period saw the nation returning to trends more typical of the pre–World War II period. From the mid-1940s to the mid-1960s the nation experienced a decline in the age at first marriage, a rise in the birthrate, and—at least for a portion of that period—a leveling off of the divorce rate. Now the American population resumed patterns that had been the norm since the mid-nineteenth century: marriage age and the divorce rate were on the rise while the birthrate was on the decline. In several respects, then, the lives of young adults in the 1970s resembled more their grandparents' experiences of the 1930s than their parents' experiences of the 1950s.[41]

One way in which young people of the 1970s resembled those of the 1930s was in their greater acceptance of single adulthood as an alternative to marriage. While people who came of age in the first twenty-five years following World War II understood marriage as the only suitable lifestyle to pursue, young people of the 1970s—like their grandparents in the prewar era—believed that for some people remaining single was a better option. Many members of the prewar generation viewed the choice to remain single as a financial necessity because Depression conditions made setting up a household impractical. Economic pragmatism rather than any type of ideological shift had caused a greater number of young people in the 1930s to view the choice to forgo marriage as a responsible adult decision. In contrast, changed attitudes toward marriage rather than economic conditions caused more members of the 1970s generation to view single life as an acceptable alternative to marriage. The era's high divorce rate and other recent challenges to the institution of marriage left young adults of the 1970s with what social scientists termed a more "neutral" attitude toward married life. As a result, they recognized that for some people single life was preferable. Whereas a national mental health survey in 1957 indicated that 46 percent of Americans in the 21–29 age range held a negative attitude toward persons who did not marry, a follow-up study in 1976 showed that only 22 percent of persons in that age group harbored negative feelings toward people who remained single. Analysts noted that this "increased tolerance of people who reject marriage as a way of life" represented the most dramatic difference between responses to the 1957 survey and answers to the 1976 study. In particular, the extremely negative attitude that single women themselves once held toward their unmarried status and failure to conform to the postwar ideal had significantly dissipated by 1976. In summarizing survey results, scholars surmised that the "loosening of the normative necessity of being someone's wife or husband in order to be a valid adult undoubtedly has had and will continue to have profound effects on other reactions to marriage."[42]

A final demographic trend among young adults of the 1970s that challenged the ideas and practices of their parents was their increased rate of nonmarital cohabitation. While demographers admitted that information regarding cohabitation prior to 1970 was scanty, existing evidence indicated that it had been a relatively uncommon experience prior to that time. That situation, however, changed drastically during the next decade. Census Bureau statistics indicated that the number of cohabiting couples more than doubled between the years 1970 and 1979 to reach a figure of 1,346,000. The largest increase occurred among childless couples under the age of 25. For members of that population group, the number of couples living together rose from 29,000 in 1970 to 274,000 in 1979—an eightfold increase. By 1975, 18 percent of 20-to-30-year-old men who participated in a national survey reported that they had lived for six months or more with a female partner to whom they were not married. In total, the number of cohabiting couples rose 40 percent in just the two years between 1977 and 1979. By decade's end, cohabitation had become a trend that could not be ignored.[43]

Noting the dramatic social changes around him, humanist author and lecturer Khoren Arisian was one of the first to advise that wedding ceremonies should also evolve. The various ideological, legal, and economic assaults on marriage in the 1970s found expression in Arisian's *The New Wedding* (1973), a sort of etiquette book for marriage-minded bohemians. Inspired by the ideas of the 1970s counterculture and second-wave feminism, Arisian offered advice to free thinkers who may have dropped out of many conventional social practices and institutions but still apparently harbored an attachment to monogamous, heterosexual marriage. Criticizing traditional marriage as a "death trap for individual self-development" and charging that the "'happily ever after' myth [had] been one of humankind's grossest moral deceptions," Arisian set out to confront the "well-meant hypocrisy of the old" wedding and replace it with a wedding "conceived of as a humanistic celebration." The author encouraged readers to create their own wedding ceremonies that deleted such sexist practices as the father "giving" the bride to the groom and the bride promising to "obey" her new husband. Instead, Arisian counseled that couples with a heightened consciousness should employ practices and language that reflected their own more egalitarian values, morals, and politics. Sample real-life ceremonies described in the book included an anarchist-feminist wedding, in which the couple voiced their rejection of the state's authority over their union and denounced "the traditional and legal authority of man over woman" as having "no legitimate moral basis."[44]

But another book published in 1973, magazine writer Marcia Seligson's *The Eternal Bliss Machine*, indicated that most couples ignored Arisian's prescriptions and embraced the happily-ever-after Cinderella myth. Seligson's study of the American wedding industry demonstrated that the era's assaults on traditional marriage and the commercialized white wedding had not prevented most brides and grooms of the 1970s from marrying in a conventional and expensive manner. Reflecting the fact that even most cohabitors who could afford a white wedding eventually had one, Seligson found that the same percentage of Americans who had traveled to the altar in the early 1960s were now heading there in the early 1970s. And once they arrived at that destination, they were dressed in formal attire. Forgoing the handmade invitations, homemade apparel, organic food, and outdoor settings of the archetypal New Wedding, most 1970s couples continued to rent the reception hall and tuxedo, hire the caterer, buy the lacy bridal gown, and recite the standard wedding vows (Figures 1.7–1.9). Few clergy members at the time reported requests for deviations in the conventional ceremony, and only 25 percent of women who responded to a *Bride's* magazine survey of the period reported that they had requested a presiding officiant to change the customary wedding ceremony in any way. Of the 25 percent of brides who did ask for ceremonial innovations, most had made requests involving musical selections rather than changes in the traditional wedding script. Admittedly, women who read *Bride's* and the other wedding magazines were already self-selected adherents of the so-called Old Wedding and therefore saw little problem with wearing a virginal white gown and being given away by a father who would probably pay for the day's festivities. With more than four out of five brides of the period consulting such magazines, however, it was a pretty safe bet that the majority of the nation's brides desired familiar ritual rather than do-your-own-thing innovation.[45]

As Seligson's book indicated, the 1970s wedding industry successfully relied on the continuing loyalty of Baby Boomers who had grown up in the postwar era thinking of marriage and formal white weddings as the norm. It also counted on parental expectations to quell most acts of New Wedding rebellion. The wedding industry in fact continued to develop new schemes to ensure that the young adults of the 1970s continued to marry in 1950s style. A major way in which members of the industry marketed their vast array of white wedding goods to customers of the 1970s was through bridal fairs—such as the Madison Square Garden event invaded by feminist protesters—which allowed consumers to inspect numerous wares from a variety of sources.

Dozens of booths filled with wedding supplies seemingly mocked the fact that the nation faced a period of economic turmoil in the 1970s. The world of the bridal fair also appeared to scoff at the nation's rising divorce and cohabitation rates, its changing labor force, and its evolving notions about the appropriate roles for husband and wife. In fact, however, bridal fair participants were not oblivious to the realities of life in 1970s America. Brides and grooms of the period largely remained adherents to the kind of wedding celebrations they had known since child-

FIGURE 1.7. *Although they were members of the 1970s counterculture, this young couple donned formal attire and participated in all the conventional white-wedding rituals, including posing with the minister and marriage license . . .*

hood, but evidence showed that the meanings they attached to marriage and the commercialized white wedding had begun to change.

A key influence in young people's modified view of marital relationships in the 1970s turned out to be their own parents. These were the same middle-aged people who urged their offspring to follow their lead and get married in white-wedding ceremonies. Parents of middle-class brides and grooms nevertheless also played a part in encouraging their children to view marital roles in ways that differed from their own youthful outlooks. These men and women had followed the strict gender-role prescriptions of the early postwar years but were ultimately disappointed with the results. Mothers particularly wanted their daughters to learn from their own mistakes and thus encouraged them to combine marriage, motherhood, and employment. One woman who did not want her daughter to "end up" like she had summarized the position of many others who had married in the early postwar era: "I think everybody should

FIGURE 1.8.
... *cutting into a multi-tiered cake* ...

FIGURE 1.9 ... *and sitting down to a formal banquet. (Author's collection)*

have something besides another person. In other words, I made another person my career, which is very wrong. . . . I always should have had something that was just me and not completely wrapped my entire life up in a man." Like many other women of her age and class, this woman now believed the pathway to stability and self-fulfillment lay in combining workplace and domestic activities.[46]

Along with their words, middle-aged mothers of the 1970s used their actions to encourage daughters to adopt a dual married woman/working woman identity. The decade witnessed a continuing rise not only in the nation's general divorce rate but in the middle-aged divorce rate as well. This situation caused many women in their middle years to seek out new educational and job opportunities in order to become self-supporting. The period also saw a significant reentry into college and the workplace of middle-aged women whose marriages remained intact. With their children now grown, women who had put their working lives on hold early in their marriages now sought employment in midlife. These plans for middle-aged reemployment contributed significantly to a growing interest in job reentry among all American homemakers. In 1957 only 16 percent of American housewives held ambitions for reemployment, but a 1976 survey of full-time housewives indicated that 30 percent ultimately intended to return to paid employment. The desire to go back to work was particularly strong among college-educated women in the 35–54 age range. Whereas in 1957 only 23 percent of middle-aged, college-educated housewives had intended to return to work, by 1976, 50 percent of women in that category held reemployment plans.[47]

The employed mothers of the 1970s offered a different kind of blueprint for life as an adult female. Middle-aged women of the period who combined work and marriage—whether it was a first marriage begun in youth or a subsequent one begun in middle age—signaled to their sons and daughters a new view of married life. These mothers of the Baby Boomers, who had married young and completed their reproduction in the early years of their marriage, now had the second half of their lives to lead and were often doing so within more equitable married relationships. Employed middle-class, middle-aged women who remained married in the 1970s, or who divorced and remarried during this time, found that increased earning power usually translated into increased power and say-so within their marriages. And middle-aged husbands, at the height of their own earning capacity, frequently welcomed the opportunity that a second family income provided to upgrade consumer purchases. Middle-class, dual-income couples who no longer had child-rearing expenses could purchase nicer homes, vacations, and cars. Survey evidence showed that men of this generation also appreciated the fact that their employed wives had become more worldly and interesting spouses. Reflecting back on his role-based expectations of marriage the first time around, a man happy in his second marriage to a successful executive spoke for many members of his generation when he stated, "That [stay-at-home] kind of woman would no longer interest me." Another man noted that his sons were not "stuck with 'the nurturing female image'" that he had harbored as a young man. Instead, he believed the woman his wife had become in middle age was the kind of partner his sons would start a family with: "Their image of a mother is a high-powered woman executive, tough and smart, who knows how to move up in the corporate world. They're used to a mother who travels more than their father, who's out drinking and socializing evenings with her confreres, who never worried about saying, 'I'm coming home late; cook yourselves dinner.'" Men as well as women who married in the immediate postwar years were revising their views on gender roles within marriage and influencing those of the next generation in the process.[48]

Young wives and husbands of the 1970s did not immediately pick up on new parental cues regarding marriage. The decade's earliest brides and grooms had lived their childhoods in the 1950s and 1960s with the idea of the husband as provider and the wife as consumer, and they entered marriage with those notions intact. As one young wife of the period phrased it, "Here I was with the thought that I was going to obviously get married and have children at a young age and do all those nice things that my mother did." The realities of middle-class life in the 1970s, however, quickly transformed expectations and behavior within these marriages and made these couples more open to their parents' modified gender role signals. In order for these couples to achieve the middle-class standard of living they desired and were used to, both husband and wife had to earn salaries.[49]

Whether or not they themselves were enthusiastic adherents of early 1970s feminism, young wives were able to take advantage of new job and educational opportunities that feminist reformers procured through Title VII of the Civil Rights Act of 1964 and Title IX of the Higher Education Act of 1972. In a classic case of ideology following reality, they and their husbands had to rethink marital gender roles after the fact. With both partners working in time- and energy-consuming positions outside the home, husbands of necessity took on some of the household duties. As one Chicago husband described housekeeping arrangements within his marriage, "We don't consciously say that we're going to share [the housework], but it just turns out with both people working you can't have one do everything. If one of us were relying on the other to fix meals, we'd both starve." Middle-class couples found that the husband-provider/wife-consumer model of marriage that they had grown up with in the 1950s ultimately did not have practical application in the 1970s.[50]

In contrast to their older siblings, younger Baby Boomers—those who were born after the boom reached its peak in 1957—began to rethink traditional marital roles even before they entered marriage, in part as a result of the words and examples of their own parents. Younger boomers began marrying at the end of the 1970s, and their awareness of the era's rising divorce rate and its expanding lifestyle options significantly informed their attitudes by the time they wed. Typically, these couples knew the potential perils of marriage but believed that they could "beat the odds." In comparison to their parents, whom they believed had been subject to "compulsory marriage" back in the 1940s and 1950s, these brides and grooms reasoned that they were thoughtfully choosing marriage over the other lifestyle options available to them, such as serial monogamy, long-term nonmarital cohabitation, or remaining single.[51]

In comparing their marriages to those of their parents, younger middle-class Baby Boomers believed that their unions demonstrated a greater level of equality between husbands and wives from the very beginning. In fact, for a significant number of these couples, the less "gendered" nature of their marriages accounted for their confidence that they would beat the odds. Their recipe for marital success was a relationship that allowed its partners a certain level of freedom to explore varied roles and responsibilities both inside and outside the couple's shared living space. In commenting on the dynamics of her marriage, one Baby Boomer wife noted: "There's no really set role of who does what, you know, everyone does everything." For this woman and many other members of her class and age group, marriage—ideally and practically—was no longer a role-based institution.[52]

Greater equity between husbands and wives had become the marital ideal by the end of the 1970s. In reality, middle-class Baby Boomer wives continued to do a greater share of the housework than their husbands—a fact they shared with wives in over 80 percent of dual-earner marriages nationwide—and they continued to earn a lesser average salary than their husbands. These brides and grooms nevertheless still reported working toward the goal of gender equality within marriage. For them, the gender rules that had characterized the early years of their parents' marriages no longer applied. While a minority of Baby Boomers—such as some members of the Christian Right—continued to subscribe to the old rules of patriarchal marriage, most couples now publicly voiced the desire for more equitable relationships. Those 1970s couples who married in white-wedding ceremonies, which accounted for at least 75 percent of all couples who married in the decade, did not necessarily view the ritual in the same way that their parents had a generation earlier. For young women in particular, the apparently dependent role that the bride played in the conventional ceremony as she passed from the arm of her father to the arm of her groom was not automatically the one she would play in her marriage.[53]

The 1970s witnessed change not only in the ways young adults thought about marriage and gender roles but also in the ways boys and girls learned to become men and women. Acknowledging the growing participation of women in the arena of paid employment, critics of the American educational system charged that schools were not doing enough to prepare female students for the likelihood that they would grow up to become members of the American workforce. Educational and feminist reformers worked throughout the decade to persuade schools to abandon textbooks that portrayed men and women in limited, stereotyped roles and to discontinue tracking boys and girls into courses that similarly reflected traditional gender role expectations, such as all-male industrial arts classes and all-female home economics classes. Reformers also persuaded guidance counselors to broaden the range of courses and future job possibilities that they advised female students to consider. At the same time that American schools labored to instill in girls a more work-oriented personal identity, many of the nation's voluntary youth organizations also pursued this goal. For example, in the 1970s the venerable Girl Scouts organization dropped its heavy emphasis on homemaking skills and instead adopted a program that stressed a greater diversity of activities.[54]

As a result of these changes in socialization, girls growing up in the 1970s began to think of their futures in a new way. The results of a 1980 random survey of girls ages thirteen through nineteen showed that nearly 75 percent of those not yet in college planned to attend an institution of higher learning, and their main reason for doing so was to prepare for a high-paying job. Giving voice to the new feminine ideal, less than 10 percent of the survey participants said that they looked forward to college in order to meet a man, and only 1 percent admitted that they were going to college as the result of parental pressure. These teenagers expressed the belief that a single wage-earner could not sufficiently support a growing family, so most of them planned to combine child rearing and employment in their adult years. In summarizing the survey's findings, a writer for *Seventeen* magazine noted, "The surveyed girls are not Susy-Stay-at-Homes: 87 percent say they will probably work after marriage, and well over half plan to work after having children." The nation's future brides were no longer looking ahead to an adulthood in which they would accept a primarily home-centered persona.[55]

The changing attitudes of girls during this period, along with federally mandated educational and workplace reforms, ensured that a greater proportion of young people who trained for middle-class professions in the 1970s and 1980s would be women. For example, in 1969 only 9 percent of first-year medical students were women, but that proportion rose to 37 percent by 1987. Women took home 8 percent of the law degrees awarded in 1973 but earned 36 percent of the nation's law degrees a decade later. And whereas only 4.9 percent of MBA graduates in 1973 were female, that figure rose to 28.9 percent by 1983.[56]

To sociologist Rosanna Hertz and other observers of the period, young women were adopting a new version of the marriage fairy tale.

Commenting on the youth of the late 1970s and early 1980s, Hertz noted: "Earlier generations of young girls grew up on Cinderella and Snow White, dreaming of princes to carry them off so they too could live happily ever after. Young girls today dream a different plot. There is still the prince, but happily-ever-after now includes a career." Young women of the late twentieth century aspired to a life that ideally included a workplace identity.[57]

Young men of the period also expressed a greater desire to marry partners who were significant wage earners. By the mid-1980s, surveys of male college students showed near unanimity in their desire to marry wage-earning wives. In order to afford the upper-middle-class lifestyle that most college students aspired to, a two-wage family was virtually mandatory. With feminist reforms now opening up high-paying jobs to women, both spouses could benefit materially by the wife's employment. For men, they could expand the parameters of their consumerist lifestyle and unburden themselves of the sole support of a middle-class household. For women, they too could now achieve middle-class status through their own employment efforts rather than betting on the chance of marriage to a good provider. Nevertheless, those individuals who most sought and benefited from the dual wage-earner ideal were members of the upper middle class. As more and more women entered medical, law, and business schools in the 1970s and 1980s, they met and married the male colleagues that they found at those locations. For the majority of the nation's working women, who still labored in female-dominated clerical and service positions, the kind of marriage and material success touted as the new national ideal did not exist.[58]

In other words, the group of consumers whose business the wedding industry most depended on was the very segment of the population that was most thoroughly revising its notions about the ideal marriage: upwardly mobile members of the middle class. In the 1970s and 1980s wealthy couples could still maintain a life of material comfort on a one-income marriage. And lower-middle-class and working-class couples continued to rely, as they often had before, on two incomes just to afford the basics of postwar consumer society. Young professional couples of the period, though, were charting novel territory. As they had for a quarter century, middle-class and upper-middle-class brides and grooms continued to be the nation's most faithful purchasers of the accouterments of a formal white wedding. The paraphernalia and practices of the white wedding, however, no longer symbolized for these couples what they had for their parents. The ceremony no longer necessarily inaugurated the marital relationship of a senior wage-earning partner and a junior housekeeping partner. The wedding industry continued primarily to pitch its wares to members of the white, straight, upwardly mobile middle class, but the greater flexibility of spouses' roles within middle-class marriage and the attendant reinterpretation of the white wedding's potential meaning prompted men and women who resided far outside Caucasian Middle America to become industry patrons. Couples who did not come from a tradition in which one member identified largely as the financial provider and the other as the home-oriented consumer began to purchase the trappings of the formal white wedding in greater numbers. For instance, economic realities and black popular culture had taught African American Baby Boomers that men and women shared wage-earning responsibility within marriage and that even the middle-class black wife should not necessarily aspire to full-time homemaking. With the white-wedding ceremony no longer literally serving as a symbol of role-based marriage, and with more blacks now able to afford a professionally produced celebration, the elaborate, capital-intensive wedding gained a greater following among the nation's African American population.[59]

The white wedding was not a new phenomenon for African Americans; numerous elite and upper-middle-class urban blacks had been hosting such events since the late nineteenth century. But the significant growth of the black middle class that resulted from desegregation laws and affirmative action policies, and the decoupling of the white-wedding ceremony from the notion of a role-based marriage, meant that more and more African Americans could now afford and were opting to hold such celebrations. At a time when most members of American society still automatically associated African Americans with the poor or working classes, members of the black middle class often worked diligently to display the indicators of middle-class status, and the white wedding was one such hallmark. Conspicuous consumption of this sort enabled African Americans to "separate themselves from a 'degraded past.'"[60]

Wedding business persons were quick to note the willingness of middle-class African Americans to spend freely on wedding celebrations in the 1970s. At a time when identity politics was leading to greater market segmentation, wedding professionals began specifically targeting black consumers. Barbara Boggs, a professional wedding consultant who ran a Washington, D.C.–based business called Wonderful Weddings, noted that although white families might be scaling back a bit on weddings as a result of recession conditions, African American families were not. As she told an interviewer in 1973, "The big money these days is being spent on black middle-class affairs. . . . Among . . . blacks . . . we see more and more tented weddings for five hundred. For them, it's the period of social arrival." The growing African American market for formal weddings, however, not only provided white business people like Boggs with an expanded customer base but also gave African American entrepreneurs some new opportunities. For example, influenced by the Black Power movement of the era, designers Renee and Larry Greer opened a shop in New York City called the Where Did You Get That At Boutique, which sold Afrocentric wedding apparel. In Chicago, members of the Institute of Positive Education, an organization that created alternatives to Euro-American rituals for members of the black community, designed a wedding ceremony performed in both Swahili and English that blended elements of African and Western traditions and incorporated the talents of local black designers to create African-inspired wedding garb.[61]

Although the era witnessed the invention of some alternative rituals to the Euro-American nuptial celebration, most African American couples who wed in a formal ceremony in the 1970s followed the dominant integrationist ethos of the era and adopted the standard elements of the middle-class, commercially produced wedding. Throughout the decade, black couples and white couples largely purchased identical goods and services. As journalist Marcia Seligson noted at the time, "Black kids—whatever their personal goals and politics—do not, statistically, don the dashikis and bone up on African tribal rites for their nuptials; they rent a catering hall, spread out the roast turkey and potato salad and the band plays 'Theme from Dr. Zhivago.'" Regardless of a couple's cultural background and gender politics, the tangible markers of the formal white wedding largely remained in place. Wedding clothing, food, and music still generally conformed to the patterns that the white middle class had established in the early postwar period, and even the black press played a role in perpetuating these standards. The adjectives and imagery of the wedding features frequently published in *Essence*, the leading black women's magazine, paralleled those found in *Bride's* or *Modern Bride* and urged the African American bride to think of herself as a consumer-Cinderella: "It's your show and you're the potential superstar. . . . You ask yourself: What is my lifelong wedding fantasy?"[62]

Another group of Americans who expanded their presence as wedding consumers in the 1970s was the gay and lesbian community. In contrast to its developing efforts to woo black customers, the established wedding industry did not yet attempt to acquire the patronage of gays and lesbians. Nevertheless, when gay customers resisted police harassment at New York's Stonewall Inn bar in 1969, they launched a high-profile gay and lesbian liberation movement that spurred some same-sex couples to announce their partnerships in public commitment ceremonies. Once again the strength of the postwar white wedding ideal reared its head, as, lacking any other paradigm for such occasions, gay and lesbian couples of the 1970s modeled their commitment rituals on the white, middle-class, heterosexual wedding ceremonies they had known since childhood. One popular location for such celebrations was Los Angeles's Metropolitan Community Church, where gay and lesbian couples who had acquired floral bouquets, wedding gowns, and tuxedos from the usual wedding industry sources repeated their vows in front of family and friends. Although the wedding industry had not solicited their business, these couples nevertheless contributed their dollars to industry coffers.[63]

The experiences of the 1970s demonstrated that the commercialized white wedding had become such a central feature of American society that it could successfully overwhelm all challenges in its path. Rather than defeat it, traditional outsiders in American culture—African Americans, gays and lesbians, and bohemians—largely adopted it as their own. A minority of black couples constructed their own dashikis and recited vows in Swahili, but many more members of the African American middle class paid for white gowns, tails, and banquet halls. A few hippie-era youths wore jeans and wrote their own ceremonies, but many more young people bought muslin peasant dresses at stores that featured counterculture-inspired fashions, such as a New York emporium called the Barefoot Bride, or purchased more conventional frocks at traditional locations. Within the gay and lesbian community, some couples purchased elaborate bouquets and wedding banquets and marched down the aisle in white gowns or rented tuxedos. Although the social and political forces of the 1970s had altered some of the details of the wedding business, its basic parameters remained intact, and its product—the commercialized white wedding—continued to attract new adherents as the nation moved into the 1980s.[64]

But the wedding industry of the 1980s would have to modify some of its practices in order to retain its most prized consumers—young heterosexual upper-middle-class women. Many women in this category were now beginning to delay marriage until their middle or late twenties in order to prepare for and establish themselves in demanding long-term careers. The wedding industry thus had to adjust its marketing campaigns and products to the desires of increasingly older brides. The industry also had to come to terms in the 1980s with the continuing impact of Baby Boom consumers. The first half of the 1980s marked the entrance into the marriage market of the youngest members of the Baby Boom generation. In fact, 1984 marked a high point for members of the bridal trade; they had the opportunity to sell their wares to approximately 2.5 million brides.[65]

The record number of brides who purchased wedding industry products in 1984, a number of high-profile celebrity weddings in the 1980s, and a mid-decade upswing in the U.S. economy caused more businesspeople to enter the bridal trade and promote the concept of formal weddings. In 1986 fewer than fifty wedding-gown manufacturing companies existed in the United States; within the next decade, that number quadrupled. The number of bridal-wear retailers doubled in that same time period, from approximately 3,500 wedding apparel shops across the country in 1986 to about 7,000 a decade later. Annette Gerhart, owner of a Hershey, Pennsylvania, bridal boutique known appropriately as the Cinderella Shoppe, succinctly summed up the reason behind expansion of the bridal-wear business in the 1980s: "Everyone just said, 'Let's jump on this gravy train.'" The 1980s thus saw dramatic expansion of the wedding industry and increased consumer adherence to the industry message that bigger weddings were better weddings.[66]

Complicating the chances of success for newcomers to the bridal-wear trade and other wedding businesses was the simple fact that by the late 1980s, supply was exceeding demand. In 1985 the annual number of weddings in the United States began to decline as the last of the Baby Boomers had first weddings and then moved on to other stages in the life cycle. From a peak of 2.5 million weddings in 1984, the number declined within nine years to only 2.3 million new marriages a year—the lowest number in nearly a twenty-year period. In the overextended wedding gown business, that meant each of the nation's bridal wear manufacturers and retailers had to work ever more diligently to capture business.[67]

The key to staying in business in the 1980s bridal-wear trade became to sell formal attire to women who had not previously been inclined to buy such apparel. That meant capturing the business of women who were not the young, relatively prosperous bridal magazine readers that made up the industry's chief target market. Retailers now had to begin aggressively selling their wares to less affluent women, older brides, and those who were not marrying for the first time. In a business where marketing had always been central to the process, promotional strategies became even more important. In such a specialized market, however, the usual schemes for pushing sales would not work. As one industry insider noted, "No one says, 'Honey, the Bridal Boutique is having a sale—let's get married.'" Instead, the industry had to attempt to sell a formal white gown to every woman who was already planning to get married.[68]

Marketing schemes of the period included not only the expansion of long-existing strategies but also the creation of some controversial new approaches to selling wedding products. The already hefty number of advertising pages in the existing bridal magazines became even more formidable until, in the words of one industry veteran, the typical bridal magazine began to look "like a phone book." A single bridal gown manufacturer might have forty or fifty pages of advertising in just one issue of a given magazine; it was a costly investment, but a company had to familiarize the consumer with its name and product. At the same time, bridal magazines began to ease up on their advice that only first weddings should be large, expensive affairs, opening the way for what the industry was now calling "encore brides" to become second- or third-time consumers of formal wedding gowns and bridesmaid dresses.[69]

In a world where glamour, personal attention, and custom fittings had been the norm, the late 1980s also witnessed a more downscale approach to the selling and buying of wedding gowns. An increasing number of retailers sold gowns right off the rack and in sparsely appointed surroundings that allowed low overhead costs. To traditionalists in the bridal-wear trade, these new discount merchants were anathema. In a business that had generally prided itself on attention to detail and the careful fitting of each gown to each bride, the ready-to-wear mentality of the bridal discount houses threatened the marketing strategies of more traditional stores that promoted their ability to pamper brides in an elegant atmosphere. Nevertheless, the lack of expense, muss, and fuss entailed in buying a dress at a discount house certainly appealed to many of the new customers that the bridal-wear industry was trying to attract. For the working-class woman on a very limited budget, the older career woman whose professional life allowed her little time for shopping, or the divorcee busy juggling work and childcare, a discount venue might be the ideal place to purchase a wedding gown.[70]

Doing their part to attract new customers to the purchase of formal wedding gowns, bridal-wear manufacturers also attempted beginning in the late 1980s to respond better to the needs of women who fell outside the industry's traditional target market. In an effort to reach brides who were not the aerobicized 20-year-olds typically portrayed in the bridal magazines, manufacturers began producing more plus-sized gowns. Most of these frocks, however, continued to sport an abundance of lace, bows, and flounces. At a time when women's median age at first marriage had risen to 23.2 years and the average age of all American brides (first and multiple marriages combined) was 28.6 years, the bride over the age of 25 or 30 who wanted to dress her age still had difficulty finding appropriate formal wedding attire.[71]

In neglecting to focus more attention on the creation of designs that would appeal to the older bride, the bridal-wear business was in danger of losing its most potentially lucrative market segment—the growing number of upwardly mobile professional women who delayed marriage

in order to establish their careers. Women in this category had a significant amount of disposable income and were becoming aware that bridal
magazines and other industry sources now touted the formal wedding as
appropriate for older first-time or "encore" brides. One of the first people to realize that the product gap needed to be filled was Ralph Lauren
designer Vera Wang, who as a 40-year-old first-time bride in 1989 could
not buy appropriate attire for her posh 400-guest wedding. (She ended
up with a $10,000 custom-made gown.) A year later, with financial back-
ing from her wealthy father, she opened the Vera Wang Bridal House,
Ltd. Wang dropped the bows and ruffles and focused instead on sensu-
ous simplicity in her bridal gown designs. As Wang herself explained, "I
felt the market was trapped in a certain kind of formula—a corded-lace
bodice with a shantung skirt and lace trim on the bottom. And if they
could load it with crystals, bows, beads and flowers, they did. I brought
a sense of modernity." At a time when the nation's growing income gap
caused many businesses to abandon the working and middle classes in
favor of an upscale market, Wang intended her gowns for the cosmo-
politan bride with money to spare. But her designs nevertheless helped
make sleeker gowns the dominant trend in bridal fashions for all pocketbooks and regions of the country.[72]

Women of all backgrounds now seemed drawn to elaborate weddings
and willing to pay top dollar for them. In the early 1990s, at the time of yet
another economic recession, polling of more than 4 million *Bride's* readers revealed that they and their families and fiancés were spending an
average $16,144 on their wedding celebrations and engagement and hon-
eymoon expenses. That *Bride's* readers and others continued to enjoy
formal, commercially produced weddings during a recession came as no
surprise to Eileen Monaghan, vice president of the Association of Bridal
Consultants, based in New Milford, Connecticut. She observed that
while weddings were not entirely recession-proof, they were "recession-
resistant." As always, the key to success in the wedding business remained marketing. While in flusher times wedding professionals had
touted their services as convenient for the harried bride who wanted a
"dream wedding," they now emphasized that they were at the bride's
disposal to help her stay "on budget" in her wedding plans. For instance,

New York floral designer Valorie Hart reported that her first question to bridal customers in the 1980s had been "What is your fantasy?" Now in the early 1990s it was "What is your budget?"[73]

Continued efforts to woo black bridal customers also contributed to the health of the 1990s wedding industry. In January 1992, Howard University graduate Andrew Sawyer introduced *Brides Today*, the first national magazine targeted specifically to the black bride. Like other bridal magazines, a significant portion of Sawyer's venture—45 percent—was devoted to bridal fashion and accessory layouts. But recognizing that existing bridal magazines focused comparatively little attention on the black bride, the publisher announced that his new periodical would also present articles on how to incorporate African-inspired fashions, customs, and traditions into African American wedding celebrations. A year after Sawyer announced his publication, Harriette Cole, *Essence* magazine's fashion editor, published *Jumping the Broom*, the first comprehensive wedding advice book for African American brides. Taking her title from the antebellum slave custom of a couple jumping over a broom at the end of their wedding ceremony—a practice the popular television miniseries *Roots* helped reintroduce in the late 1970s—Cole's book, like Sawyer's magazine, included advice on how to plan a white wedding that included references to traditional African American culture. Her wedding planner included information on how to go about finding and patronizing black wedding professionals, and it concluded with a six-page "Resource Guide" that provided contact information for clothiers, jewelers, caterers, wedding consultants, stationers, musicians, gift shops, and florists that specialized in goods and services for African American weddings. Cole also provided information on how readers might contact the Washington, D.C.–based Black Bridal Expo, Inc., an organization of black wedding professionals that conducted wedding fashion and trade shows around the country.[74]

The 1990s also witnessed growth and change in the world of same-sex weddings. While same-sex marriages still did not have legal standing in the United States, more gay and lesbian couples than ever before were choosing to make public declarations of their relationships in ceremonies involving family and friends. While not all same-sex couples saw such rituals as desirable, a larger segment of the gay and lesbian community participated in these events and pushed for reforms that would give same-sex unions comparable legal standing with heterosexual marriages. Even some activists who had once decried marriage as an innately sexist and heterosexist institution now saw gay and lesbian marriage as a means to counteract high-profile attacks on same-sex relationships by the Christian Right, which frequently characterized gays and lesbians as promiscuous and unable to provide stable households for children. Some feminist and gay/lesbian legal theorists now championed legalized same-sex marriage as a development that could once and for all dismantle the traditional sexism of heterosexual marriage because same-sex unions would have "enormous potential to destabilize the gendered definition of marriage for everyone." Such legal scholars also reasoned that if same-sex couples could profit from the various perquisites of legal marriage—such as next-of-kin benefits and privileges—they could then also take advantage of the legal and emotional supports that went along with the formal, legal dissolution of a marriage. In the words of one gay lawyer, "I used to say, 'Why do we want to get married? It doesn't work for straight people.' But now I say we should care: They have the privilege of divorce and we don't. We're left out there to twirl around in pain." With increasing acceptance of marriage within their ranks and with a higher average income than the population in general, lesbians and gays were financially capable of supporting their own small-scale wedding industry, which included a growing how-to literature that provided ideological underpinnings for same-sex ceremonies. For example, a couple's vows might not only reflect their commitment to one another but also their solidarity with the larger gay and lesbian community.[75]

Even with the greater acceptance in the 1990s of public commitment celebrations among members of their community, most gay and lesbian couples did not avail themselves of formal ceremonies to acknowledge the creation or continuation of long-term relationships. Same-sex weddings, however, did achieve a higher profile in American popular culture. In 1994 television's first gay wedding occurred when a tuxedoed male couple in fictional Cicely, Alaska, married amidst dozens of hothouse flowers in an episode of *Northern Exposure*. And on a 1996 episode of the hit situation comedy *Friends*, one of the main characters attended his ex-wife's "marriage" to another woman. In an instance of stunt casting, the episode even featured real-life lesbian activist Candace Gingrich, the half-sister of conservative Speaker of the House Newt Gingrich, in the role of the officiant who presided over the white-wedding ceremony.[76]

Although same-sex ceremonies may have acquired greater visibility as fictional entertainment, in real life the wedding industry establishment still focused its sights on heterosexual couples and did not go out looking for gay and lesbian customers. After all, the Cinderella story that was the industry's major marketing theme was a fantasy firmly rooted in heterosexual romance. As the 1990s proceeded, most of the prescriptive literature, retail establishments, and popular culture cues devoted to wedding ceremonies continued to function alongside the nation's marriage laws in maintaining heterosexual privilege. A few months after the *Friends* episode aired, the U.S. Congress overwhelmingly passed the Defense of Marriage Act, which defined marriage exclusively as "a legal union between one man and one woman." When the legislation reached his desk, President Bill Clinton, who had run for office as a gay-friendly candidate, quickly signed it into law.[77]

As the twentieth century neared its end, the success of the national wedding industry still relied on one major premise: convincing women that the Cinderella fantasy was theirs for the buying. Continuing trends begun in the 1970s and 1980s, the typical wedding industry customer of the 1990s was older than her counterpart of the first postwar generation. By the early 1990s, the median first-time marriage age for American women had risen to 23.9 years. As a bride with more maturity, the prototypical bride of the 1990s did not want—in the words of an industry old-timer—a wedding dress covered in "froufrou." She instead desired the sophisticated, updated version of the princess look that Vera Wang and less pricey wedding gown creators provided. In a 1996 interview at the upscale Suky Rosen bridal shop in Philadelphia, the store's bridal buyer commented, "We never see a 21-year-old bride anymore." Instead, the store regularly attracted women in the 28- to 32-year-old age range. These were women who had established careers, traveled, finished their college educations, perhaps earned advanced degrees, and known their fiancés for several years. The older, more worldly bride, however, was not simply the product of a well-heeled urban environment. For instance, at Hope's Bridal Boutique, in the middle of an Iowa cornfield, proprietor

Diane Niebuhr noted that most of her customers were several years out of school and had already established their jobs or careers. In her words, "We don't have a lot of 20-year-old brides anymore." Nevertheless, when the older bride of the 1990s walked through the door of the bridal shop, she still expected to find a dress that would transform her from an ordinary citizen into honorary royalty.[78]

The bride of the late twentieth century was a different Cinderella from the one who had fantasized about fairy princess dresses a generation earlier. In many ways, she was actually a throwback to the more assertive Cinderella who existed before her domestication in late nineteenth-century picture books and twentieth-century film treatments. As folklorists have noted, in the versions of the Cinderella story told and written prior to the late Victorian era, the protagonist was a young woman actively involved in her own transformation from house servant to princess. She went looking for her own magical tokens, invoked her own spells, or, at the very least, advised the fairy godmother on how to go about converting a ragged girl into a beautiful lady. Brides of the 1990s reclaimed that sense of agency, but they used their own purchasing power—rather than magical amulets or incantations—to effect the transformation from ordinary woman to princess bride.[79]

In the waning years of the 1990s, the Roper Organization conducted a survey that found that women who were planning a formal wedding were accomplished career women. The average age of survey respondents was 26, and 65 percent of these women were college graduates. Respondents to the poll in fact were 20 percent more likely than their fiancés to have attended college or graduate school. Seventy-two percent of respondents worked full time, with 41 percent of them earning as much or more than their husbands-to-be. Eighty-four percent said that they never wanted to be financially dependent, and almost a third reported that they would maintain their own separate bank accounts after marriage. Looking at the poll's results, Nina Lawrence, the publisher of *Modern Bride* and the person who had commissioned the survey, noted that women marrying in the late 1990s were more affluent than the brides of previous years because they had developed careers and significant earning power. Thus, when it came time for these women to organize their weddings, they felt that they deserved "the best of everything."[80]

With numerous etiquette books now telling engaged couples that they should feel free to pay for their own wedding celebrations rather than rely strictly on funds from the bride's family, many financially secure brides wanted to spend their own abundant resources on the best weddings that money could buy. These women were not necessarily from wealthy families but were at least at a point in their lives when they had access to a significant amount of disposable income—before mortgage payments, child-rearing expenses, and other obligations of married life were upon them. If they chose to spend money on themselves by purchasing an elaborate wedding, the industry was willing to oblige.[81]

For this generation of affluent, educated "have-it-all" women, when it came to weddings, "the best of everything" still meant the Cinderella fantasy. And women of the late 1990s expended a great deal of time and effort in pursuit of that identity. After trying on and rejecting fifty-nine different dresses at the annual bridal gown sale at Filene's Basement in Boston, one hard-to-please bride of the period told a reporter exactly what she was looking for in a bridal dress: "I want the fairy tale." As the 1990s came to an end, most American brides still wanted the fairy tale—not only in terms of their wedding-day wardrobe but in reference to all other aspects of the nuptial celebration. They wanted to travel by limousine (a modern-day version of Cinderella's ornate coach), to surround themselves with fragrant flowers, and to be feted by hundreds of guests at an elaborate party. Although men had increasingly joined women in other family-oriented shopping, organizing and shopping for the wedding festivities remained a largely female pursuit. The bride was the powerful, knowledgeable purchaser who sought counsel not from her groom but from female friends and relatives and the (often female) wedding professionals. Whereas men considered their relatively limited wedding shopping a chore, women saw their more extensive shopping as a largely pleasurable activity that would yield storybook results.[82]

Among the many sources that promoted this version of the late-century wedding was the popular "Vows" feature that began appearing in both the local and national editions of the Sunday *New York Times* in 1992. Located in "Sunday Styles," a section of the paper intended primarily for a female audience, writer Lois Smith Brady's weekly story described a real-life recent courtship and wedding. Unposed documentary-style photographs of the couple's ceremony or reception illustrated each story and created the impression that readers were receiving an intimate look at a stranger's wedding. Another prominent feature of each "Vows" profile was Brady's background story about the bride and groom, including information about their education and employment. And since most of the weddings Brady covered were upscale affairs, degrees were often from Ivy League schools and the jobs prestigious ones. The most prominent feature of each "Vows" story, however, was its love-conquers-all narrative. Regardless of a couple's age or whether either had been married before, their story was filled with romantic imagery. In December 1998 Brady detected a castle motif in the decorating scheme of a couple who held their wedding in Philadelphia's Memorial Hall. In Brady's words, the event "definitely" conjured up "a fairy-tale Snow White and Prince Charming feeling." A week later, in describing the wedding that comedienne Joan Rivers organized for her daughter at New York's Plaza Hotel, Brady noted that the celebrity mom purchased 100 white-painted trees and 30,000 white flowers to turn the wedding site into a winter garden scene straight out of *Dr. Zhivago*. Brady let the mother of the bride describe the decorating plan herself: "This wedding is going to be romantic. I want it to be a fairy tale. No reality."[83]

Another "Vows" story concerned a bride who had hopelessly mooned over her future groom at their Michigan prep school. Brady noted that the young woman was an "unassuming, insecure daughter of a steel broker . . . [who] spent many Saturday nights at home, Cinderella-like, sewing her own clothes." In contrast, her future husband, the great-grandson of a famous industrialist and philanthropist, was "flirtatious, dashing, dramatic." According to the bride, he also had "dark brown wavy hair like someone on the cover of a romance novel." Unfortunately, however, he only had eyes for a "Barbie doll" with "flippy hair and frosty lipstick." Many years later, when the bride was studying fashion design in New York and the groom was working in the city as an actor, they met once more, developed a friendship, fell in love, and eventually married in an elaborate church ceremony where the bride wore an "off-white satin wedding dress that . . . shimmered like the polished inside of a conch shell." Brady closed the story by referring to the bride as "a contemporary Cinderella—another talented seamstress and underdog who finally got the guy." Brady's brides were the new Cinderellas—resourceful, well educated, and accomplished women whose talents helped them attract ideal mates and organize storybook weddings.[84]

At the end of the century, this was the image of the American bride that the wedding industry assiduously promoted through an expanding variety of media. From black-and-white print ads in the "Sunday Styles" section to razzle-dazzle Web sites, the savvy Cinderella bride sold all the necessities for an ideal wedding. The 1990s witnessed a proliferation of magazines devoted to apprising brides-to-be of the latest wedding trends, styles, and shopping opportunities. With 700 advertising pages and 405,000 readers per issue by decade's end, *Bride's* remained the nation's most influential bridal magazine, followed by its venerable competitor, *Modern Bride*, which enjoyed a per-issue circulation of 371,294. They had been joined on newsstands by an overwhelming array of newer publications with names like *Elegant Bride* (300,000 readers per issue) and *Bridal Guide* (250,000 readers). For TV-generation brides who would rather follow instructions from the video screen than the printed page, the 1990s also witnessed the release of dozens of instructional videotapes, wherein bridal-wear retailers, caterers, florists, photographers, invitation designers, and others in the wedding business touted their wares and services. By the second half of the decade, computer CDs that presented similar prescriptions were also available. And in the closing years of the decade, the Internet, which was transforming many aspects of American life, also became a major player in the commercialized wedding. Wedding photographers used the new technology to present bridal couples with samples of their work, gift registry services went online, and Web sites appeared where brides could purchase a discount wedding dress or reserve the services of a neighborhood caterer. For many Information Age brides, the ease with which they could learn about and act on available consumer options was a godsend. As one bride preparing to marry in November 1999 put it, "I can't see how you would do it without the Internet. I don't know how my sister did this in 1985." As the century ended, the scope of the ideal wedding was so vast that it entailed the intelligence gathering and planning of a major corporate merger.[85]

It was against this backdrop of constant wedding publicity—and women's positive reaction to it—that the editors of *Ms.* published their special issue on marriage and weddings in 2000. Many veterans of 1970s feminism were frankly puzzled by the situation and voiced their concerns in the magazine. One Baby Boomer explained, "Many young feminists, whatever their orientation, still prize marriage, still seek and idealize a love that will last till death." And these young women frequently chose to celebrate committed relationships in "cream-puff weddings" that featured "lesbians walking down the aisle in two white dresses or two tuxedos" and heterosexual weddings that continued "to come with many of the traditional trappings, no matter how 'liberated' the couple." In response to criticism of their choices, young feminists quoted in *Ms.* said they knew achievement of a successful marriage would be difficult, but they were willing to try. As one young woman admonished Baby Boomer naysayers—in words similar to those Molly Jong-Fast would share with her mother three years later—"Your generation saw a lot of marriages that trapped women. But many of us grew up with divorced parents. So maybe it's one thing we want to do better than you." A new generation of feminists enthusiastically prepared to carry on America's love affair with the white wedding, but in the pages of *Ms.* and elsewhere many second-wave feminists scratched their heads in bewilderment.[86]

Among those who provided a plausible answer was Susan Schnur, a psychologist and rabbi who had officiated at the weddings of more than a hundred couples. Schnur reasoned that contemporary women needed the familiar practices and objects of a white wedding to provide stability as they entered a new and challenging stage of life. In an era when a large proportion of the nation's marriages failed, a woman embarking on a change of marital status in the year 2000 might especially crave the comforting reassurance of established rituals and the public support of numerous wedding guests. Elaborating on Schnur's explanation, a young woman who had recently become engaged hypothesized that "vocal feminists" continued to eye the white wedding "with appreciation" because they viewed it as a female-centered celebration that connected them with previous generations of women. Contemporary brides had grown up with firsthand knowledge that their mothers' weddings did not necessarily culminate in happily-ever-after marriages, so they did not seek their "fairy tales" among members of the Baby Boom generation. Instead, the young woman observed, brides in 2000 spoke of using the white wedding to achieve a greater sense of kinship with their grandmothers.[87]

American women continued to find merit in the elaborate white wedding because it provided them with a sense of stability and continuity. The ritual provided connection to tradition and the "good old days" when their grandmothers formed strong, loving unions with their grandfathers. Many of these grandmothers married in the formative years of the postwar wedding, when a "traditional" celebration was becoming one in which consumers paid professionals to provide abundant floral displays, tables full of food, and factory-produced wedding gowns. In fact, one way in which a year 2000 bride could achieve "a greater sense of family connection" was to restore and wear her grandmother's postwar gown, a process that could cost as much as $4,000. In discussing this increasingly noticeable trend, a professional costume restorer noted that the kind of dresses their grandmothers would have worn—"beautiful romantic 1950s gowns with the portrait necklines and the full skirts and crinolines that flattered the waist"—were particularly popular garments among contemporary brides.[88]

To the bride of 2000, her grandmother's 1950 wedding dress possibly served as a symbol of marriage the way it was "supposed to be." For young women like those quoted in *Ms.*, who believed that the norm for their mothers' generation was separation or divorce, the intact marriages of their grandmothers seemed ideal. While these young women insisted that they did not romanticize marriage for themselves, some of them idealized their grandmothers' unions. A young feminist who felt conflicted about conforming to the white-wedding ideal as she organized her massive summer 2000 celebration found herself longing for the simplicity of weddings and marriage in her grandmother's time, "when there were rules, stability, and well-defined sex roles." Behind the apparently placid postwar marriages of her grandmother's generation, however, lay the bitter truth that many couples had simply stayed married to conform to social standards and had frequently compromised opportunities for individual growth and happiness in the process. Mothers of the Baby Boom generation taught their daughters to learn from their mistakes and not sacrifice their personal identities on the altar of marriage. Daughters of the Baby Boomers often only saw the broken marriages of their parents' generation and did not know that their divorced mothers were acting on feelings and concerns that their grandmothers had also harbored—but had frequently not dared to put into action.[89]

The white wedding that the bride of 2000 organized indeed looked very much like the one her grandmother held fifty years earlier. The major props remained the same, although their symbolic meaning likely altered. In particular, the defining element of a capital-intensive formal wedding, the glamorous white bridal gown, no longer communicated information about the bride's sexual history. Yet, in many ways, women's motivation for donning that gown and showcasing the other elements of a grand formal wedding had not changed. Elaborate wedding celebrations still allowed a woman and her loved ones to advertise material success and to proclaim publicly a change in marital status. In fact, at a time when social mores allowed American women a greater variety of acceptable lifestyles outside the institution of heterosexual marriage, a white wedding could serve a very practical purpose: it alleviated any public ambiguity about the marital status of a woman who had previously cohabited with a partner or sampled other nonmarital living arrangements.

No single influence created and sustained the popularity of the white wedding during the six decades of economic, ideological, and political change that followed World War II. Media and advertising images, parental and peer expectations, and the advice of political pundits and etiquette experts all played a role in shaping the ritual and aiding its adaptation to changing times. Throughout its evolution, however, one characteristic of the white wedding remained intact: its display of family togetherness and material abundance indicated that the bride at its center had achieved "the best of everything." When seven months into her pregnancy Molly Jong-Fast donned the standard white bridal costume and took the arms of both her mother's third and fourth husbands, she announced her conformity to a new feminine ideal. She expected "to have it all": a strong relationship with her family of origin, a comfortable domesticity with her life partner, and an independent identity that found expression in her personal choices. Those choices included early motherhood, a career as an author—and holding an elaborate wedding. In perhaps the ultimate statement of her identity as the new Cinderella who combined domestic and professional ambitions, Jong-Fast even went on to publish several essays about her experiences as a bride and young mother.[90]

For Molly Jong-Fast and many other twenty-first-century brides, formal weddings serve to demonstrate—or, at least, create the illusion of—financial, professional, and social success. Although the ritual no longer symbolizes adherence to the mid-twentieth-century values of premarital virginity and postmarital housewifery, the capital-intensive white wedding remains an event advertising a couple's prosperous status and places a woman indisputably at the center of public celebration and acclaim. In the twenty-first century, such female-focused events are all too rare, and the fact that white weddings allow women this unchallenged starring role also contributes to their continuing popularity. And through the use of photographs, video recordings, and scrapbooks, the formal wedding is a vacation that a woman can take again and again in years to come. For the bride at the beginning of a new century, as for the bride who emerged in the aftermath of a world war, a variety of messages, hopes, and dreams continues to be pinned on her wedding day—even if, in an era when the bridal industry increasingly promotes white weddings for second and third marriages, it might not be her only time to don the fairy princess gown.

CHAPTER 2

LOOK LIKE A PRINCESS

The Wedding Gown

Halfway through *Here Comes the Bride* (2001), a 428-page indictment of marriage and the American wedding industry, feminist author Jaclyn Geller describes infiltrating a Brooklyn bridal salon disguised as a prospective bride. Despite her disdain for the formal white wedding, a glimpse of herself in the salon mirror draped in an Oleg Cassini gown prompts a momentary reassessment of her contempt.

> For a moment I don't recognize myself. I'm a New Yorker with short, spiky brown hair who consistently wears black—but only because there's no darker color. A graduate student and college instructor, I wear pants and sweaters, pantsuits, the occasional skirt if I'm giving a conference paper. No white, no satin, no beading, no long dresses. In this A-line gown, with its long smooth skirt, I look like a different person, the heiress to the throne of a small country, a duchess, or the protagonist of a Harlequin romance novel. I actually think to myself, "I look amazing. I look like a queen. It would be worth getting married just to be seen in this dress for a few hours. I will never take this dress off."[1]

That even a hardened wedding critic like Geller could succumb to the lure of the white wedding dress is an indication of American women's indoctrination into the cult of the princess bride, a process that began in earnest at the end of World War II. For more than sixty years, the constant barrage of images of brides in elaborate, sweeping gowns has not only thoroughly familiarized Americans with the concept of the formal white wedding but also has communicated the idea that the only "real" bride is the one wearing the long white dress produced by bridal-wear manufacturers and sold in bridal salons. Without the gown and head-piece, a genuine wedding celebration simply does not exist. And al-though the wedding industry periodically attempts to popularize bridal finery in colors other than white or ivory—perhaps to cut into the un-profitable practice of brides passing along heirloom gowns to the next generation—those efforts have been largely unsuccessful. It is a *white* wedding dress that stands as the centerpiece of a wedding. The cut, length, and look of that dress determine the level of formality—and thus often the expense—of the entire wedding ceremony. The dress is also how a woman sets herself apart from her wedding guests and attendants and ensures that she will be the center of attention on "her day." One bridal gown designer notes that customers invariably want gowns that make them look like "fairy princesses." Another designer observes that every bride wants to feel "like a star on an MGM set—her dress is the ul-timate costume." Thus the wedding gown has become highly sacralized. Many women fantasize about the "perfect" wedding gown beginning in early girlhood and are apt to recall the experience of finding the "right" dress as a magical process (see Figure 2.1). After the wedding, women often go to great trouble and expense to preserve and store their gowns, even if they never intend to pass their dresses along as heirlooms.[2]

Brides of diverse class and cultural backgrounds and varying political persuasions now take for granted the notion of a white gown worn only on the wedding day. As scholars of consumer behavior note, "the influ-ence of mass culture and/or the desire to be 'bridelike'" lead most Amer-ican brides—as well as many brides elsewhere in the world—to purchase such a garment automatically. But that was not always the case. The gar-ment that names the entire white-wedding ritual only became fashionable when Queen Victoria wore one for her 1840 marriage to Prince Albert. Even then, not all women of fashion followed her lead. Only at the end of the nineteenth century did a white gown become the preferred garment for elite and upper-middle-class brides on both sides of the Atlantic. By this time, popular belief also equated the gown's color with the bride's maidenly status. Whereas earlier in the century brides had often reworn their white gowns, this new symbolism now made them less likely to do

FIGURE 2.1. *In the 1970s the Bride Game helped girls nurture their bridal gown fantasies as players pretended to buy wedding dresses, cakes, rings, and other white-wedding accouterments. (Author's collection)*

so. And since the vast majority of brides could not afford the expense of a shimmering gown worn only once, financially comfortable women remained the primary consumers.[3]

Even those who could afford to hire a dressmaker to create a once-in-a-lifetime gown still had to make a number of shopping trips to a variety of retail venues to procure the other elements of a formal wedding. Creation in the 1930s of specialized "bridal services" in upscale department stores began to ease the well-to-do bride's organization of her wedding celebration and her acquisition of the necessary material goods. Chicago's Carson, Pirie, Scott, and Company claims to have originated this practice in 1935 when it opened a salon where staff members exclusively created and sold bridal clothing and provided other wedding accouterments, but similar facilities surfaced in a number of other high-end, big-city department stores at about the same time. By the late 1930s, for instance, New York's Lord and Taylor store employed a staff of "bridal consultants" who provided brides with their wedding gowns and also helped them procure their wedding flowers, bridesmaids' dresses, bridal trousseaus, and wedding pictures.[4]

Department stores unveiled their new strategies for selling wedding paraphernalia at an inauspicious time. The Great Depression forced most brides and grooms to marry in unostentatious fashion and caused tens of thousands of engaged couples to postpone or cancel their marriages altogether. Their dwindling consumer base prompted the makers and sellers of wedding accouterments to target well-to-do brides more aggressively than ever in an attempt to capture the business of each and every consumer who could still afford an elaborate wedding. The one-stop-shopping system that exclusive department stores provided with their bridal services strategy ensured that they could advise a prosperous bride to purchase a variety of wedding and household items in one place and at one time. The consumer base for such goods and assistance, however, remained necessarily small throughout the Depression and war years of the 1930s and early 1940s.[5]

The notion that every American bride should be "all dressed in white" emerged only with the democratization of the formal wedding gown in the 1940s, when a handful of enterprising individuals established their own independent firms to design and manufacture wedding dresses for a broader range of bridal consumers. The Depression was ending, the United States was on the brink of war, and getting married was becoming the popular and patriotic thing to do when Alfred Piccione established the Philadelphia-based Alfred Angelo company in 1940. Piccione based his new enterprise on smaller-scale operations already in existence in the Italian neighborhoods of several U.S. cities. The best-known of these tiny bridal shops were located in New York City, where immigrant seamstresses custom-made bridal gowns piece by piece, with one woman making the sleeves, another the bodice, a third the skirt, and the trio then assembling the dress. Piccione moved this process into a factory setting to produce custom-fit wedding dresses more quickly, on a larger scale, at less cost. His factory produced several copies of a gown and sold one to each retail client. When a shopper tried on one of the sample gowns at a store and liked it, the store's personnel measured her and ordered a custom-fitted gown. Piccione thus applied an assembly-line approach to the creation of customized, luxurious wedding gowns. This ingenious method of producing and marketing wedding dresses soon came to dominate the bridal-wear industry and enabled its rapid expansion in the years following World War II.[6]

Piccione was not the only innovator at work in the bridal gown trade. In the first half of the 1940s, the Nania family in St. Louis also adapted the practices of the small Italian American bridal shop to create Bridal Originals. And in the decade's second half, Priscilla Kidder, a former department store buyer and bridal consultant, founded a Boston-based business to design, manufacture, and sell wedding gowns using the same principles.[7]

These innovations in the 1940s resulted in the establishment of a truly national bridal-wear business that became the centerpiece of a larger postwar wedding industry. Middle-class women now had access to the custom-fitted luxury that elite women had been enjoying for decades. Brides from coast to coast had access to an identical series of wedding dresses originating from the same few bridal gown factories, albeit feeling custom-made. The people who made and sold these gowns were particularly committed to the postwar expansion of the lavish wedding. While the other entrepreneurs in the wedding business—jewelers, florists, caterers, bakers, photographers, and stationers—were not solely dependent on weddings, the manufacturers of wedding dresses were. They had to ensure that weddings would be a stable industry. The bridal fashion industry could exist only if a significant portion of the nation's middle class believed that spending money on a stylish, custom-fitted, national-brand wedding dress was requisite behavior.

To promote their interests, members of the fledgling bridal-wear industry created a professional organization, the Association of Bridal Manufacturers, which achieved an early victory when it persuaded Congress and the War Production Board to exempt makers of wedding clothes from World War II fabric restrictions. Arguing that the war was being fought to protect American institutions like marriage, the association urged that U.S. weddings be allowed to utilize at least some silk and satin clothing to boost national morale. One association member recalled the wartime crusade:

We concentrated on key congressmen, and told them that they should put pressure on the Administration to release fabric to us for morale purposes. We told them, "American boys are going off to war and what are they fighting for except the privilege of getting married in a traditional way? They're fighting for our way of life, and this is part of our way of life and the government is taking it away."[8]

By invoking "tradition" to justify its exemption from wartime restrictions, the association actually promoted a new cultural norm. The association's wartime argument served two of the chief purposes of an invented tradition: it established the legitimacy of a particular institution, and it socialized the public in the values and conventions of that institution. According to the association's argument, bridal clothing was so meaningful, so integral to cultural values, that its manufacturers should be exempt from the rules that applied to other members of the garment industry. Without a factory-produced bridal gown, a "real" wedding simply could not take place, and the nation's bridal-wear manufacturers made a commitment to the proposition that a "formal wedding . . . [be] within the reach of *every* Bride."[9]

The production method, lobbying organization, and invented tradition that would sustain a national wedding gown industry were all established in wartime, but only postwar conditions allowed the industry to thrive and grow. Increased incomes, pent-up consumer demand, and an end to wartime rationing enabled the dramatic growth of postwar retailing, including the wedding gown trade. The biggest factor in creating widespread consumer demand for wedding gowns, however, was the era's domestic ideology. One groom spoke for other members of his generation when he recalled: "I married marriage. I had been in the service and finally felt that everyone was supposed to get married and settle down and I felt that was my function. . . . I had no roots and in 1946 I felt that was the thing to do." Millions of others also believed getting married was "the thing to do" in 1946, boosting the nation's marriage rate to a record 16.4 per 1,000 population.[10]

Members of the World War II generation were attracted not only to marriage but to jobs in the wedding industry. With a national bridal-wear trade now in place, the popularity of marriage at an all-time high, and domestic-oriented spending on the rise, a growing number of young Americans sought their fortunes in the wedding gown business. Newly discharged from the military, former ladies' ready-to-wear buyer Willie Dolnick became a sales representative for the St. Louis–based Bridal Originals company in 1947. Traveling by train throughout his five-state sales territory, Dolnick transported in burlap bags samples of the six different dress styles manufactured by the young firm. The nation's total advertising expenditures tripled in the decade and a half following the war, and wedding gown companies were among those that spent heavily on advertising. Dolnick recalled that even in the early, small-scale days of the 1940s, bridal wear was a "marketing business." And the chief advertising strategy was to emphasize the wedding gown's special nature: it transformed an ordinary woman into a glamorous princess bride.[11]

With her bridal crown and floor-length gown, a woman looked like the princesses she saw in books and movies. And like them, she now held an exalted position. She was assuming her sanctioned postwar role by becoming a wife. But her costume also yielded significant information about her family of origin. Like the real-life or storybook princess she now resembled, a woman dressed as a formal bride automatically communicated notions about family status and legacy. Her wardrobe advertised that her family could afford the luxury of a white wedding and cared enough about the bride to bestow her one.

Reflecting the unprecedented postwar popularity of marriage and family-oriented spending, department stores with a predominantly middle-class clientele now emulated more elite establishments and organized bridal service sections to aid brides in their quest for the ideal wedding and wedding gown. Philadelphia's Strawbridge and Clothier store provides an excellent case study of the new policies and floor space plans developed in department stores around the country. Founded in 1868, Strawbridge and Clothier opened its new bridal shop in March 1949 staffed by bridal consultants who were "responsible for coordinating the bridal services, managing weddings, and checking on a million and one minute details . . . involved in elaborate wedding preparations." Like other bridal salons of the era, the Strawbridge and Clothier shop was more elaborately furnished and decorated than the store's other departments, creating an atmosphere of elegance where customers could purchase a custom-fit gown and receive other special services.[12]

Although the bridal consultants' main task was to provide the bride with her wedding gown and clothe the other female players in the wedding, the store's management also encouraged the bridal shop staff to engage in "interselling." Bridal consultants accompanied prospective brides to other store departments to expose them to a "threefold must-buy market," encouraging each young woman to buy items for the wedding day, the honeymoon trousseau, and the new home. As they escorted consumers through the store, Strawbridge and Clothier bridal consultants portrayed themselves as helpful and trusted experts who could choose the bridal party wardrobe and honeymoon trousseau, suggest reception menus and entertainment, advise on etiquette, and register the bridal couple for the "most acceptable gifts." The staff of the store's other departments also offered their "free . . . expert advice" to ensure a *"carefree* bride" who avoided disappointment and embarrassing mistakes. Experts were there to help couples formulate the ideal wedding and domestic life. In the home furnishings department, the interior decorator advised the bride on color schemes, and an expert in the engraved stationery department counseled her on the appropriate wording of her invitations and announcements. Marketing strategies like this convinced consumers that the formal wedding and wedding dress were paths to the middle-class ideal. If they could be proper middle-class Americans on their wedding day, they could be so every day.[13]

By the mid-1950s, if sales personnel did their jobs correctly, a department store could encourage a single bride and her entourage to spend $3,300 on its premises. This was at a time when an expensive new car cost $2,730. At Philadelphia's Strawbridge and Clothier, brides purchased trousseau items and registered for shower gifts in the lingerie department; registered for shower and wedding gifts in the linen, silverware, china, and glassware departments; ordered wedding cakes and reception sandwiches from the store's restaurant; procured invitations, announcements, and reception cards from the engraved stationery department; bought flowers from the store's florist; booked honeymoon trips through the store's travel service; purchased suitcases in the luggage department; arranged for wedding portraits at the store's photo studio; made appointments for the bridal party to have their wedding-day hairdos created in the store's beauty salon; purchased household items in the home furnishings and housewares departments; and visited the store's fancy dress department to purchase the bride's trousseau and her mother's wedding day wardrobe. As Strawbridge and Clothier's ambitious interselling agenda indicates, a single wedding had a significant ripple effect throughout the retail economy. The mid-twentieth-century wedding single-handedly enhanced the meaning and importance of the urban department store.[14]

Strawbridge and Clothier attracted the Philadelphia-area bride and her potential $3,300 worth of business via several techniques. To familiarize brides, their mothers, and their bridesmaids with the store's range of goods and services, Strawbridge and Clothier sponsored public fashion revues to showcase gowns advertised in the latest bridal magazines and publicize products associated with domesticity. To ensure a large turn-out, staff from the bridal shop and public relations department appeared on the local *Homemaker's Notebook* television program offering a tantalizing preview of featured products.[15]

In addition to marketing to its middle-class clientele, Strawbridge and Clothier worked to convince its own employees, many of whom came from decidedly working-class backgrounds, to purchase at least a few wedding items from the store. Its employee magazine, *Store Chat*, published elaborate photo layouts of employees wearing the bridal gowns they had purchased at Strawbridge and Clothier. Ads exploited a Cinderella theme, calling on "starry-eyed brides of [the] Store Family" to patronize Strawbridge and Clothier when it came time "to choose the gowns for their day of days." Even with an employees' discount, however, Strawbridge and Clothier wedding goods remained beyond the means of many employees and their families. African American employees, who worked largely in the housekeeping and cafeteria departments, frequently appeared in formal garb in employee magazine wedding announcements but never appeared in layouts that explicitly showcased brides who had purchased their dresses or registered for wedding gifts at Strawbridge and Clothier. While some of the store's African American employees were obviously marrying in white-wedding attire, they were apparently not purchasing that clothing at Strawbridge and Clothier. Whether as the result of expense or of segregation customs, African American members of the "Store Family" seemingly did not shop in the emporium's glamorous bridal salon.[16]

Other components of the postwar wedding-industrial complex continued to aid department stores in using the bridal gown as a magnet to attract customers to additional wedding and household purchases. The January 1962 issue of *Modern Bride* sandwiched numerous pages of promotions for various household goods between its usual wedding fashion layouts. Representatives of the magazine then arranged a series of "bridal forums" at department stores that carried the advertised merchandise, including Strawbridge and Clothier's flagship emporium in Philadelphia and its new suburban branch store in Cherry Hill, New Jersey. In order to ensure that Strawbridge and Clothier received its share of the Philadelphia area's annual $50 million in wedding expenditures, the bridal forums promoted "all of the appurtenances of the wedding itself," including invitations, floral bouquets, jewelry, footwear, intimate apparel, trousseau fashions, wedding gifts, home furnishings, men's wear, and bridesmaids' fashions, gifts, and accessories. After attracting prospective brides and their mothers to its January bridal fashion show, the flagship store then lured them back later with bridal forum speakers. The editor-in-chief of *Modern Bride* delivered information on wedding bills and budgets; a representative of the Crane Paper Company discussed wedding invitations and stationery; a spokeswoman for Cannon Mills lectured on coordinating bath, bedroom, and table linens; *Modern Bride's* travel editor discussed honeymoon travel and wardrobe planning; and Strawbridge and Clothier personnel provided information on how to use the store's bride's shop and bridal service. Other speakers presented lectures entitled "How to Select and Coordinate Your Table Appointments," "Planning and Decorating Your First Home and Kitchen," and "Beauty and the Bride." With similar activities scheduled at the Cherry Hill branch store, the manufacturers, promoters, and retailers of "wedding appurtenances" made sure that Philadelphia-area brides knew where and how to spend their money.[17]

In the 1950s and early 1960s, Strawbridge and Clothier was only one of hundreds of stores around the country that used its bridal salon as the gateway to other departments and purchases. Distinctly middle-class notions of gender and family shaped these department store strategies. When a woman visited the bridal salon and purchased one of the gowns currently in fashion—with its exaggeration of the female silhouette—she confirmed her commitment to the middle-class feminine ideal (Figure 2.2). The garment she would wear on her wedding day advertised her marriage, class status, and—with its emphasis on hips and bust—her potential ability to bear and nurse children. And on her mandatory trek through the entire store to purchase goods for her wedding, the bride viewed the furniture, appliances, and children's clothing she would return to buy as a wife. The department store thus acquainted her with the elements of both the perfect white wedding and the idealized middle-class household.

Purchase of the flowing white gown was not only the first step toward acquiring all the other elements of a formal wedding but was a major step toward becoming an American housewife.[18] As the pivotal enterprise in a growing wedding industry, the modern bridal wear business went to great lengths to ensure that the American bride maintained a sentimental attachment to the special garment that transformed her into the American wife. As was noted earlier, during the war the Association of Bridal Manufacturers fought rationing restrictions to make the long, formal gown synonymous with being a bride, and in the 1950s the industry focused its energies on stamping out the popular midcalf-length wedding ensembles based on Christian Dior's "New Look" for postwar street dresses. With their small waists and full skirts, these dresses were the height of fashion, but—at least according to the bridal-wear industry—they were the wrong length for wedding gowns. And in the early 1960s when these garments followed street-dress trends and their skirts rose to knee-level, the outcry was louder still (Figure 2.3). Arguing that only floor-length gowns were truly "maidenly," bridal-wear manufacturers advised that shorter lengths only be worn for a second or third marriage. Fueling this etiquette was the fact that shorter dresses cost less than floor-length gowns and could be sold in regular dress shops. Members of the industry also feared that women who purchased shorter gowns had less formal weddings with fewer attendants and thus fewer bridesmaid dresses. To their dismay, every time a celebrity like Audrey Hepburn donned a street-length gown,

FIGURE 2.2. *The dress this 19-year-old California bride wore in 1960—with its exaggeration of the female silhouette's bust, waist, and hips—represented the height of bridal fashion. (Author's collection)*

FIGURE 2.3. *Despite bridal industry attempts to maximize profits by promoting more expensive floor-length gowns, wedding frocks that featured mid-calf or knee-length skirts were nevertheless popular with many fashion-conscious brides of the 1950s and early 1960s. Among those who chose such a costume was this 1962 Kansas bride, who poses on the farmhouse porch alongside her similarly clad bridesmaids, her parents, and the family dogs. (Author's collection)*

as Hepburn did both in the film *Funny Face* (1957) and when she married in real life, she ensured that bridal gown manufacturers grudgingly included at least a few such frocks in their collections.[19]

Bridal-wear advertisements publicized the bride in a long white gown surrounded by organdy-clad bridesmaids in a variety of imaginative ways, but one promotional campaign in particular not only provided women around the country with access to the ultimate "fairy princess" gown but also illustrated the complicated inner workings of the wedding wear industry. Bringing together fabric and clothing manufacturers, retailers, and the media to create the notion of obtainable fantasies, the Miss America wedding gown campaign demonstrated the power and scope that the wedding gown industry had achieved by the early 1960s.

It also demonstrated the industry's reliance on—and consumers' positive response to—dominant middle-class gender prescriptions.

The Miss America campaign was part of the postwar attempt by the makers of synthetic fabrics to market their wares as ideal material for wedding dresses. Although chemical and textile companies initiated the large-scale manufacture of synthetic fibers and cloth in the late 1930s, as the war approached they shifted from consumer to military production, concentrating largely on the manufacture of material for parachutes. With the loss of that market in the postwar era, the nation's synthetics manufacturers argued that artificial fabrics made ideal wedding dresses because they were easier to maintain and less expensive than traditional silks, satins, and velvets. Hailing nylon as a "product of chemical research that [had proven] its versatility in scores of life-protecting uses during the war," Du Pont announced that the fiber was now available for "its return to civilian uses." To enhance this announcement, the company exhibited a wedding gown made of Du Pont nylon in the June 1946 issue of *Science Illustrated* and on the cover of the Du Pont company's own employee magazine (Figure 2.4). As the decade progressed, Du Pont continued to promote better wedding dresses through chemistry by advertising nylon fabric as "strong, slow to wrinkle, hard to tear, the last word in wedding gowns!" By the early 1950s, the Celanese Corporation of America likewise promoted synthetic-fabric wedding gowns, advertising its acetate product as "the beauty fiber" and boasting that most of the nation's bridal gowns were now made of it[20] (Figure 2.5).

The Joseph Bancroft and Sons Company, manufacturer of rayon goods marketed under the trade name Ban-Lon, also popularized synthetic wedding gowns. Engaging the services of the Craig Advertising Agency, the Bancroft Company and *Modern Bride* magazine jointly launched an ambitious campaign to sell Ban-Lon wedding gowns as part of their Miss America "dream wedding" sales promotion. The rayon manufacturer and the bridal magazine informed the nation's bridal salons that only two days after her September 1959 crowning, Miss America 1960 would be photographed for *Modern Bride* wearing her "dream" gown of Ban-Lon lace. Each participating store arranged two window displays of the dress and related merchandise and publicized the apparel in local newspaper ads with prominent mention of *Modern Bride*

FIGURE 2.4. *DuPont's postwar campaign to popularize wedding garments made of synthetic fabric paved the way for the elaborate Miss America wedding gown promotion of the early 1960s. (*Du Pont Magazine *cover, June–July 1946, Hagley Museum and Library)*

For beautiful fabrics to live in and
live with—Acetate, the beauty fiber

Do you know why most bridal gowns are made of acetate? Because no other fiber makes fabrics that are quite so lovely, that fall into such fluid lines, or drape with such luxury and elegance.

But glamour isn't the *only* thing you can expect from fabrics made of acetate. You'll find that acetate suits and blouses stay fresh-looking throughout the day, that acetate lingerie washes easily and dries *very* quickly.

You'll find acetate fabrics make handsome draw draperies, practical glass curtains, wonderful

bedroom ensembles, and that acetate is used in the most modern rugs and carpets. *For beautiful fabrics to live in and with,* look for the tag that says "Made of Acetate, the beauty fiber" when you shop.

What is acetate? Acetate is the man-made textile fiber, cellulose acetate, pioneered by Celanese Corporation of America. Acetate has a unique combination of characteristics that make fabrics wonderfully soft and comfortable. You will find acetate fabrics in all kinds of beautiful blouses, suits, lingerie, sportswear, dresses and evening gowns.

**Acetate fabrics look lovely, feel wonderful, drape gracefully, launder easily
—dry quickly, dry-clean perfectly—AND acetate helps wrinkle recovery.**

Celanese CORPORATION OF AMERICA · 180 MADISON AVENUE, NEW YORK 16, N. Y.

135

FIGURE 2.5. *The Celanese Corporation of America touted its synthetic acetate product as the ideal fabric for wedding gowns. (Life, 9 June 1952, p. 135)*

and Ban-Lon. In exchange, each store enjoyed the publicity associated with the Miss America name and earned a listing in *Modern Bride* as its city's exclusive retailer of the Miss America gown. Noting that the Miss America pageant garnered 60 million television viewers and nationwide newspaper headlines the previous year, and forecasting similar media attention in 1959, the brochure promised bridal shop managers that they could "capitalize on this important 1st in bridal promotion by [spotlighting] Miss America's 'dream wedding'" in their stores.[21]

As the creator of Miss America's "dream" dress, the Philadelphia-based Alfred Angelo company's logo was prominently displayed throughout the promotional campaign. The Angelo company's dress became the epitome of bridal fashion. It conformed to New Look dictates and exaggerated the bust, waist, and hips of the female form. It featured a bodice embroidered in seed pearls and a billowing bell skirt covered in Ban-Lon "bridalace" (Figure 2.6). Since the bridal fashion world was making one of its periodic attempts to popularize colored wedding dresses, Angelo produced the dream dress in blush pink and ice blue as well as white. Retailing for about $175 ($1,217 in present currency), the dress cost the stores participating in the Miss America promotion $89.75. As part of their agreement with Ban-Lon and *Modern Bride*, stores pledged they would showcase the pink version of the gown.[22]

Alfred Angelo's creation made its public debut in the holiday edition of *Modern Bride* in November 1959. Pictorials and advertisements throughout the magazine featured Miss America Lynda Lee Mead wearing the pink dress with matching bridal crown and veil. Layouts also featured bridesmaid attire, mother-of-the-bride dresses, and Vassarette and Munsingwear lingerie made of Ban-Lon lace. In a narrative that introduced this sequence of photographs and drawings, the makers of Ban-Lon stressed both the fairy princess aspect and the practicality of artificial fabrics:

Every girl cherishes the dream of a beautiful wedding, the never-to-be-forgotten joy of a day so specially hers. Lovely Lynda Lee Mead, Miss America 1960, dreams of her wedding too. But Lynda Lee is not permitted to marry during her reigning year. She must content herself for now with plans for the future and thoughts of a dream wedding.

"Dream Wedding" for Miss America 1960

FIGURE 2.6. *Miss America 1960 models her Alfred Angelo "dream gown" of Ban-Lon "bridalace." (Hagley Museum and Library)*

. . . True to tradition these dreams include a romantic wedding gown and luxurious trousseau, elegantly enhanced with the beauty of "Ban-Lon" lace. Lynda Lee loves the cloud-soft touch and beautiful, clear patterns of feminine "Ban-Lon" lace. Filmy and fragile looking, it is completely durable and stays lovely looking and easy to care for in the years to come.[23]

The "dream wedding" campaign transformed the fantasy figure of single womanhood—Miss America—into accessible reality for every American Bride. The premise did not overtax the imagination of American consumers. The televised Miss America pageant had for years organized its program to showcase contestants as young women who possessed the appropriate skills to be ideal middle-class wives.[24]

In the two months that followed the campaign's initiation, retailers enthusiastically touted its success. Although it did not yet even have the Miss America dress in stock, the San Francisco Macy's store received seventeen telephone requests for the $175 dress by mid-December 1959—a particularly remarkable occurrence because the store typically sold wedding gowns for under $110. At the end of January, a representative from Pollard's department store in Lowell, Massachusetts, reported that since the gown's debut at the store's January 12 bridal fashion show, customers had purchased sixteen copies of the dress—ten on the evening of the fashion revue. One Newark, New Jersey, emporium sold three dresses within a week of its local fashion show debut. Another retailer told *Modern Bride's* promotion merchandise manager that the Miss America gown contributed to days when the store's bridal sales figures reached $2,000. The Miss America campaign was heralded as a nationwide success, as brides from Paducah, Kentucky, to Riverhead, New York, mailed detailed descriptions of their Ban-Lon wedding gowns to local society page editors, using the preprinted cards provided by the Angelo company with each Miss America gown.[25]

Many factors contributed to the success of the Miss America wedding dress campaign. The garment itself was accessible to the expanding pool of formally clad brides. Made of synthetic fabric that cost much less than natural-fiber silk or satin, it was a gown that more women could afford. The costume's bouffant skirt and abundant decorative flourishes appealed to the era's brides, who fell almost exclusively between the ages of 18 and 24. Just as American marketing and design equated color with modernity, a dress in multiple hues also seemed particularly fashionable. Responding to the color-it-modern message, consumers were beginning to replace black-and-white television sets with color TVs and to discard white kitchen appliances for machines in pink, blue, and yellow. Although most brides of the era still bought white dresses, the pink and blue versions of the Miss America gown may have turned the heads and opened the pocketbooks of women who considered themselves in the vanguard of fashion.[26]

The young woman who modeled the dress epitomized the ideal American woman. Young, virginal, white, middle-class, college-educated, and with a physique and personality pleasing to American men, Miss America 1960 was the ideal unmarried woman who wanted to become a married woman. In her Ban-Lon gown, Miss America was the perfect role model for the burgeoning population of bride-consumers.

In the aftermath of its successful effort, the Bancroft Company and *Modern Bride* joined forces again the following year to create another Miss America "dream wedding" campaign. This time they engaged Priscilla of Boston—a company known for more classic and sophisticated gowns than Alfred Angelo—to manufacture a Ban-Lon gown. At a suggested retail price of $245 ($1,675 in current dollars), it cost considerably more than the previous year's Miss America gown. This time the bridal magazine and Bancroft targeted stores in twenty big-city markets for the most intensive publicity efforts. As in the previous year's campaign, this promotion included a layout in the holiday issue of *Modern Bride*. The fashion spread showcased photographs of 18-year-old Miss America Nancy Anne Fleming in her Ban-Lon "dream" gown, pictures of models in Ban-Lon bridesmaid dresses, and photographs and sketches of Ban-Lon lingerie items.[27] The layout again opened with a narrative designed to tap into women's fairy princess fantasies, a ploy also employed in Bancroft Company press releases:

Standing on tip-toe watching the bridal party emerge from a village church has always been dear to the heart of every little girl, and from those moments comes the special dream of her own wedding in the future. . . . Miss America, a representation of American womanhood, personifies the dreams of all young women. . . . In her dreams she sees a lovely feminine trousseau, a regal wedding gown etched and appliqued in luxurious "Ban-Lon" lace, bouffant skirt studded with crystals and graceful Watteau train. Priscilla of Boston has created this exquisite wedding gown, a snow-white confection with petal-like bodice, for the lovely Miss America.[28]

Following the cues of *Modern Bride* and the Bancroft Company, participating retailers employed the epitome of girlhood fantasies—beauty queens and princess brides—in their local publicity campaigns. The Woolf Brothers store in Kansas City promoted its December 1960 bridal fashion show with newspaper ads touting the "dream dress" of Miss America 1961—"the girl chosen to symbolize beauty and charm in this country." *Modern Bride*, the Bancroft Company, and Priscilla of Boston, Inc., monitored local publicity efforts closely, not only to make sure that stores incorporated the "dream wedding" theme in their advertising but to ensure they used all available publicity avenues. Atlanta's J. P. Allen store presented Miss America's "dream gown" and "dream trousseau" as part of a televised bridal fashion revue. Best's Apparel in Seattle placed a copy of the Miss America dress in its largest window and hosted 400 women at a fashion show featuring all the merchandise from the *Modern Bride* layout and a special appearance by Priscilla Kidder, the founder of Priscilla of Boston.[29]

Stores that did not adequately promote the gown risked displeasing the promotion's sponsors. By late February 1961, Lord and Taylor, designated to serve the campaign's entire New York City market, had sold only five copies of the dream dress. Representing his wife's firm, James Kidder penned advice to Lord and Taylor's bridal-wear buyer:

> I am sure you realize that we are channeling all inquiries in the New York area to you, and helping you wherever we can to merchandise the dress. However, is there a possibility that you might use this dress in a window? If I remember correctly, you do promote a bridal window at about this time of year, and it occurred to me that the Miss America dress might be used and further promoted in this way. . . . I am sure you realize that we are most happy for you to have this

promotion, but one of the requisites was that this dress be given some promotion and backing.[30]

Yet window displays, appeals to girlhood fantasy, and elaborate fashion shows could only go so far in convincing brides to purchase the 1961 Miss America "dream gown." In late February 1961, James Kidder acknowledged that the current Miss America campaign had not been as successful as the previous year's effort. He also noted, however, that his wife's company never expected "to duplicate [1960's] fine results as regards the number of units sold, since [the Priscilla] dress [was] a different type of dress, . . . [selling at] a higher retail price." Although Kidder voiced satisfaction that the gown, placed in more than forty major marketing areas, resulted in over $10,000 worth of sales, he also noted that "the retail price of the dress worked against complete distribution." In these years before extensive reliance on credit cards and a marked upscaling of Middle American tastes, middle-class consumer values still differed from those of the upper class; for the typical bridal customer, price considerations trumped the desire to emulate the wearers of high fashion.[31]

In their second Miss America campaign, the Bancroft Company and *Modern Bride* misjudged postwar sensibilities. Flushed with the success of the previous year, they pushed the envelope by centering the promotion on an expensive dress at a time when most gowns cost between $95 and $125. And Priscilla of Boston designed a sleek gown in classic white that did not fit the fairy princess image as well as the Angelo design, with its hoop skirt, taffeta roses, and multiple color-scheme options. At a time when half the young women buying formal wedding gowns were teenagers, the Priscilla of Boston dress was perhaps not only too expensive but too sophisticated for their tastes.[32]

As the bridal apparel industry attempted to appeal to the masses, the 1961 Miss America campaign was curiously misguided. Perhaps emboldened by the previous year's success, those behind this second campaign believed they could define fashion sense and appropriate dress. They learned a valuable lesson. The makers and marketers of bridal wear could set the general parameters of cost and style, but they could not stray from the desires of their youthful consumers when it came to details.

While the makers of Ban-Lon may have backed the wrong dress for 1961, they did not feel that they backed the wrong advertising campaign. As the 1960s unfolded, Miss America remained the archetypal All-American Bride clad in Ban-Lon. There she was, Miss America 1964, this time in the pages of *Bride's* magazine safely garbed in an Alfred Angelo gown. As in previous campaigns, the 1964 title holder, 21-year-old Donna Axum, was mentioned only in passing by her given name. With her veil held in place by a regal crown and her gown dripping with Ban-Lon "bridalace," she was much more than Donna Axum—she was Every Bride on the way to the wedding of her dreams. The 1964 campaign showcased Miss America and her dream gown and featured pageant runners-up wearing less elaborate wedding dresses. The message was clear: If the Miss America dream gown did not match a bride's taste or budget, another Ban-Lon lace dress would.[33]

The Miss America campaign demonstrated how various institutions in one branch of the wedding industry joined forces to sell a product to American brides. Fabric manufacturers, dress makers, advertising agencies, bridal magazines, and retailers acted as a well-oiled machine to use print, radio, television, and store-site publicity to sell bridal gowns by playing on dominant middle-class gender notions. The bride-consumers, however, were not mindless automatons. Items had to meet their style and price requirements.

Brides of the period not only sought the right style of dress at the right price, they also sought the right kind of shopping experience. Industry marketing taught them that buying this special garment should be a memorable event. Whether they purchased the garment in a department store salon, the bridal section of a women's clothing store, or a stand-alone bridal shop, the surroundings should be elegant. Plush carpets, rich draperies, and ornate mirrors were typical features. Brides should also surround themselves with the appropriate shopping companions. The woman or women nearest and dearest to the bride should accompany her on this important shopping trip.[34]

Twenty-year-old Memphis resident Elizabeth Cleghorn was the typical bride of the era, and she participated in every magical aspect of the wedding gown experience. From the moment she and Ramsay Wall Jr. became engaged on New Year's Day 1964, her mother, Rosa—"a walking etiquette book"—began organizing the September wedding. The starting point was a trip to the bridal department at Helen of Memphis, a "rather exclusive ladies' shop," where Rosa and Elizabeth selected a bouffant-skirted gown of silk taffeta. This purchase was a central episode in the story of family success and generational legacy that Elizabeth's wedding represented. When Rosa married Elizabeth's father in 1943, "everything was fairly small"—in part because the groom was soon shipping out for military duty in the Pacific. In contrast to her own restrained wartime ceremony, Rosa and her daughter wanted everything about Elizabeth's wedding to be "the way it was supposed to be." Helping her daughter select a stylish wedding gown—and paying for it—was one way in which Rosa Cleghorn showed that she and her husband, John, could provide their offspring with luxuries they themselves had lacked. John's salary as an executive with the Holiday Inn hotel chain allowed them not only to purchase the glamorous wedding gown but to procure the services of a professional florist, photographer, caterer, and a seamstress who constructed six bridesmaids dresses in just the right shade of gold—a "very 'in' color" in 1964. The Cleghorns also rented formalwear for all the male participants and purchased dozens of candles to light the sanctuary of Memphis's Second Presbyterian Church. In total, they spent between $4,000 and $5,000 on their daughter's wedding, a figure in line with the era's budget recommendations for a wedding of that size and translating into somewhere between $26,000 and $33,000 today.[35]

The wedding gown and other purchases that Rosa and Elizabeth Cleghorn chose together did not merely symbolize their household's prosperity. These items—and the gown in particular—represented the goals and values the mother and daughter shared. Rosa and Elizabeth accepted advertisers' portrayal of the wedding gown as a symbol of family cohesion and a token of parental affection. Purchasing the gown together demonstrated the women's close relationship and reflected Rosa's approval of and active participation in Elizabeth's transformation from daughter to wife. But the Cleghorns also perceived the white wedding in explicitly religious terms, a theme the wedding gown business could not emphasize with any specificity and still appeal to a diverse consumer audience. Rosa had prayed for the man her daughter would someday marry since the day she was born and had always counseled the girl to "marry the man God chose" for her because nobody else would make her happy, "no matter how wonderful" he might be. Both women viewed marriage as a Christian commitment that all generations of the family—particularly the female members—should play a role in launching. As they made arrangements for Elizabeth's wedding, Rosa sought suggestions from two main sources: Emily Post and her own mother. With her mother, grandmother, and the Lord all sanctioning the event, Elizabeth recalled, "By the time I walked down that aisle there was not one shred of doubt in my mind that this was the man I should marry, and I thoroughly enjoyed my wedding."[36]

Elizabeth's elaborate wedding, and her mother's role in creating it, gave her confidence as she entered a new stage in life. With an eye toward someday providing a similar experience for other female relatives, Elizabeth paid an annual fee at Nunnery's—Memphis's "premier" dry cleaning establishment—to have her wedding gown vacuum-packed. As a result, years later a younger cousin could proudly wear the pristine gown by updating it with 5,000 seed pearls. And after several more years of storage at Nunnery's, Elizabeth's daughter wore the dress at her wedding in the early 1990s. Once again, the gown provided an important link between female generations and was a means of demonstrating shared familial values. To Elizabeth, her daughter Beth's decision to wear the gown—like her choice of the same silverware pattern that both Elizabeth and Rosa owned—indicated that the women possessed similar, "very traditional" tastes. Elizabeth was pleased that Beth also chose to marry at the Second Presbyterian Church, sharing her belief that a "Christian wedding" was the "only way" to establish a "Christian home." But the wedding dress served as their primary touchstone and featured prominently in all the wedding photos. Purchasing a fashionable gown in an elegant setting and then bequeathing the artifact to later generations enhanced Elizabeth Cleghorn Wall's memories of her wedding day and prompted her to say decades later that her wedding was a meaningful and enjoyable experience.[37]

A year after the Cleghorn-Wall wedding, the Bridal and Bridesmaids Apparel Association commissioned a study to demonstrate the supposed long-term advantages of wearing a white wedding dress. Researchers asked 2,000 women what they had worn at their weddings, and the results could not have pleased the wedding industry more: when brides wore white gowns, 5.9 percent of marriages ended in divorce; when they wore street dresses or suits, 12.3 percent disbanded. The association announced that a bride clad in a formal white dress had more than double the chance of staying married as other brides. The association's study attributed the staying power of expensive white-wedding marriages to several of the elements that Rosa and Elizabeth Cleghorn believed the ceremony represented, including the "deep psychological commitments which are formalized in a formal wedding; serious investments in time and money which accompany the formal ceremony as opposed to the quickie wedding; an important sense of responsibility to the family; and religious commitments."[38]

While subsequent studies have not replicated the association's self-promoting results, research has indicated that the longer the bride and groom know one another before the wedding, the better their chances of avoiding divorce. Couples who invest months in the planning of a formal wedding must have known one another for at least those number of months. In contrast, at least some of those brides and grooms who have "quickie," less formal weddings make spur-of-the-moment decisions to marry after knowing one another only briefly. Nevertheless, by publicizing its study, the Bridal and Bridesmaids Apparel Association ensured that, according to one estimate, 85 percent of American brides in the mid-1960s purchased formal wedding gowns. Even the popularity of the minidress did not threaten the formal bridal gown. While the skirts of a few dresses got shorter, the veils and trains designed to accompany them often got longer. Thus the bridal wear industry did not have to face the specter of less fabric and lower profits[39] (Figure 2.7).

But the times they were a-changin'. By the late 1960s, the sparkling white wedding gown symbolized something new. Radical feminists sounded the call for change at the 1968 Miss America pageant. Most famously, the Miss America protesters organized a Freedom Trash Can into which they deposited false eyelashes, curlers, wigs, girdles, and bras. Demonstrators also issued a manifesto denouncing Miss America as a "Degrading Mindless-Boob-Girlie Symbol" whose image of idealized virginity contributed to a Madonna-Whore complex that degraded all women. Protesters accused Miss America of being part of a

FIGURE 2.7. *To ensure that the fashionable minidresses they created included enough fabric to warrant selling the gowns at a profitable price, bridal designers of the 1960s often attached lengthy scarves, veils, and trains. In 1968, model and future actress Ali MacGraw wore such an ensemble in* Bride's *magazine. (Gianni Penati/*Bride's, *December/January 1968, p. 113)*

"consumer con game." According to feminist critics, she was an automaton willing to endorse any commodity her handlers set before her: "Wind her up and she plugs your product on promotion tours and TV." A year later, the product that Miss America had endorsed—the white wedding dress itself—received similar treatment when feminist demonstrators disrupted the Madison Square Garden bridal fair with their white mice, black veils, and protest slogans.[40]

While feminist protesters condemned Miss America, the American bride, the American family, and other national institutions, social surveys indicated that few young women conformed to their mothers' sexual mores. In the 1950s, polls indicated that only a quarter of Americans found no fault with premarital sex. By the 1970s, however, three-quarters of the population tolerated the practice. Historical circumstance contributed to this change in attitudes. The introduction of an oral contraceptive in 1960 and Supreme Court decisions in 1965 and 1971 that overturned state laws banning birth control allowed young women opportunities for sexual expression without the fear of unwanted pregnancy. Women's increased participation in higher education—from 38 percent of college-aged women enrolled as full-time students in 1960 to 49 percent in 1970—resulted in delayed marriage and thus the greater likelihood of sexual activity before marriage. The counterculture's mantra, "If it feels good, do it," along with feminist criticism of patriarchy and the sexual double standard, also made it acceptable for fewer brides to reach the altar as sexual innocents. Surveys on the nation's college campuses showed that women were indeed closing the sexual activity gap between themselves and their male peers.[41]

The increase in women's paid employment in the 1970s further undermined postwar ideas and practices regarding marriage. Women who earned a wage of their own were less reluctant to end unhappy marriages, and the nation's new no-fault divorce laws eased the path to dissolution. The American divorce rate increased 90 percent between 1960 and 1980. Many divorced Americans eventually remarried, but second marriages had an even greater record of failure than first marriages. According to some estimates, by the end of the 1970s half of all American marriages were ending in divorce.[42]

In the changing cultural landscape of the 1970s, a white gown did not necessarily symbolize a woman's virginity, her adoption of a primarily homemaking role, or her lifelong commitment to the man she married. Nevertheless, the white wedding had become so central to the act of getting married that brides in the 1970s were more likely than ever to buy a formal white gown. In the early 1970s, 87 percent of American brides wore floor-length gowns. Ninety-four percent of those garments were white or ivory. As counterculture weddings featuring brides in tie-dyed T-shirts captured media headlines, the overwhelming popularity of formal attire prompted the publisher of *Modern Bride* to observe: "The vast number of first-time brides get married in an unaltered traditional fashion. . . . Each year there is even a higher rate of white wedding gowns sold than is accounted for just by the increase in the number of marriages. More and more people are having formal weddings every year. It astonishes even me." The wedding wear business even managed to co-opt elements of countercultural style, producing a few muslin, cotton lace, and eyelet dresses; hats rather than veils; Mexican wedding dresses of embroidered white cotton; and medieval-style caftans and hoods. Most American brides wanted a stylish wedding ensemble, whether it conformed to "traditional fashion" or followed bohemian trends. At an average cost of $164 ($794 in today's currency), a bridal costume could be purchased at a significant but not excessive price in the early 1970s.[43]

With 21 the median age of a first-time bride, designers in the early 1970s continued to create dresses with a youngster in her late teens or early twenties in mind. No bridal gown firms of the era produced apparel appropriate for the bride over age 25 or 30, even if she were making her first trip down the aisle. Instead, the entire industry was geared toward selling to very young first-time brides, with the pitch that they were headed toward a once-in-a-lifetime experience. Ignoring rising divorce and remarriage rates, the wedding industry maintained the fiction that a wedding was a one-time proposition for the typical American woman. While bridal magazines had finally begun to give advice on how to organize second wedding ceremonies, they counseled that the affairs should be simple, include only a short guest list, and under no circumstances should second-time brides indulge in the luxury of a white wedding gown. Bridal retail establishments thus remained an environment geared only to the young, first-time bride—even though 25 percent of people marrying each year were doing so for the second or third time. As one bridal wear buyer noted, "We just *can't* stock appropriate dresses for the divorcee or widow. . . . It would take a lot of glory out of it for the young bride to see, for example, a short beige cocktail suit hanging next to a heavenly white lace gown. It's sort of depressing for her." Regardless of changing social standards, the wedding industry of the 1970s continued to play by the rules established in the early postwar era.[44]

The wedding industry developed innovative strategies to encourage young adults of the 1970s to continue marrying in 1950s style. A typical promotional event held in Pennsylvania at the Valley Forge Music Fair theater in March 1974 attracted nearly 18,200 people—mainly brides, their mothers, and assorted members of their bridal parties—who visited a hundred different booths displaying merchandise from area florist shops, travel agencies, furniture stores, stationers, and formal-wear shops. It also featured dancing models attired in the latest fashions for the bride, bridesmaid, and flower girl. One of thirty such bridal megafairs held that year throughout Canada and the United States, the Valley Forge event ensured a large turnout of wedding consumers by holding drawings for extravagant free gifts—including new automobiles and a Jamaican honeymoon.[45]

During the next two decades, the bridal industry continued to attract new customers by employing schemes that were more controversial than dancing brides and free cars. Old-timers considered the package deals offered by some newcomers to the bridal trade—in which the retailer sold a bride her wedding dress with the promise of a discount on her catering or flowers—to be the height of poor taste. And most participants in the industry were appalled by the attempt of a few businesses to rent the bride her gown "after six other sweaty women had worn it and spilled champagne on it." Their concerns, however, proved to be unjustified. The industry had achieved great success in communicating the notion that each bride deserved her own unique dress, and by the late 1980s, 96 percent of brides still purchased their gowns. Changed attitudes about marriage and female gender roles had not dampened the desire for a dress that still had the power to make a woman the center of attention and announce her secure position in American society. In fact, the informalization of etiquette and dress codes in the late 1960s and early 1970s rendered the singular white gown more precious than ever. In a society where blue jeans had become acceptable attire for both sexes on most occasions, the formal wedding allowed a bride the increasingly rare opportunity to dress in an elaborate manner that set her apart from everybody else.[46]

Not only the white dress but the process of acquiring it remained central to the experience of being a bride. Twenty-two-year-old Ann Hardy and her mother, Jean, purchased the dress for Ann's 1985 wedding at a Lincoln, Nebraska, emporium called Sassi's, located "in a neat old house that had been redone into a wedding shop." But the unique location was not the only aspect of the shopping experience that made it memorable. Years later, the bride fondly remembered spending the day with her mother, who had traveled to eastern Nebraska from the other side of the state in order to help her daughter select a gown and other wedding items. Although her sister lived in Lincoln and she had numerous friends in the city, Ann chose Jean as her shopping companion because she and Ann's father were paying for the gown and because "it was just kind of fun" to make wedding plans and purchases with her mother. For Jean, the trip to Sassi's and purchase of the dress represented meaningful involvement in her daughter's wedding experience.[47]

In several respects, the Hardys' 1985 shopping excursion resembled that of the Cleghorns two decades earlier. A special location, an opportunity for mother-daughter bonding, and the chance for a parent to bestow a special gift—the white wedding dress—characterized both events. And many aspects of Ann Hardy's wedding to Steve Vrana echoed Elizabeth Cleghorn's wedding to Ramsay Wall Jr. Both brides chose ceremony sites and participants that reflected their personal experiences and values. Elizabeth Cleghorn married in Memphis's Second Presbyterian Church because she was a long-time member and she and her fiancé had worshiped there together during their engagement. She asked the senior pastor to preside because he was a good friend who would set the foundation for a Christian marriage. Similarly, Ann Hardy married in a picturesque Lincoln park because she and her fiancé had often walked there, and her Church of Christ minister from "back home" officiated in order to establish a Christian marriage. Their fathers gave both brides away, and their sisters served both brides as honor attendants.[48]

But there were key differences between the marital expectations of the bride of 1964 and the bride of 1985. Elizabeth Cleghorn dropped out of college and was living with her parents in the months preceding her wedding. Planning and shopping for her wedding became her full-time job, and when she and her new husband returned from their honeymoon at a friend's North Carolina vacation home, she devoted several more months to setting up their new apartment. Once she had put the myriad wedding gifts in place and finalized other domestic details, Elizabeth took a secretarial job in the office of a family friend. It was the kind of employment that brought in extra money but did not challenge her bookkeeper husband's role as chief breadwinner and could be easily set aside with her first pregnancy. In contrast, Ann Hardy was a couple of years older than Elizabeth and living hundreds of miles away from her parents at the time of her wedding. She maintained her full-time paralegal job while planning her wedding and immediately resumed it after her Caribbean honeymoon cruise. She waited ten years to start a family and in the interim shifted career paths, earned an advanced degree, and as a school librarian became her household's chief wage-earner. And once the children were born, her husband, whose employment was more seasonal in nature, became their primary care-giver. Like Elizabeth Cleghorn, Ann Hardy came from a conservative religious tradition that regarded the husband as household head, and she did not call herself a feminist. Nevertheless, like most others of her generation, she possessed a strong—and permanent—workplace identity that second-wave feminism helped make possible. Only two decades after Elizabeth Cleghorn donned a white gown to become Mrs. Wall, Ann Hardy wore a similar garment to become Mrs. Vrana. But the expectations that she and the rest of American society now held for the marital relationship had significantly changed.[49]

Wearing a delicate white dress and standing alongside her groom under a city park gazebo, Ann Hardy was the new Cinderella. Her dream included a groom and a workplace identity, and her wedding celebrated both aspects of this ideal. In conformity with new etiquette guidelines, she chose to pay for a portion of the wedding expenses from her own salary. But a sense of parental duty and affection made her parents insist on some purchases themselves—including the all-important wedding dress (Figure 2.8). Fraught with meaning, the purchase and wearing of a white gown remained central to the experience of being an American bride and central to the fantasies of American girlhood. Participating in a consumer focus group a few years after Ann Hardy's wedding, another Midwestern bride summarized her standards for selecting a wedding dress: "I always imagined myself, ever since I was little, in, you know, the perfect huge white gown. . . . It's not something that I could settle for, it had to be the one."[50]

The wedding dress maintained its mystique, but in deference to changes in demography, social mores, and consumer demand, the industry began producing more styles appropriate for brides over age 25 and started promoting the idea of elaborate weddings and white gowns for women who were not first-time brides. Even the venerable Emily Post organization acknowledged changing times when granddaughter-in-law Elizabeth L. Post published a 1991 etiquette guide for second weddings, explaining, "The preponderance of second-time brides today has created the need for a fresh look at old attitudes about getting married the second time around." By the end of the 1990s, encore brides could also seek wedding advice from the quarterly magazine *Bride Again*. Here and elsewhere, the seasoned bride learned that an encore wedding could still be a storybook fantasy—if she purchased the right props to distinguish it from her previous nuptial celebration. Thus, if she chose to wear white, she could not simply recycle her first wedding gown, which, after all, was now the symbol of a failed relationship. Instead, to demonstrate her confidence in the new marriage, she might purchase an even grander gown for her second wedding. After choosing a sequined white gown for her 2002 marriage to a divorced 50-year-old, a 56-year-old second-time bride proudly proclaimed, "We are doing everything we would have done and then some, as if we were getting married at 23 years old." If older, more affluent brides were willing to spend big money on second wedding gowns—or even third, fourth, and subsequent gowns—the bridal-wear business was now ready to oblige. As a Florida bridal shop proprietor

FIGURE 2.8. *In 1985, Ann Hardy was the new Cinderella who combined marriage to Prince Charming (Steve Vrana) with a strong workplace identity. Her mother traveled hundreds of miles to the city where Ann worked in order to help the bride select the all-important white gown. (Author's collection)*

noted with satisfaction, "We have one bride we have done seven weddings for already, and every time, the dress gets whiter and the train gets longer."[51]

Another consumer receiving more attention in the late twentieth century and the early years of the twenty-first was the African American bride. Industry efforts to woo her business in this period were unprecedented in scope, but they were not new. Images of the white-gowned bride had been prevalent in the black press since the early postwar era. She appeared on the cover of the June 1947 issue of *Ebony*, and the white gown itself received significant treatment in both *Ebony* and *Jet* in the postwar years. A 1953 *Jet* feature noted that brides dreamt of the "glory, pomp, and splendor of the traditional June wedding—and the selection of the bridal gown [was] one of the biggest thrills of their lifetimes." An *Ebony* fashion layout that year anthropomorphized the all-important white gown, noting that at a proper wedding it marched "down the aisle as the star of the big show." The elaborate, Euro-American–style garments pictured in these features reflected the magazines' integrationist message of the period: Adopting the consumer habits of the white middle class would take upwardly mobile blacks one step closer to full citizenship in the American republic. Only in the late 1960s, under the influence of the Black is Beautiful movement, did the African American press begin to promote African-inspired wedding celebrations and clothing. But the price tags for these items still suggested their intention for an upscale consumer.[52]

In the mid-1980s, as the bridal industry reached out to a wider market, more African American entrepreneurs entered the trade to serve the desires of the growing black middle class. Now constituting approximately 25 to 30 percent of the nation's African American population, middle-class blacks who had grown up during the Black Power years of the late 1960s and early 1970s frequently preferred to patronize black-owned businesses for their wedding purchases. Within a few years, *Essence*, the leading black women's magazine, began listing the names and addresses of black-owned clothing boutiques, including those that sold bridal wear, and publicized guides such as the *Diaspora Design Directory* and *Style Noir* that advised readers on how to locate and patronize African American designers. In comparison to earlier decades, fashion layouts and designer interviews in the black press now included a greater focus on Afrocentric themes, but more than half the wedding gowns pictured still resembled the white frock commonly recognized as the one true American wedding dress, and some black designers even expressed a preference for these Euro-American–style designs (Figure 2.9). One of the most successful African American bridal-wear designers of the late 1990s, Jamaican immigrant Harold Clarke, told *Essence* that he expressly patterned his creations on Euro-American gowns of the Victorian and Edwardian periods. The magazine also published profiles of couturiers like Therez Fleetwood and Cassandra Bromfield, who created gowns using African fabrics and updating the loose design of traditional African wedding clothing, but purchasing Afrocentric wedding attire could prove costly. Bromfield's wedding dresses started at $800 in the late 1990s, and Fleetwood's creations ranged from $1,025 to $2,350 apiece.[53]

The most controversial developments in the wedding gown trade were not about attracting affluent customers but those on more modest budgets. From the 1980s onward, the growing gap between the have's and have not's caused most American retailers to target either an upscale or downscale market. The bridal-wear business, which had previously coaxed working-class and middle-class customers to spend like those higher on the socioeconomic scale, now bowed to the inevitable and began marketing to the discount-minded. Businesses that experimented with renting gowns or selling used dresses that did not yet have "vintage" or "antique" cachet met with limited success. The industry had simply been too successful in nurturing the mystique of the one-time-only wedding dress. Years of promoting the idea that each woman deserved a wedding gown that was uniquely her own—unless she chose to wear a family heirloom—meant that businesses targeting the budget market had to focus on selling new dresses at lower prices. Women walked into a discount bridal house willing to spend more on a wedding gown than they would on any other article of clothing, but they trusted it to cost less than at a more conventional bridal shop. In exchange for lower prices, the customer received relatively little service and did without the elegant surroundings and custom fittings that had previously defined the national bridal-wear trade. In contrast to Priscilla Kidder's advice in the early 1970s that bridal-wear saleswomen spend 42.5 hours ministering

FIGURE 2.9. *Even after the introduction of Afrocentric wedding attire in the late twentieth century, many African American designers and most African American brides preferred the conventional white gown for formal ceremonies. (Courtesy of Michael DiBari Jr.)*

to each customer, an increasing number of retailers—led by the David's Bridal chain—sold gowns right off the rack in sparsely appointed warehouse surroundings that allowed low overhead costs. To industry veterans, the rule of thumb had always been, "If a dress costs $50 wholesale, you retail it for a hundred." But the sales philosophy of the bridal-wear discounters enabled them to retail their gowns for much less than the usual 100 percent markup rate.[54]

The seriously bargain-minded bride might make due with Filene's Basement or a warehouse setting, but others wanted to purchase their special garments in special surroundings and wanted the saleswomen's undivided attention. One 1990s bride noted, "When you go shopping for regular clothing like jeans and stuff, you don't want people bothering you. . . . But I think for wedding gowns, it's completely different. People should really give good service." As the bride's most important acquisition, the white gown deserved even greater attention than her other

wedding purchases. Another bride of the period believed "salespeople need to be more helpful when you're finding your wedding dress.
Because you're the most important person on your wedding day. And
you're the one that needs to look the best . . . so, it's more important than
shopping for other wedding items." For women with this mind-set, where
and how they purchased their dream gowns still mattered. The decline
of multipurpose department stores in the 1980s made it less likely for a
bride to purchase her gown in a glamorous department store salon, but
there were other out-of-the-ordinary shopping experiences. Thousands
of bridal shops around the country still resisted the off-the-rack discount
mentality and shared the philosophy of the Brooklyn-based Kleinfeld
emporium: "We believe the day you choose your wedding gown should
be as joyful and memorable as the day you wear it."[55]

Hope's Bridal Boutique—located on a working Iowa farm in a converted dairy barn painted an attention-grabbing pink—provided what
for many was the ideal wedding gown shopping experience (Figure
2.10). Even in the recession of the early 1990s, proprietor Diane Niebuhr
reported that brides were willing to plunk down an average $550 ($793
in current dollars) for a wedding dress. While Niebuhr noted they might
trim back the reception budget or other wedding expenses, her customers were not "cutting back on the bridal gowns . . . [because] that gown
seem[ed] to be important to them." Conforming to national trends, the
typical Hope's customer was in her midtwenties and already had her own
"job or career established." In contrast to the norm a generation earlier,
teenage brides or those in their early twenties were a rarity. But when the
older, more worldly, and self-sufficient bride of the 1990s walked into the
lushly carpeted boutique, she still wanted a unique shopping adventure
that included pampering by saleswomen and seamstresses who checked
and rechecked the fit of a gown. Since purchasing the farm and boutique
from its founder Hope Kolsto in the mid-1980s, Niebuhr and her husband had turned it into one of the top five bridal businesses in the Midwest and provided employment for over two dozen local women who
fussed over customers and complimented their selections. In a rural area
with few attractive wage-earning options, this was "a fun type of job,"
and the employees were genuinely "excited for any bride." The personal
attention a bride received at Hope's Bridal Boutique was a major reason

FIGURE 2.10. *Shopping at a unique location like Hope's Bridal Boutique—located in a converted Iowa dairy barn—made the bride's selection of her wedding gown all the more memorable. (Author's collection)*

for shopping there. As Niebuhr proudly noted, "We want our customers to know that we have a big city selection and big city service but a small-town atmosphere." Many of Niebuhr's customers had fantasized about shopping at the boutique ever since Hope Kolsto established the business in the early 1970s. Whenever Diane Niebuhr heard customers say, "I've always wanted since I was little to shop at the pink barn," or "I've always dreamed that I would get my gown here," she knew she would make a sale. As Niebuhr explained, "Those people that come in with that attitude are bound and determined that they are going to buy their dress here."[56]

But for Niebuhr and other bridal-wear retailers, only the "'Oh, Mommy' moment" confirmed the sale of a particular dress. This was when a customer looked in the mirror, saw herself wearing a gown that lived up to all her girlhood fantasies, and exclaimed to her mother, sister, or other shopping companion that she had at last found the perfect dress. As one bride explained: "When I found that dress, I mean I put it on . . . I started crying, 'cause I was like, 'Lisa, this is my dress!' . . . It just, it just was a really overwhelming, I guess, type of feeling."

The joy of experiencing the "'Oh, Mommy' moment" in an elaborately appointed bridal shop was becoming less common as customers increasingly shopped at bridal discount stores and fell victim to what Bridal Originals representative Jerry Smale called the "Wal-Mart effect." But Smale reasoned that even though discounters were "creeping in" to the bridal-wear business, there would always be room for what he proudly referred to as "true retailing" in an industry that since World War II had promised elegance for the masses. While consumers might save money by purchasing other items at discount stores, they were still "willing to put those dollars into a wedding." Proving Smale correct, even David's Bridal stores eventually acquiesced to industry custom and consumer demand by upgrading their interiors, placing greater emphasis on service, and selling some special-order gowns.[57]

The synthesis of old and new trends in the bridal-wear business was readily apparent at the October 1995 National Bridal Market, held in the cavernous Chicago Apparel Center. Here, buyers for retail bridal shops chose the merchandise they would sell to customers the following spring. From the designated Bridal Originals suite, two committed believers in "true retailing"—Jerry Smale and his septuagenarian colleague Willie Dolnick—worked diligently to promote their company's gowns to the hundreds of retailers streaming into the Apparel Center. With microphone in hand, the younger man narrated a fashion revue showcasing the company's latest products while Dolnick held court behind the runway, greeting old friends and clients and sharing the wisdom garnered from forty-eight years in the business. As they listened to the rules of the game that Dolnick helped establish as a young World War II veteran, visitors recognized some obvious changes in the bridal industry. In an increasingly global economy, most of the wedding gowns modeled at the Bridal Market were now manufactured in Asia. Literature distributed throughout the Apparel Center advertised seminars on "How to Combat Warehouse Operations" and publicized survey results showing that traditional bridal retailers had successfully combated discounters by "stressing service, holding sales, lowering prices, and providing free alterations." A one-page profile of a successful Kentucky boutique noted that its proprietor attracted business through TV infomercials and an annual fashion show featuring 300 gowns. But the story concluded by citing the real secret of the man's success: his ability to steer a customer toward a wedding gown that made her "look like a princess."[58]

Over the course of the next decade, the trends apparent at the 1995 Bridal Market continued. The hourglass-shaped configuration of American retailing remained in place as merchants sought either upscale or discount-minded consumers, with David's Bridal continuing its dominance of the discount trade. After its acquisition by the May Department Stores Company in 2000, the David's chain continued to expand and within three years accounted for a full 20 percent of the nation's bridal gown sales. As one observer noted, with a fifth of all American brides now purchasing their gowns at the discount chain, the nation truly witnessed the "democratization of princessdom." And although smaller, independent stores continued to compete with David's by emphasizing service and glamour, David's now also attempted to give its customers a taste of the royal treatment with its upgraded store interiors and a few special-order gowns. As the chain's chief executive officer noted, even a discounted wedding dress was still likely to be the most expensive clothing a woman ever bought. And under those circumstances, he noted, "She wants to feel special. She is living her dream, in many ways."[59]

David's Bridal was also a key player in the May Company's attempt to attract younger customers and thereby extend the department store's life into a new millennium. In an updated version of the postwar interselling process, every bride who purchased her dress at David's received discount coupons for the bridal registry at May's department stores. Hoping to build the continued consumer loyalty of brides, grooms, and the wedding guests who bought them presents, a May's executive explained, "The number of brides [David's] can put through our door is a lead generator for all the processes after." In the average sixteen months between engagement date and wedding day, brides and grooms were now responsible for sales of $4 billion in furniture, $3 billion in housewares, and $4 billion in tableware.[60]

When the twenty-first-century bride walked through the door at David's Bridal—or any of the 3,000 independent bridal shops that continued to compete with the big-box bridal store—she was not the youthful housewife-in-training that retailers envisioned sixty years earlier. But for most first-time brides, the average $800 they invested in the wedding gown still ushered in an unprecedented spate of spending on other wedding clothing and on catering, travel, and household purchases. And in the era of the encore wedding, even the purchase of a gown for a second or third ceremony could still function as the gateway to a round of massive—albeit not unprecedented—consumer spending. Like her counterpart of the early postwar era, a bride on the search for her dream gown was still the retailer's dream consumer. When she took her coupons to the housewares department at her local May's store, however, she was just as likely to make a side trip to peruse briefcases as she was baby cribs. And because she was now more likely to be spending her own money than her parents', she often spent without restraint or guilt. For wedding industry merchants, the ideal Cinderella bride of the 2000s was someone like the 27-year-old Connecticut attorney who unashamedly spent nearly $3,000 on her enormous gown, reasoning, "This is the only time in my life I'll be able to wear a big dress."[61]

If outfitting one extravagant Cinderella was a dream come true, clothing a pair of free-spending brides was even better. When the Massachusetts Supreme Court ruled in November 2003 that same-sex marriage was constitutional, members of the wedding industry lost no time in promoting their wares. Although civil unions had been legal in nearby Vermont for three years, Massachusetts was the first state to recognize full marital rights for gays and lesbians. Demonstrating the extent to which Americans now automatically paired the concepts of marriage and the white wedding, the state's clothiers, caterers, and jewelers for the first time enthusiastically courted gay and lesbian customers. With the option of a real marriage now available to the state's more than 17,000 same-sex couples, the wedding industry hoped to build on the base of gay and lesbian customers who were already modeling their extralegal commitment ceremonies on the white wedding. A Waltham, Massachusetts, proprietor who typically dressed two same-sex couples a year now hoped such customers would make up a full 10 percent of her business, reasoning, "Two dresses are better than one." Whereas a single bride might spend $3,000 at the woman's shop, she had recently clothed a lesbian couple for $2,500 apiece. National chains also hoped to profit from the state court's ruling. In Boston, Bloomingdale's welcomed 200 consumers to an invitation-only same-sex wedding expo billed as "The Pink Event." Recognizing that same-sex couples were older and had more discretionary income than their straight counterparts, the event's organizer noted that these consumers usually headed "straight for the luxury goods."[62]

Extending the wedding gown's magic to lesbian brides entailed controversy as well as profit. Businesses that welcomed same-sex couples risked alienating their heterosexual consumer base, even in communities where gay and lesbian commitment ceremonies had been common for decades. The producer of a 2002 documentary on same-sex unions ruffled feathers when he filmed subjects buying bridal wear in a wealthy Los Angeles neighborhood because the shop's employees worried the couple "might freak out other customers." And a well-known Boston jewelry store ran eight months of focus group and other market research before risking its venerable reputation on gay-oriented advertising. The discomfort of straight consumers, however, did not deter those same-sex couples who believed that the trappings of a white wedding bestowed greater public legitimacy on their relationships. Massachusetts residents Carole Allen and Nancy Scannell chose to marry in white gowns at a posh estate because they viewed it as "a once-in-a-lifetime event" that they wanted to "be special" (Figure 2.11). When presiding at the elaborate wedding of another lesbian couple in white silk gowns, the officiating rabbi reminded the many guests, "We still live in a world where it is often dangerous emotionally, and sometimes physically, for Jill and Kriss to be open with their lives and their love. The importance of your presence as family and friends cannot be underestimated."[63]

While same-sex marriage supporters used the white dress as an emblem of acceptance, opponents employed it as a symbol of rejection. In the wake of the Massachusetts ruling, campaigns soon arose to amend the constitutions of other states to prevent similar interpretation of their marriage laws. In states where the issue was on the fall 2004 ballot, amendment proponents displayed yard signs and posters that used the white wedding as a shorthand symbol of heterosexual marriage, pairing a female figure in a white gown and veil with a male figure in a black tuxedo. Conservative candidates used their support of anti–gay marriage amendments as a major theme in their 2004 campaigns and often

FIGURE 2.11. *Massachusetts residents Carole Allen and Nancy Scannell visit a bridal salon to shop for their 2004 wedding. The state's supreme court opened up a lucrative new wedding gown market when it recognized the legality of same-sex marriage late in 2003. (Courtesy of Robert Spencer)*

incorporated images of the formally clad bride and groom in their litera-ture. In a campaign that received national attention for its vitriol, Ohio State Senator Joy Padgett employed this strategy to rebuff a challenge by journalist and former Middle Eastern hostage Terry Anderson. Issuing a flier with the words "One Man, One Woman," and the photograph of a tuxedo-clad man and a woman in white gown and veil, Padgett success-fully conveyed her message that she was the only candidate in the race who opposed same-sex marriage (Figure 2.12). That November, Ohio and ten other states passed amendments banning same-sex marriage, and President George W. Bush's support of such measures helped earn him another four years in the White House.[64]

With controversy continuing to surround the issue of same-sex mar-riage, most retailers continued to focus on the heterosexual bride. Re-gardless of the size of the pocketbooks they targeted, the merchants' message was the same: a bride should buy a dress that lived up to her

FIGURE 2.12. *Same-sex marriage opponents throughout the nation used images of the white-gowned bride to win office in 2004. Ohio State Senator Joy Padgett distributed this flier in her successful campaign to defeat Democratic challenger Terry Anderson. (Courtesy of the Ohio Republican Party)*

romantic fantasies. For middle-income brides, this usually meant spending beyond their means at a time when, as marketing consultants noted, consumers had "no aspiration to be middle class." Instead, most Americans wanted to shop like they were "at the top," in a development that analysts dubbed "the mainstreaming of affluent attitudes." The thriving economy of the late 1990s and the continuing influence of Baby Boomers on the nation's consumer habits contributed to this upscaling of middle-class tastes. Reaching the height of their earning power and entering their empty-nest years, the oldest Boomers were spending on themselves as never before. And many younger consumers followed their lead, even as the economy weakened again in the early twenty-first century. Under these circumstances, brides who had heavily invested in their gowns sometimes reassessed their notion of a wedding dress as a garment worn only once. A *New Yorker* cartoon satirized this phenomenon, picturing a bride in strapless gown and veil jogging through Central Park and remarking to a more appropriately attired companion, "I paid three grand for this dress—I'll wear it wherever I want!"[65] (Figure 2.13).

With Internet commerce revolutionizing the way Americans bought and sold goods, brides could now use this technology to recoup a portion of their substantial investment in a high-end wedding ensemble. By 2005, when nearly one-third of the nation's brides and grooms financed their weddings entirely on their own, brides frequently attempted to ease their financial pain by selling their gowns on the Internet auction site eBay. Having recently been bridal-wear customers themselves, eBay sellers knew the language that would resonate with other wedding consumers. An Illinois bride set the opening bid at $550 for a gown Marshall Field originally sold for nearly $4,000 and pushed her product with familiar imagery and the status appeal of an exclusive brand name: "Look like a princess on your day! . . . For those of you dying to wear Vera Wang at your wedding, here is your chance!! Get this AMAZING dress here for a mere fraction of it's [sic] retail price!!!" A New York bride added another tried-and-true advertising strategy, the celebrity endorsement, when she suggested that a popular First Lady would have admired the wedding gown she now offered to eBay bidders. After spending $6,600 at a Manhattan boutique for the strapless gown she listed as a "Vera Wang Luxe Wedding Dress Gown Cinderella 2005," the bride then added thousands of dollars of Swiss netting and lace to give it a more "Jackie O look." Noting that she had only worn the "magnificent" dress for five hours before having it "professionally cleaned and stuffed right after the wedding," the bride reasoned that "it would be a shame for no one to ever wear it again." But most brides who could afford to make a bid approaching the gown's actual value probably looked elsewhere for wedding attire. If a bride wanted a high-end dress and was paying for it herself, she usually heeded the bridal industry message and purchased a dream gown that was all her own—even if that meant adding to her credit debt or taking out a loan.[66]

When asked to name the most consistent feature of the bridal-wear business during her forty years in the trade, an industry veteran noted, "Once a bride-to-be sets her heart on a dress she usually buys it, no matter what the cost." The bride's eternal quest for the perfect fairy-tale gown—even in the face of financial sacrifice—sustained the wedding

"I paid three grand for this dress—I'll wear it wherever I want!"

FIGURE 2.13. *In this* New Yorker *cartoon, a bride rejects the notion that an expensive wedding gown should be worn only once in a lifetime. (Carolita Johnson/* New Yorker, *8 May 2006, page 32)*

gown business through changing times. Attempts to undermine the industry through acts of civil disobedience—such as the Madison Square Garden protest in 1969—had little long-term impact. The equity branch of second-wave feminism had used the 1964 Civil Rights Act and other legal reforms to secure greater workplace equality for women, transforming Cinderella into a woman who happily combined employment and marriage. Radical feminism, however, had not succeeded in dismantling the Cinderella myth altogether. By the early twenty-first century, the white wedding gown was more popular than ever.[67]

Surveying American popular culture in the mid-1960s, journalist Kitty Hanson observed, "In popular fiction, in drama and television and movies, in newspapers and magazines and advertisements in all media, the bride is portrayed as a radiant creature in a long white gown and floating veil. The subliminal message seems to be that bridal radiance is produced in direct proportion to the length of the bridal gown." In the two decades following World War II, the bridal-wear industry successfully used innovative marketing techniques, the mass media, and conventional notions of female beauty to convince Americans that the floor-length wedding gown was of almost magical significance. The wedding gown conferred upon its wearer instant glamour and a place in the idealized postwar middle class. Its allure remained intact even in the face of feminist criticism and the changing social standards and tolerances of the late 1960s and the 1970s.[68]

While the white gown no longer indicates compliance with the narrow gender-role prescriptions that emerged after World War II, it still represents the achievement of material success and emotional security. Whereas it once announced that the bride's family could afford to demonstrate their affection for her by purchasing a special dress for a one-day celebration, it now frequently advertises the bride's own ability to purchase the elegant, distinctive garment. Widespread adoption of the white wedding in the early postwar decades contributed to the myth that America was a middle-class nation—even as approximately 20 percent of the population continued to survive on an income that the federal government defined as at or near poverty level. The postwar image of the United States as a land of universal prosperity coupled with the American propensity toward constant self-improvement left many Americans by the beginning of the twenty-first century believing that the appearance of middle-class status was not good enough. Instead, Americans ratcheted up their expectations and material goals, attempting to demonstrate their financial security and self-satisfaction through the purchase of more elaborate cars, houses, vacations—and weddings. Creation of an ever-more-upscale facade was the norm as the new century began.

The bridal-wear industry contributed to this scenario with its message that every bride deserved at least one day in her life when she and her loved ones could show their ability to dress in ways that approximated those perched higher on the socioeconomic ladder. And if they could achieve that level of apparent success on the day of the wedding, perhaps they could do it in other aspects of their lives as well. Pulling off a successful white wedding was one way to demonstrate the desire and potential ability to achieve the entire American success story. In the quarter-century following World War II, most brides purchased formal gowns to celebrate their accomplishment of the middle-class dream:

marriage to a good provider and creation of a comfortable and secure household. During the next several decades, the white gown evolved into a garment worn by women who sought achievement of an updated and expanded dream: professional success, egalitarian marriage, and the chance to act like a rich and famous celebrity for at least one day. For African American and same-sex consumers, the gown could also represent an improved level of acceptance and participation in mainstream American culture. Regardless of the fantasy's dimensions, the white gown retains the power to convince brides that they have realized some piece of it.

CHAPTER

LIKE A ROYAL WEDDING
The Celebrity Wedding

The December 11, 2000, cover of *People* magazine breathlessly announced "Michael & Catherine's Wedding Album: The stars, the cake, the dress—14 pages of photos!" Accompanying the headline were pictures of movie stars Michael Douglas and Catherine Zeta-Jones slicing their wedding cake and Zeta-Jones modeling her cleavage-revealing gown. Inside the magazine, readers learned more about "the stars" who attended the event (including Goldie Hawn, Jack Nicholson, Russell Crowe, and UN Secretary General Kofi Annan), "the cake" (a six-foot, ten-tier vanilla and buttercream concoction covered with thousands of sugar flowers), and "the dress" (a $140,000 Christian Lacroix creation with a six-foot train). Readers found out that the 350-guest bash at New York's Plaza Hotel featured 20,000 cream-colored roses, a forty-member Welsh choir, a lamb and lobster dinner, and Art Garfunkel as the wedding singer. Scrutinizing the photo captions, they learned the couple's three-month-old son attended the ceremony in a sailor suit after his mother rejected a lace gown that "made him look like a girl." *People* reported that Zeta-Jones envisioned the occasion as a "homespun wedding—no gimmicks." But according to one guest, "The ceremony felt like a royal wedding." The bride even held her veil in place with a sparkling tiara.[1]

Like other celebrity weddings, the Zeta-Jones–Douglas extravaganza offered fans the opportunity to compare their own wedding memories, model their own nuptial plans, or simply enjoy the performance of an epic pageant with a familiar plot line. With a little imagination, *People* readers could even put themselves in the movie stars' shoes. Most brides could not afford a designer original, but they still donned a white gown—even if, like Zeta-Jones, they were already mothers. Unlike images of the Douglases' wedding, most wedding pictures did not result in a $2 million magazine deal or a lawsuit against a tabloid—but they did make a splash in family photo albums and the local newspaper. And most couples who held weddings in 2000 did not spend the $2 million that the Douglases paid for their celebration—but they still spent a significant sum, by non-celebrity standards, when they invested an average $20,000.[2]

Glitzy celebrity weddings reaped countless benefits, and the Zeta-Jones–Douglas celebration was no exception. Weddings gained positive press for the celebrities; enabled the media to sell more newspapers, magazines, and television air time; and provided free advertising for dressmakers, pastry chefs, hotels, and other segments of the wedding industry. (Or at least until the early twenty-first century, when some businesses began paying celebrity brides and grooms in kind or cash to endorse their products.) But these successful outcomes all stemmed from the same root causes: Americans' acceptance of weddings as visual entertainment and their vicarious enjoyment of the social lives of the rich and famous.[3]

Celebrity culture, like consumer culture in general, revolves around the notion that people can bring meaning to their lives through consumption of the right products. People habitually consume the image of a famous person on the movie screen or magazine page to achieve a sense of community and shared experience with the celebrity or the celebrity's other fans. And consumers can often achieve these same goals by purchasing products that a luminary uses or endorses. Advertising campaigns built on celebrity endorsements suggest that a "celebrity's aura [will] rub off on a consumer who use[s] the favored products," placing that purchaser "on the other side of the glass with the celebrity." A fan can also dive into these "swirls of vicariousness" through connection to a celebrity's personal style. The celebrity watcher can claim affinity with the object of her interest "by sharing a gesture, a hairstyle, . . . a piece of clothing"—or a style of wedding.[4]

The consumption of celebrity images and celebrity-endorsed products and practices has a long history, but Americans' fascination with fame and their imitation of persons who have achieved it intensified measurably in the second half of the twentieth century. The rise of television and its ability to bring celebrities right into the nation's living rooms enhanced consumers' impression that they intimately knew persons of renown and achievement. And postwar prosperity allowed consumers greater power to emulate their heroes and heroines through the purchase of the right products. Time, Inc., furthered the nation's fascination with celebrity when it launched *People* magazine in 1974, bringing full-time celebrity reporting out of the shadowy world of cheap tabloids and movie magazines and into the mainstream. Other glossy celebrity-centered magazines followed and helped nurture the achievement of a full-blown American celebrity culture.[5]

As celebrity culture and the American wedding industry grew up side by side in the six decades following World War II, numerous movie stars, heads of state, wealthy socialites, and other celebrities hosted weddings that captured the attention of press and public. From the 1969 *Tonight Show* wedding of novelty entertainer Tiny Tim and his bride Miss Vicki to endless coverage of Tom Cruise and Katie Holmes's 2006 ceremony in a romantic Italian castle, the spotlight shone brightly on celebrity weddings. But four weddings and the brides who starred in them achieved iconic status. Each of these brides possessed a public image that closely matched the gender prescriptions of her era, and each celebrated a wedding that showcased and further popularized dominant wedding industry trends. Grace Kelly, Tricia Nixon, Diana Spencer, and Carolyn Bessette were ideal bridal role models for their times and thus significantly influenced the way Americans thought about and enacted white weddings.

The 1956 marriage of actress Grace Kelly to Prince Rainier of Monaco was not the first union to achieve widespread coverage in the American press. Several stylish and photogenic Gilded Age and early twentieth-century brides received extensive attention in the print media of their day, including Frances Folsom when she married President Cleveland (1886), Consuelo Vanderbilt when she wed the Duke of Marlboro (1895), and first daughter Alice Roosevelt when she married Congressman Nicholas Longworth (1906). With the arrival of film, a style-setter like Wallis Simpson—who as an encore bride became the Duchess of

Windsor in 1937—now received an avalanche of publicity in the movie newsreels as well as in print.[6]

The Kelly-Rainier marriage was not even the first wedding to become a global media event in the postwar era. That honor went to the marriage of Britain's future queen and her groom, Philip Mountbatten. Occurring only two years after the war's end, the marriage of Elizabeth and Philip gave the British people and their American cousins a taste of royal pageantry for the first time in nearly a decade. As author Rebecca West noted at the time, "People are tired of sadness, they need a party; they are tired of hate, they need to think of love." Radio broadcasts from Westminster Abbey carried the royal wedding to a worldwide audience, and the event even inspired a Hollywood musical starring Fred Astaire and Sarah Churchill (Sir Winston's daughter). Nevertheless, as *Life* magazine noted in its thirteen-page photo essay on the wedding, it was an occasion of "pomp and straitened circumstance." Taking place in the ninth autumn of war-imposed consumer rationing in Great Britain, the celebration featured party menus that "showed no trace of luxury" and included "only a small array of flowers" at the Abbey altar. It also occurred before the era of mass television broadcasting, featured a bride known more for her common sense and sense of duty than for her fashion sense, and took place at a time when the coast-to-coast American wedding industry was in its infancy and not yet ready to exploit the marketing potential of a celebrity wedding to its fullest. For all these reasons, the royal wedding of 1947 failed to make a lasting impression on American consumers.[7]

In contrast to Elizabeth and Philip's marriage, the royal wedding of 1956 included every embellishment, occurred in the age of television, featured plenty of Hollywood glamour, and had a well-established wedding industry ready to bask in its reflected glory. Grace Kelly was the daughter of a wealthy Philadelphia family and an Oscar-winning actress known for playing sophisticated upper-class roles in films like *Rear Window* and *High Society*. Her already enormous popularity with the American public increased further when her engagement to a prince made it seem she was living out a real-life Cinderella tale. Shortly after the 26-year-old blonde announced her engagement in January 1956, members of the wedding industry made plans to capitalize on interest in her story. Bridal- and formal-wear manufacturers planned to create and sell replicas of the couple's wedding clothing. Linen makers intended to manufacture handkerchiefs emblazoned with the seal of Monaco. Toy makers hatched plans to manufacture dolls that replicated the bride and groom in their wedding attire. Plans to exploit interest in the wedding caused the Kelly family attorney to run an ad in *Women's Wear Daily* warning manufacturers that the names and seals of Kelly and Rainier could not be used "for commercial purposes or to further the sale of merchandise" without explicit permission. Even with this legal obstacle, purveyors of wedding goods still found ways to cash in on the wedding of Grace Kelly and Prince Rainier. Stanley Marcus, for instance, secured significant publicity for his Dallas emporium when he arranged for Neiman-Marcus to provide the bridesmaid dresses.[8]

By the day of the April 1956 wedding, interest in Grace Kelly's nuptials had reached such a fever pitch that over 1,600 reporters converged on the tiny principality of Monaco. In contrast, observers noted, only a thousand journalists had traveled to Geneva the previous year to cover an important U.S.-Soviet diplomatic summit. Thirty million television viewers in nine European countries watched the ceremony live, and Americans viewed it on TV several hours later or in vivid color the following month when Metro-Goldwyn-Mayer (MGM) released a moviehouse production entitled *The Wedding in Monaco.*[9]

Still photographers and newsreel and television camera operators were particularly eager to capture images of the glamorous bride in her wedding gown. As she broke from American tradition and preceded her seven elegantly dressed bridesmaids down the aisle of Monaco's St. Nicholas Cathedral, Kelly and her wedding dress did not disappoint their audience. Created by MGM costume designer Helen Rose, the ivory-colored, bell-skirted show-stopper was valued at nearly $7,300 (over $54,000 in present currency). Its intricate design and construction had required 25 yards of peau de soie, 25 yards of silk taffeta, 100 yards of silk net, 300 yards of Valencienne lace, and three crepe and taffeta petticoats. Antique lace and thousands of pearls decorated the accompanying headpiece and veil (Figure 3.1). Kelly's bridal ensemble was such a hit with fashion professionals and the public that it later went on permanent display at the Philadelphia Museum of Art, where it soon became the institution's most popular attraction, and inspired the creation of similar gowns around the world. In the United States, bridal gown manufacturer Alfred Angelo circumvented legal complications by creating and selling an "interpretation" of the famous frock rather than an exact copy. Kelly's dress ultimately achieved such popularity that more than ten years after her death in a 1982 car accident, a panel of fashion experts including Hollywood costumer Susan Becker, etiquette consultant Letitia Baldrige, and bridal designer Vera Wang rated it their favorite celebrity wedding gown of all time. And in 2006, in honor of the fiftieth anniversary of the Kelly-Rainier wedding, Yale University Press and the Philadelphia Museum of Art even published a new book about the creation and long-term impact of Grace Kelly's celebrated dress[10] (Figure 3.2).

According to one report, the wedding that transformed Grace Kelly into Her Serene Highness Princess Grace of Monaco cost her wealthy father $2 million. Following the 1956 extravaganza, the bride never returned to her successful career as an actress and instead, by her own description, devoted the rest of her life to charity work, Monacan public relations, and raising her husband's heirs. With her father providing a lavish ceremony for her wedding and her groom providing a lavish palace for her home, Grace Kelly ultimately played the role of both ideal bride and ideal housewife. Women's magazines of the era told and retold the story of how Grace Kelly abandoned Hollywood to become a full-time wife and—within a year of her marriage—a mother.[11]

Most of Kelly's movie fans willingly sacrificed her presence on the screen in exchange for the storybook fantasy that her wedding and new royal status seemed to represent. Not only Kelly's gown but other aspects of her wedding, from the style of her flower girls' dresses to the type of gloves her bridesmaids wore, inspired imitation around the world. In Kelly's native United States, members of the wedding industry considered her highly publicized nuptials the best free advertising they could ask for and credited her with creating even greater demand for commercially produced formal weddings. The typical wedding consumer might not be as wealthy, talented, or conventionally beautiful as Grace Kelly. She might not be marrying a man as rich or socially prestigious as Prince Rainier. She might even have to make do with one or two

FIGURE 3.1. *Actress Grace Kelly's 1956 marriage to Monaco's Prince Rainier was a media event that furthered the popularity of elaborate formal weddings and bell-skirted gowns. (Associated Press)*

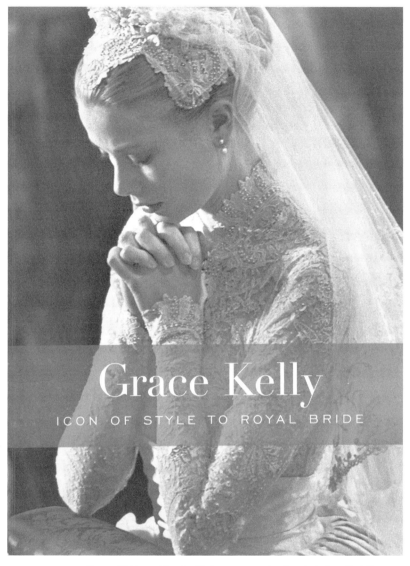

Grace Kelly

ICON OF STYLE TO ROYAL BRIDE

FIGURE 3.2. *Grace Kelly and her bridal gown remained so popular that they were the subject of a book published fifty years after the wedding in Monaco. (Philadelphia Museum of Art)*

bridesmaids rather than the seven that attended the new princess. She could still, however, approximate the pomp and circumstance of Grace Kelly's wedding on a more modest budget. In the wake of Kelly's marriage, the nation witnessed the establishment of dozens of new bridal salons eager to sell bell-shaped gowns, ranging in price from $49.75 to $139.75, to women who wanted their own downsized version of Kelly's "Wedding of the Century."[12]

While Grace Kelly's wedding story featured an upper-class cast of players and a multi-million-dollar budget, it nevertheless neatly conformed to middle-class notions about appropriate gender roles within marriage and the family. As was typical of celebrity coverage at the time, the popular press told Kelly's story as an appealing middle-class domestic saga. The press quoted Kelly as saying that she chose to marry the prince because, like other American women, she preferred to marry up the socioeconomic scale: "I've always thought that a man who marries a famous woman, a woman more famous than him, can lose his own identity. I didn't want a future Mr. Kelly, if you see what I mean. I didn't want to take a husband. I wanted to become someone's wife." For his part, the 32-year-old Rainier, like so many other men of his generation, believed that marriage was simply "the thing to do" once people reached a certain age: "We knew we could make our lives together, and that now was the time to do it. . . . That's what decided us to go ahead. It wasn't irrational, it was very thought out, but it was also very romantic."[13]

According to fashion designer Oleg Cassini, who had a serious romance with Kelly before she met Rainier, the actress married the prince because she was the "dutiful daughter" of a high-powered family that was a "thoroughgoing patriarchy." Knowing that her difficult-to-please father was never impressed with her acting career, Kelly sought to make him happy by marrying a titled man of wealth. Jack Kelly demonstrated how seriously he took his patriarchal duties when he flouted royal protocol and declined to seat himself before Prince Rainier arrived at the altar. Instead, after escorting his daughter down the aisle, he remained standing to hand her directly to the entering groom. Grace Kelly was no longer a movie star romantically linked to some of Hollywood's most virile leading men. Dressed in virginal white, she was now a dutiful daughter leaving her father's protection to become her husband's loyal helpmate.

In portraying her wedding and marriage in this fashion, the media publicized Grace Kelly's nuptials in a way that guaranteed the public's widespread approval and imitation during the height of the postwar domestic ideal.[14]

The escapist glamour of her wedding—coupled with media exploitation of a familiar domestic plot—ensured that Grace Kelly remained America's most famous and emulated bride for a decade and a half. Although numerous celebrities married in well-publicized ceremonies, none of them captured the public's imagination in the way that Kelly did. Even when the ceremony sported powerful players and a dramatic storyline, a wedding did not achieve iconic status if it lacked the appropriate role-model bride as its centerpiece. The weddings of several presidential daughters in the 1960s, for instance, failed to translate into the wedding industry marketing coup that Grace Kelly's wedding had been.

As actress Edie Adams noted at the time, when Luci Baines Johnson married in 1966, "only the immediate country was invited." The 19-year-old convert to Roman Catholicism—whom a *New York Times* reporter described as "a theatrical, romantic girl"—chose as her wedding venue the nation's largest Catholic church, the Shrine of the Immaculate Conception. When she walked down the aisle on President Lyndon Johnson's arm in her Priscilla of Boston gown, Luci Johnson traversed a distance thirty feet longer than a football field and did so before an audience of 700 invited guests. She and her 23-year-old groom, Patrick Nugent, had a total of twenty-four attendants—with the bridesmaids dressed in shocking pink—and they married to the strains of a 100-voice choir and a million-dollar carillon. Afterwards, at their White House reception, the Nugents and their guests feasted on cold sirloin and a seven-tier, 300-pound wedding cake. The president gratefully acknowledged that his only contributions to the extravaganza were wearing a formal suit and paying the exorbitant bills. In financing his daughter's spectacular, the architect of the Great Society appropriately played the role of provider. The monumental pageantry that LBJ bankrolled, however, could not guarantee a happily-ever-after ending for his daughter and her groom; their marriage ultimately ended in divorce.[15]

In comparison to her sister's festivities, Lynda Bird Johnson's wedding the following year was practically a restrained affair. Her December

1967 ceremony, however, was actually the first to occur within the walls of the White House since Woodrow Wilson's daughter Eleanor married there in 1914. The wedding's location, and the fact that Lynda's Marine captain bridegroom would be leaving for service in Vietnam only three months after the ceremony, ensured that the event made up in drama what it lacked in pageantry. Media interest in Lynda Johnson's nuptials remained high, and journalists tracked every aspect of the wedding's planning and execution. Less than three weeks after the president's 23-year-old daughter announced her engagement, *Women's Wear Daily* reported that she had ordered $4,000 worth of coats, suits, and dresses for her wedding trousseau. The White House abruptly denounced the report as "absurd." Speculation then moved to what the first daughter would wear at the wedding itself. A *New York Times* reporter took a stab at guessing what a young woman of Lynda Johnson's size, coloring, and tastes would choose for her bridal apparel. Describing the president's daughter as "a slim (size 8 or 10), tall (5 feet 9 inches) brunette partial to somewhat more make-up and hair than [were] currently fashionable," the journalist then went on to predict who among the nation's major designers would receive the honor of creating the gown for the White House wedding. All bets were off a few weeks later when the White House announced that Geoffrey Beene would design both the wedding gown and the bright, Christmas-red bridesmaid dresses.[16]

All the breathless prewedding publicity risked turning the White House ceremony itself into an anticlimax. The flamboyant Johnsons, however, did not disappoint. Even though it lacked the scope of her sister's celebration, Lynda Johnson's marriage to 28-year-old Charles Robb did not lack pomp and circumstance. The formal military ceremony, presided over by an Episcopal priest, boasted 500 guests and a total of fourteen attendants for the bridal couple. *Women's Wear Daily* noted that the total cost for the wedding and honeymoon was approximately $62,850 ($380,863 in current dollars). The trousseau and flowers each cost $10,000, and the champagne and honeymoon were $5,000 apiece.[17]

The first White House wedding in over fifty years snagged major air time on the era's three television networks. Broadcast on a tape-delayed basis, Lynda Johnson's wedding first appeared on the National

Broadcasting Company (NBC), which ran footage of the ceremony only an hour after it commenced in "real time." Along with beating the Columbia Broadcasting System (CBS) and the American Broadcasting Company (ABC) onto the air, NBC also outpaced the other networks in negative critical reviews. Titling its broadcast of the military wedding *Candle-Light and Crossed-Swords*, NBC interspersed its coverage with commercials for beauty and grooming products rather than airing it commercial-free, as ABC did, or with "a clear and distinct separation of the ceremony from the commercials," as on CBS. Television critics charged that NBC's coverage of the $62,850 affair had "commercialized" the Johnson-Robb wedding celebration. In the words of a *New York Times* critic, "Since a radiant bride is synonymous with feminine beauty, the opportunity to inject plugs for cosmetics, presumably, was irresistible. But old-fashioned as the idea may be, it would seem reasonable that a happy occasion at the Executive Mansion should be declared out-of-bounds as a peg on which to hang spot announcements. The hard sell should stop at the White House gates."[18]

For members of the 1960s wedding industry, the "hard sell" did not end at the White House gates; it began there. Capitalizing on the first daughter's high-profile nuptials, the Alfred Angelo company announced only three days after Lynda Johnson's wedding that it was shipping out "unauthorized" copies of her gown to stores throughout the nation. Noting that it had also done successful copies of the gowns worn by Monaco's Princess Grace in 1956 and Britain's Princess Margaret in 1960, the Angelo company predicted that its $135 Lynda Johnson gown would be a big hit and eclipse the 2,000 copies it had sold of her sister Luci's dress the previous year. The bridal buyer for New York's Gimbel's store agreed, observing that copies of Lynda's dress would sell better because her gown was prettier than the one her younger sister had worn in 1966.[19]

As the hoopla surrounding Lynda Johnson's wedding died down, members of the wedding industry undoubtedly regretted losing all the free publicity that a first family wedding provided. Luckily for them, in less than a year another man with marriageable daughters was elected president. Considered more photogenic than the Johnson sisters, Julie and Tricia Nixon served as particularly appealing advertisements for the white wedding. Announcing her engagement to David Eisenhower a few days before Lynda Johnson's wedding, Julie Nixon set her New York nuptials in December 1968, only weeks before her father's inauguration. Looking doll-like in a puff-sleeved Priscilla of Boston gown and white mitts, the 20-year-old bride had chosen youthful attire that momentarily inspired other young women to rush to their local bridal salons in search of dresses that resembled the Julie Nixon gown.[20]

For all the coverage these first daughter weddings of the 1960s received, none of them captured the public imagination in the same way that Grace Kelly's nuptials did, and none of the brides achieved superstar status. Unlike Kelly, the Johnson sisters and Julie Nixon did not remain the subject of conversation and imitation for weeks, months, and even years following their wedding ceremonies. Within a matter of days, the fanfare surrounding their nuptial festivities quickly subsided.

For the Johnson sisters, the role of ideal bride perhaps eluded their grasp because they did not conform neatly to the demure and obedient dutiful daughter role. While in reality Grace Kelly had a much more turbulent relationship with her parents than either of the Johnson sisters had with theirs, this fact was not widely known until after the former actress's death. During Kelly's lifetime, most Americans viewed her in terms of her patented movie persona: the refined and loyal wife, daughter, or girlfriend. Luci and Lynda Johnson had no such screen image to fall back on, and the public was fully aware of their real-life acts of daughterly rebellion, including Luci's religious conversion and Lynda's romance with B-list movie actor George Hamilton. The sisters' larger-than-life Texas style—exemplified by their "too much" hair and makeup and their less-than-subtle choices in bridesmaid attire—additionally worked against their playing the role of demure, retiring bride. The sisters' out-of-the-mainstream fashion sense also made their wedding accouterments more difficult for the wedding industry to copy and market to other brides of the 1960s.[21]

In contrast to her immediate first bride predecessors, Julie Nixon's wholesome public image epitomized the dutiful daughter. Even before the votes were counted in the close 1968 presidential race, she had embroidered her father a replica of the presidential seal. This and numerous other acts of her daughterly devotion received wide television and print coverage. At the time of her wedding, however, Julie Nixon worked diligently to avoid the press and downplay what she characterized as a family event rather than a national pageant. She chose to sidestep the built-in publicity attached to a White House wedding by marrying before her father took office. Her nuptials ended up being such a restrained affair that some wedding industry members openly criticized the celebration for not adequately showcasing their wares. The florist for the wedding's Plaza Hotel reception even accused the Nixons of being "cheap" because they spent only $700 on flowers ($4,071 in today's currency). One reason, therefore, that Julie Nixon did not qualify as a superstar bride was that her bridal style—in direct opposition to the Johnsons'— was too subtle to grab the nation's attention in a way that could be fully exploited by the wedding industry. Another reason that Julie Nixon may have failed to assume the role of ideal bride was that, like the Johnson sisters, she was a brunette at a time when the reigning symbols of bridedom—from Disney's Cinderella to bridal magazine models—were overwhelmingly blondes.[22]

Regardless of the era's civil rights crusade and its emerging feminist movement, the model bride of the 1960s remained what she had been in the 1950s: a well-to-do white woman whose blonde hair further emphasized her privileged racial status. She was also someone who subsumed her identity and ambitions to those of the men around her. Blonde Grace Kelly, who abandoned Hollywood and married a prince to win her father's approval, still fit society's image of an ideal bride.

While members of the wedding industry may have been disappointed that a new superstar bride failed to emerge in the 1960s, they had reason to rejoice in the early 1970s. Once again, the nation was caught up in the drama of a White House wedding, as President Richard Nixon's older daughter, Tricia, planned her June 1971 marriage to Harvard law student Edward Cox. This time, to the delight of wedding professionals, the bride seemed to be straight out of central casting. Even stodgy *Time* magazine referred to the size-4 blue-eyed blonde as a woman of "porcelain near beauty" who appeared to be the walking embodiment of the "fairy-princess stereotype." Seeing Tricia Nixon as the perfect advertisement for their wares, people in the wedding business wasted no time in attempting to cash in on her image as bride of the decade.[23]

Manufacturers of tableware, kitchen gadgets, and other popular wedding gifts were the first businesspersons who attempted to associate their products with the White House wedding. Getting wind of these plans, the first lady's office soon thwarted them by warning that the White House would summarily return any "gifts" sent to Tricia Nixon as part of a publicity stunt. The nation's pastry chefs were the next members of the wedding industry to attempt to bask in the reflected glory of Tricia Nixon's wedding. When the White House announced that three chefs would construct a six-foot-tall, 350-pound lemon-flavored cake for the occasion and released the recipe to the public, professional bakers around the country garnered publicity for themselves by alleging that the cake batter included too many egg whites and would remain "mush" when baked. Fortunately for the bride, the critics were wrong, and Tricia's wedding cake turned out to be both structurally sound and edible.[24]

As the day of the wedding approached, all eyes were on the nation's capital, where Tricia Nixon would become the first White House bride ever to take her vows in the mansion's Rose Garden. Sixteen hundred members of the news media requested credentials to cover the ceremony. National news magazines pictured the first daughter and her fiancé on their covers, the three television networks organized to provide even more thorough coverage of the event than they had of Lynda Johnson's nuptials, and the popular *60 Minutes* television program capitalized on wedding-mania by rerunning a segment in which Tricia Nixon conducted a tour of the White House. The Nixon-Cox wedding had become the major news story of June 1971. As a *Time* reporter observed, "Enough atavistic American love of royalty and appetite for pageant remain[ed], along with gossips' curiosity about the powerful, to make it a kind of minor national ceremony."[25]

Ultimately, one American in four watched the televised coverage of Tricia Nixon's wedding, and the event's impact on average citizens was palpable. A New York psychiatrist reported that for a solid week following the Rose Garden ceremony, every one of his female patients wanted to discuss Tricia Nixon's wedding—most of them in envious tones. And for days following coverage of the Nixon-Cox nuptials, wine merchants experienced a consumer stampede for the brand of California champagne the couple served at their reception.[26]

Among those who gained from the nation's interest in the latest White House wedding was President Nixon himself, whose taped conversations with aides reveal that he stage-managed the event for maximum political impact. Discussions with Press Secretary Ron Ziegler, Chief of Staff H. R. Haldeman, *Look* magazine photographer Howell Conant, and others demonstrate the president's concern that photographs and television footage showcase his family and himself in the best possible light. President Nixon considered his daughter's wedding "the biggest news story going today." Images of the beaming father of the bride escorting his daughter and flashing an "okay" sign at the ceremony's conclusion helped humanize Nixon's normally stiff media persona and noticeably improved his public approval ratings. Early the following year, Special Counsel Charles Colson noted that the "warm and appealing" portrait of the Nixons that emerged from the wedding and other recent family events might be "one of the most important political developments" of the Nixon presidency.[27]

Another eager beneficiary of Tricia Nixon's wedding was Alfred Piccione, who once again positioned his Alfred Angelo company to create copies—or rather, unauthorized "interpretations"—of a celebrity wedding gown. As Piccione watched the event on television from his Philadelphia headquarters, he saw the chaplain of the House of Representatives standing before rows of dignitaries—including former first brides Alice Roosevelt and Luci and Lynda Johnson—and waited anxiously for the arrival of the latest young woman to join their ranks. Suddenly, there she was, entering the Rose Garden on the president's arm . . . but something was wrong. Gone was the 25-year-old woman whose taste in frilly, girlish clothing once earned her the annual Goody Two-Shoes Award from a children's clothing manufacturer. Perhaps stinging from past criticism of her "too-young clothes" and flowing mane of hair, Tricia Nixon now walked into her wedding with her hair worn up and her sleeveless Priscilla of Boston gown exposing a bit of cleavage (Figure 3.3). Unlike the puff-sleeved wedding dress her younger sister wore a few years earlier, this one was too sophisticated to fit snugly into the "fairy princess" mode. Although Angelo company officials confidently announced their $170 copy of Tricia Nixon's dress three days after the ceremony, the company's founder must have been disappointed that the

FIGURE 3.3. *Although demure by the standards of a later generation, Tricia Nixon's sleeveless Priscilla of Boston gown with its deep V-neck raised some eyebrows in 1971. (Associated Press)*

first daughter did not revert to her usual tastes on the day of her wedding. With the median age of first-time brides still four years below Tricia's quarter-of-a-century mark, a "too-young" princess bride look would have been a better seller. Although Alfred Angelo Inc. ultimately sold thousands of copies of the Tricia Nixon gown, the consumer stampede that the company hoped for did not materialize. One young bridal-wear customer who rejected the gown did so telling reporters, "Let Tricia be Tricia, I want to be myself." For the typical bride of the era, being herself on her wedding day meant wearing a dress that made her look more like a ruffled Cinderella than a newly sophisticated Tricia Nixon.[28]

While Tricia Nixon's recently acquired taste in grown-up clothing may have thwarted plans to sell replicas of her dress in record-breaking numbers, her turn at playing White House bride nevertheless made a significant impact. Decades after the event, she reported meeting strangers who wanted to talk about their memories of her televised wedding (Figure 3.4). Her blonde good looks certainly helped Tricia Nixon become a bride worth watching and remembering, but the fact that she was an appropriate type for her times also contributed to her becoming a bridal role model. At a time when white-wedding resistors who married barefoot on the beach were capturing headlines, a 25-year-old woman who still lived with her parents and married in full formal regalia was the dutiful daughter that wedding professionals wanted to tout and that the majority of the era's brides wanted to emulate in some fashion. With most young women of the early 1970s rejecting the barefoot countercultural wedding and its anticonsumer ethic, they looked to Tricia Nixon as a bride who tastefully consumed what the wedding industry had to offer—even if some youthful consumers found her sophisticated wedding gown a tad too restrained.[29]

While Tricia Nixon was an appropriate role model bride for the early 1970s, she ultimately lacked Grace Kelly's staying power as a bridal icon. One reason for this situation was that the president's daughter receded into an ordinary existence following her 1971 wedding. Her life as a New York lawyer's wife was definitely not fodder for romantic fantasies or tabloid scandal sheets. Whereas Princess Grace maintained a glamorous and high-profile life that reminded the public again and again how fascinating and exciting her wedding day had been, Tricia Nixon Cox

FIGURE 3.4. *Amid a sea of middle-aged women who fondly remembered the couple's 1971 wedding, Ed and Tricia Nixon Cox celebrated their twenty-fifth anniversary by watching a revue of Priscilla of Boston gowns at the Richard Nixon Library and Birthplace. (Rhonda Birndorf/Associated Press)*

only returned to the spotlight on rare and somber occasions—such as when her father resigned the presidency. Also, while in the early years of her marriage the former Grace Kelly conformed neatly to the reigning ideology of her times by maintaining an identity as a full-time wife and mother, the former Tricia Nixon led the life of a quiet housewife at a time when the role was beginning to go out of fashion. The growing feminist movement and the perceived need for two family wage earners in the era's inflation-plagued economy caused most brides to adopt an alternative plan. A poll of *Bride's* readers in the early 1970s showed that 84 percent of respondents were employed at the time of their weddings and that even more of them—94 percent—anticipated holding jobs for at least a few years after marriage. While Tricia Nixon may have been an appropriate role model for white-wedding brides of the early 1970s, Tricia Nixon Cox was not an appropriate role model for young wives of the period. Her low-key married life caused her "Wedding of the Decade" to fade largely into the background before the 1970s even ended.[30]

Within a decade of Tricia Nixon's wedding, the American bride was in sore need of a new celebrity role model. Fortunately for members of the wedding industry, the early 1980s brought forth an old-fashioned fairy tale bride. The star of what the press dubbed yet another "Wedding of the Century" was a virginal blue-eyed blonde with a fashion model's physique, whose wedding literally transformed her into a princess and made her the most famous woman in the world for the next decade and a half.

This time the eyes of America and the world turned toward London. There, in July 1981, 20-year-old Lady Diana Spencer married Britain's Prince Charles and became the Princess of Wales. Although Americans had to rise in the wee hours of the morning to be among the 750 million worldwide viewers who watched the live television broadcast from St. Paul's Cathedral, millions of U.S. residents did so and saw the woman the British press called "Shy Di" emerge from a horse-drawn coach in a taffeta gown trimmed with bows, antique lace, and more than 10,000 pearls and sequins. Her long walk down the aisle of the cathedral on the arm of her ailing, slow-paced father, the Earl Spencer, allowed the wedding's huge international audience to gain a lingering look at the extraordinary frock. And after the ceremony, her walk down the cathedral steps with Prince Charles displayed the gown's record-setting twenty-five-foot train to great effect (Figure 3.5). A *Time* reporter described the David and Elizabeth Emanuel design as balancing "stately splendor and storybook fantasy." In reply to such descriptions, David Emanuel noted, "The fairyness was us. The regalness was her."[31]

While Buckingham Palace refused to comment on the cost of the bride's voluminous gown, or on any other expenses incurred in celebrating the "Wedding of the Century," the price-tag was obviously substantial. American journalists speculated that the cost of the wedding cake alone was probably $6,000 ($13,360 in current dollars). The realization that such extravagance was occurring in the midst of Britain's worst economy since the Great Depression incited little protest either at home or abroad. Instead, Britons seemed to welcome the pageantry as a distraction from the realities of 12 percent unemployment and worker unrest, while international viewers, including those in the United States, just wanted to sit back and enjoy a good show. In contrast to the wedding of Elizabeth and Philip thirty-four years earlier, the nuptials of Charles and Diana were unapologetically opulent. Press coverage of Elizabeth's 1947 celebration duly noted that the future queen wore a gown made of fabric she purchased with her own carefully hoarded ration stamps, but no such qualifying statements were deemed necessary in 1981. In the 1940s, the press apparently believed that even a war-weary population eager to celebrate a happy national occasion deserved an explanation of how the royal family was paying for the morale-raising splendor of Elizabeth's wedding. In 1981, journalists wasted no words explaining how or why the Windsors were using their vast wealth to throw history's most lavish wedding. After all, by this point in the twentieth century, people significantly lower on the social scale also expected to organize elaborate weddings for their offspring. Queen Elizabeth and Prince Philip were simply doing on a grander scale what millions of British parents—and their American counterparts—did all the time: they were hosting the best wedding they could afford.[32]

Just as the marriage of Charles and Diana proved that the white wedding remained popular in periods of economic strife, it also demonstrated the ritual's continuing resilience in the face of feminist protest. Feminists on both sides of the Atlantic issued numerous criticisms regarding the royal wedding, but they focused particular attention on the fact that a gynecologist had confirmed Diana's virginity as a prerequisite for the marriage, while the 32-year-old prince had obviously been enjoying an active sex life for many years. The sexual double standard notwithstanding, Charles and Diana's marriage enjoyed immense popularity around the world, including in the United States, where even the somber *New York Times* declared it "a fairy tale come to life" and where photographs of the demure Princess of Wales in her billowing gown graced the fronts of newspapers and magazines on every newsstand.[33]

In the same year that Diana's picture beamed from the nation's magazine and newspaper racks, a self-help guide entitled *The Cinderella Complex* occupied the shelves of American bookstores. In her 1981 volume, author Colette Dowling argued that even the most seemingly liberated woman probably harbored the unhealthy desire to be transformed by "something external" to herself. Raised with stories of the damsel in distress and her handsome rescuer, women of the 1980s still looked to marriage as "something external" that would help them solve their problems and provide them with a greater sense of security. Women continued to embrace this notion even as they also increasingly aspired to personal success in the workplace. Intended largely for a white middle-class audience that had been exposed in childhood to the notion of married life as a refuge from the troubled world, Dowling's book became a bestseller.[34]

Though Dowling counseled American women to break free of the Cinderella fantasy, they instead appeared to embrace it as they enthusiastically followed Diana's saga. Through the attentions of a real-life prince, a shy child of divorce could now have a chance at domestic happiness and be transformed into the most glamorous and envied woman in the world. For many women, this story was simply too compelling to resist, and they continued to read about it in heavily illustrated magazine stories and coffee table books that featured Diana enveloped in the world's most famous wedding dress.

The enormous gown worn on her wedding day by Diana, Princess of Wales, became the prototype for millions of excessively ornate wedding dresses manufactured and purchased in Britain and the United States. The first copies showed up in stores only a day after the royal wedding. The sparkling dress and the other thrilling highlights of the televised nuptials secured the popularity of elaborate white weddings for years to come. Even after the Charles and Diana saga became a fractured fairy tale of infidelity and divorce, their spectacular nuptials remained the hallmark against which all other extravaganzas were judged. To mark the twenty-fifth anniversary of the Wedding of the Century, the Emanuels— now themselves divorced and with separate designing careers—briefly reconciled to produce yet another coffee table book about Diana and her legendary frock. By the time of the book's publication, Prince Charles had been married to Camilla Parker-Bowles for over a year and Diana had been dead for nearly a decade, but discussion of their wedding and her remarkable dress continued.[35]

The vogue for lavish Charles and Di–style weddings in the United States was helped along by other events in 1981, such as the highly rated fictional wedding of the popular Luke and Laura characters on ABC's *General Hospital* series. The arrival in the White House of First Lady Nancy Reagan also played a role. When her husband took office in

January 1981, the purchasing power of the average American family was a thousand dollars less than it had been a decade earlier. In 1982, 10 percent of the country's workforce was unemployed. By 1983 the nation's poverty rate was 15.2 percent, the highest in nearly twenty years. Nevertheless, during these same years, Nancy Reagan spearheaded a fashion movement variously labeled a "style of unabashed opulence," "luxurious exhibitionism," and "excessory chic." This 1980s fashion statement also found expression in several highly popular television series, such as *Dynasty*, *Dallas*, and *Lifestyles of the Rich and Famous*, and it went hand in hand with the Reagan administration's high-profile alliance with persons of wealth and privilege. Counting well-dressed socialites and famous fashion designers among the members of her inner circle, Nancy Reagan made headlines in the early 1980s for her expensive tastes in dinner party china and designer clothing. Her inaugural wardrobe alone cost $25,000 in 1981, and she nearly doubled that price to $46,000 ($86,528 in current dollars) for her husband's second inauguration in 1985. Although the first lady's pricey elegance received criticism from some members of the press and from some of her husband's political opponents, the extravagant "Nancy Reagan look" also landed her on the top of many best-dressed lists and inspired legions of imitators. As one of her admirers noted, with the first lady as their role model, women with the financial means now knew that it was "all right to buy grand clothes again without looking out of place." Nancy Reagan quite simply helped make expensive dressing and entertaining very fashionable in the 1980s.[36]

One of Nancy Reagan's most famous social successes occurred in 1985 when she and the president hosted a visit to Washington by the young couple whose wedding she had attended four years earlier. In town to visit the National Gallery's "Treasure Houses of Britain" exhibit and a J. C. Penney show of popular fashions inspired by the British aristocracy, Charles and Diana attended a private White House dinner party that a wealthy guest described as "one of the most exciting nights in the history of the White House." As Americans watched television coverage of the lavish affair, including footage of Diana twirling across the dance floor with movie star John Travolta, they were reminded again of the breathtaking splendor of the princess's 1981 wedding. In an era when fancy dressing and glamorous escorts were fashionable, Diana remained second to no one—not even Nancy Reagan. Whether in a blue evening gown in the arms of John Travolta or in a wedding gown on the arm of Prince Charles, Diana remained the decade's unrivaled fashion icon.[37]

Diana's marriage to Charles was only the first of many high-profile celebrity weddings that captured Americans' attention in the 1980s. In the spring and summer of 1986 alone, wedding watchers not only witnessed the Westminster Abbey ceremony of Prince Andrew and Sarah ("Fergie") Ferguson but also the glamorous Hyannis Port celebrations of Caroline Kennedy and her cousin, broadcaster Maria Shriver. The celebrity impact of Shriver's wedding was doubled by the fact that she married movie superstar Arnold Schwarzenegger. It was Diana's 1981 wedding, however, that remained the ideal. No other bride could match the opulence and expense of the "Wedding of the Century," but she could wear a similarly styled dress and imitate other aspects of Diana's extravaganza on a smaller, less expensive scale.[38]

While her lavish style of adornment and celebration seemed appropriate for the 1980s, many of Diana's other qualities appeared out of place for the times. In the early months of 1981, when Diana first entered the limelight as Charles's fiancée, her public image seemed curiously dated. While her frequently voiced desire for marriage and children placed her in sync with most of her contemporaries, her lack of sexual experience and career ambition placed her outside the mainstream. Many young women wanted to look and dress like Diana Spencer and have their own versions of her Cinderella wedding, but they had difficulty relating to much of the rest of her public persona. As Diana matured and her image evolved, however, that persona came closer to the 1980s ideal: by the middle of the decade, she was a woman who successfully combined marriage, motherhood, and meaningful work outside the home. For Diana, the home was a palace and the labor was not remunerated, but her high-profile charity work on behalf of AIDS patients and others in need of a celebrity patron demonstrated that the glamorous princess had a more serious side. Her commitment to these activities continued, in fact, even after she separated from and later divorced the heir to the British throne. In a famous 1995 television interview about the breakup of her marriage, Diana discussed her commitment to what she carefully termed her "work" and resolved to remain in the public eye to benefit her

FIGURE 3.5. *The gown that Lady Diana Spencer wore for her 1981 marriage to Britain's Prince Charles epitomized the "fairy princess" style and ensured the popularity of voluminous wedding dresses on both sides of the Atlantic for the remainder of the decade. (Associated Press)*

charities. Some feminist critics now began to embrace Diana and applaud her for challenging one of the world's most famous patriarchal
institutions: the British royal family. Diana, who married at age 20 and
became a mother at 21, now for the first time began to talk about herself
in autonomous terms, saying, "I have learned much over the last years.
From now on I am going to own myself and be true to myself. I no longer
want to live someone else's idea of what and who I should be. I am going to be me." But while the Diana of this period was more work-minded
and independent than the "Shy Di" of the early 1980s, she was by this
time also a woman with a failed marriage and thus no longer the best
bridal role model. By the mid-1990s, then, women were in need of a different bridal ideal.[39]

In August 1997, sixteen years after marrying Britain's Prince Charles
in the Wedding of the Century, Diana, Princess of Wales, died in a Paris
auto accident. In the United States, *Bride's* magazine memorialized the
princess by commenting that her 1981 wedding had "transformed" the
way American women thought about weddings: "The images of that
event are so thoroughly implanted in our memories, it's hard to separate
the idea of a bride from the picture of Diana emerging, Cinderella-like,
from her glass coach. That early morning . . . we started dreaming about
the day when we, too, would promise to love, honor, and cherish." In
reality, *Bride's* magazine and the rest of the wedding industry had helped
create the expensive fairytale wedding long before Diana's 1981 ceremony. The royal wedding did not so much transform women's image of
the ideal wedding as it solidified their already existing picture of the perfect nuptial celebration. And by the time of Diana's death, nearly a year
had already passed since another woman supplanted her as America's
version of the ideal bride.[40]

Seemingly in the nick of time, a new icon emerged in 1996 who popularized a fresh look in wedding attire and provided brides with an up-
to-date prototype. In September of that year, the "world's most eligible
bachelor," John F. Kennedy Jr., married Carolyn Bessette, a public relations executive for designer Calvin Klein. Although the small, secretive
ceremony took place in an isolated country church on Georgia's Cum-
berland Island, the couple released a photograph of the event that quickly
made its way around the globe. In it, the willowy, 30-year-old blonde

was seen emerging from the church's vine-bedecked interior with her famous groom. The dress she wore was the epitome of minimalist style. Designed by one of the bride's friends in the fashion world, Narciso Rodriguez, the Paris-made, bias-cut gown of pearl-colored silk crepe made even Vera Wang's sleek bridal designs look "froufrou" in comparison[41] (Figure 3.6).

With the widespread publication of that one photograph, a different kind of princess bride emerged. She was a mature, sophisticated career woman, who also happened to have as her groom a handsome celebrity that *People* magazine once called "the Sexiest Man Alive." And she married this Prince Charming in a secluded, romantic setting, while wearing an eye-catching frock that "almost instantly" inspired imitation. Allen Schwartz, the decade's fashion "knockoff king," sold some 80,000 copies of the dress. Commenting on the gown's impact, etiquette consultant Letitia Baldrige noted, "Brides-to-be all over the world discarded their beaded, bouffant wedding dresses for the slinky slip dress worn by Carolyn." A year and a half after the wedding, one fashion writer described Bessette as a muse whose signature style "whispered" rather than "shouted" and as a "contemporary fashion icon" whose "modern elegance" was responsible in part for the current popularity of wedding dresses that featured "streamlined silhouettes and modest adornment." In discussing the impact of Carolyn Bessette's bridal gown, another writer noted that the white wedding dress had now entered the final stage in its evolution from the ostentatious styles of the 1980s to the simple elegance of the 1990s. He worried, however, that in moving "from the overblown Cinderella look chosen by the Princess of Wales . . . to the satin slip worn by Carolyn Bessette Kennedy," betrothed women around the country would turn themselves into "Robobrides" who exercised incessantly to achieve the slender physique necessary to carry off the "Carolyn look" at their weddings.[42]

The famous photograph of Carolyn Bessette and her groom communicated to its audience not only that the bride possessed a sophisticated fashion sense but that she was an independent woman of the 1990s. Unlike wedding photographs of Grace Kelly, Tricia Nixon, or Diana Spencer, this one did not feature a proud father giving the bride away or beaming on the sidelines. No benevolent paternal figure graced this

Silk Crepe
bias gown
Silk tulle
veil &
gloves

CERRUTI 1881
PARIS

FIGURE 3.6. *The eye-catching slip dress that Carolyn Bessette wore for her 1996 marriage to John F. Kennedy Jr. was designed by Narciso Rodriguez for Cerruti 1881. (Associated Press)*

photo of the happy bride and her new husband. Neither did the bride
cling demurely to her husband's arm in the typical wedding day pose.
Instead, the statuesque bride stood almost evenly with her groom, looking him squarely in the eye as he stooped a bit to kiss her hand. The image was of a bride and groom who were beginning their lives together as
equal partners (Figure 3.7).

Carolyn Bessette was a new and appropriate role model for the 1990s,
but parts of her story paralleled the tales of earlier superstar brides. Her
wedding attire and professional history differed from those of Grace
Kelly, Tricia Nixon, and the Princess of Wales, yet she resembled them
in other ways. She too was a photogenic blonde from a privileged background who married a man from a wealthy, prestigious family. In becoming the nation's latest bridal icon, she furthered the image of the ideal
bride as a prosperous white woman. And after her marriage, Carolyn
Bessette Kennedy—like her predecessors—defined herself largely as a
wife. She never went back to work for Calvin Klein, and the public only
knew her as the striking woman who attended charity events on her husband's arm. In fact, the American public never even heard the woman's
speaking voice, because her husband answered any questions that the
press shouted to the couple on such occasions. Nevertheless, for numerous brides of the late 1990s, particularly career women of a similar age,
Carolyn Bessette was the bride to emulate.

Even when—like Princesses Grace and Diana before her—Carolyn
Bessette Kennedy died in a tragic accident, she remained a role model.
After the 1999 plane crash that took their lives—on their way to the elaborate Hyannis Port wedding of cousin Rory Kennedy—the famous wedding picture of Carolyn Bessette and John F. Kennedy Jr. was flashed
around the world again and again. In its commemorative issue on the
life of JFK Jr., *Time* magazine, like numerous other publications, printed
the photo and described the event it portrayed as a "fairy-tale wedding,"
a "story-book wedding," and "the wedding of the decade." Women admired the chic wedding gown once more, and some of them set their
minds on acquiring one just like it. One 38-year-old professional woman
preparing to marry for the first time reported that she decided then and
there to scour wedding shops in search of a gown that approximated
Carolyn Bessette's. And feminist bride-to-be Kamy Wicoff, on her first

It could have been you.

FIGURE 3.7. *In January 1997, a Hingham, Massachusetts, boutique used a cardboard cutout of the groom and a mannequin wearing a copy of the bride's trend-setting dress to recreate the famous wedding photo of JFK Jr. and Carolyn Bessette. The store's owner reported that her customers were "demanding the popular dress." (Charles Krupa/Associated Press)*

trip to a wedding boutique in January 2000, immediately requested "a Carolyn Bessette kind of thing" because "every woman in the country who preferred pants to crotchless clothes thought she wanted a dress like the one Carolyn wore to marry JFK Jr. Slinky, silky, and without petticoats, it had one foot in the sexy-tough, tradition-busting door and one foot in the I'm-no-girly-girl-but-if-I'm-going-to-do-this-thing-I-might-as-well-do-it-right door."[43]

Carolyn Bessette was everything women of her generation were supposed to be. She was successful in the workplace, athletic, and sexually liberated enough to live with her groom before marriage. But the media version of Carolyn Bessette's saga—and the public's reaction to it— seemed to indicate that her greatest achievement was wearing the right dress when she became Carolyn Bessette Kennedy. As the twentieth century came to an end, playing the bride's role well still mattered. And one of the morals of the brief Carolyn Bessette Kennedy story was that a woman's wedding day still outranked all others in importance.

In her 1998 biography of the former Diana Spencer, feminist author Julie Burchill noted that a princess has "the ultimate Being, not Doing job description. Her job [is] to look beautiful and to be married to a Prince." While only two of the women considered in this chapter literally became princesses when they wed, all four of them played the role of "Princess Bride" in media versions of their wedding stories. For the four women whose weddings most captured America's attention in the six decades following World War II, their "Being" indeed eclipsed their "Doing."[44]

For each of these women, in her public life, being a celebrity bride clearly overshadowed any other task she engaged in or goal she accomplished. For Diana Spencer and Carolyn Bessette, their route to fame rested solely in the act of being a bride. Had they not become the brides of famous men, both women would have remained in obscurity. Even for Grace Kelly and Tricia Nixon, the renown they achieved by being brides surpassed what either of them had previously achieved as an actress or first daughter. And following her wedding, none of these four women— no matter what she went on to do with her life—received more acclaim than she achieved through the act of simply being a bride. Even the Princess of Wales—whose soap-opera love life, opulent wardrobe, international acts of charity, and shocking demise all received wall-to-wall press coverage—was never more famous than on the day of her wedding.

Fulfilling "the ultimate Being, not Doing job," these women became associated with the image of the smiling, white-clad bride to such an extent that it developed into a permanent identity. The extensive press coverage that accompanied each of their premature deaths focused significant attention on the wedding celebrations that Princess Grace, Princess Diana, and Carolyn Bessette Kennedy once-upon-a-time enjoyed, and photographic tributes to each woman always included wedding-day images of her in her famous bridal gown. On the rare occasion that Tricia Nixon Cox stepped back into the media spotlight in later years, such as at her father's 1994 funeral, press commentators inevitably referred to her wedding day and remembered it as the only time that President Nixon danced in the White House. In the public consciousness, even in moments of tragedy these women remained beaming brides.

Whether marrying the Prince of Monaco in 1956 or the "Prince of Camelot" in 1996, the princess bride largely achieved her exalted status for one reason: she looked like the nation's ideal image of a bride. Blonde, conventionally pretty, expensively attired, and properly posed alongside the significant male players in her wedding pageant, the princess bride looked strikingly like the professional models who simply pretended to be perfectly appointed brides in the wedding magazines. Bridal gown fashions changed from decade to decade, and wedding pictures evolved from images that emphasized a bride's deference to her father or groom to those that communicated eye-to-eye equality between the new husband and wife. Nevertheless, the princess brides seemed eerily similar to one another as they emerged onto the nation's magazine pages or television screens every ten or fifteen years. Elegantly attired and surrounded by expensive props, each of these women became connected with the notion of bride as consumer. Never more famous than on her wedding day, each of these women became associated with the idea that a woman's wedding day marked the height of her prestige. Assuming the role of wife as her primary postwedding identity, each woman relinquished her claim to a public persona that could be entirely separated from that of bride. The Princess of Wales, who had the least amount of time to develop an independent identity before becoming a bride, was the only one of the four who had some success in breaking free of her image as an eternal bride. As she approached middle age, Diana began to form an independent identity for the first time in her life, but the most widely reproduced images of her—even after her divorce from Charles—remained those wedding-day pictures in which she stood arm-in-arm with her father the earl or her husband the prince.

Curiously absent from these celebrity wedding scenes was the figure who loomed so prominently at most weddings—the mother of the bride. Aside from the bride herself, women in general remained relatively absent from media coverage of these occasions. The only other adult female who received significant media attention at any of these weddings was not the bride's mother but the groom's. As head of state, however, Queen Elizabeth II was impossible to ignore. But with the exception of Her Majesty, female friends and relatives were generally on the sidelines in these celebrity wedding stories. And their absence was the most obvious proof that these celebrations were not typical weddings. With millions of dollars at their disposal, celebrity brides did not have to rely on the constant presence of mothers, sisters, aunts, cousins, and friends to attend to the fine details of the day. Anonymous retainers could instead perform these duties.

Over the decades, the princess bride evolved in some significant ways. In the 1950s she was a twenty-something woman who very publicly renounced a fulfilling career in favor of the era's Cinderella dream: marriage and family. By the 1990s she was a 30-year-old woman who never had to make any either/or announcements regarding career and marriage. By this point in time, the Cinderella fantasy had transformed into one that simultaneously accommodated both a job and a handsome prince. In reality, however, the brief postwedding life of the twentieth century's last princess bride followed a familiar path. While at the time of her 1996 marriage Carolyn Bessette was the accomplished career-woman bride touted in 1990s popular culture, she soon adopted the role of celebrity wife as her primary identity.

Like Princess Grace, Tricia Nixon Cox, and Princess Diana, Carolyn Bessette Kennedy remained chiefly known to the public as a smiling bride in an attention-grabbing dress. After her untimely death, her famous wedding-day picture remained the most widely reproduced and recognized image of the former Calvin Klein executive. Forever a bride, this end-of-the-century fashion icon thus remained indelibly linked with her special day—the day she married John F. Kennedy Jr.

As a new century began, celebrity watchers continued to follow the wedding adventures of well-known personalities, now often taking advantage of the many Web sites that tracked celebrity marriages. Whether a site was devoted to celebrity weddings in general or to same-sex unions, African American weddings, Las Vegas–based ceremonies, or another specialized category, it invited visitors to approximate the celebrations of their heroines and heroes. Through words and pictures, Internet users learned all the details about Catherine Zeta-Jones's wedding cake, Jennifer Aniston's bridal gown, Star Jones's gift registry, and the presents Britney Spears bestowed on her bridesmaids. Most significant, they learned the names of the jewelry stores, fashion and cake designers, and other personnel who provided this paraphernalia, and they typically viewed advertisements suggesting where at less cost they too could book a gay-friendly honeymoon resort, purchase African-inspired wedding invitations, or reserve a wedding chapel with an Elvis theme. Visitors to a banking industry site learned how to "re-create that spectacular celebrity style" from a "well-known wedding consultant to the rich and famous" who assured Web surfers, "Celebrity weddings are a great source of ideas and trends that you can incorporate into your affair for much less money." By borrowing her jewelry from her grandmother rather than Tiffany's and placing decorative candles in inexpensive juice glasses rather than crystal candle holders, a bride could indeed approximate the look of a fancy celebrity wedding and "get married like a star."[45]

Recognizing that consumer interest in marrying "like a star" was greater than ever, mental health professionals worried that the nation's brides might be carrying this "wedding mania" too far. In a phenomenon that psychologists labeled the "postwedding blues," a growing number of brides reported feeling let-down and disappointed when the glamour of the long-anticipated wedding day ended and the real marriage began. Brides who looked to celebrity Web sites for inspiration and shopping advice certainly found reinforcement of the message that wedding style was more important than relationship substance. A site profiling dozens of famous weddings acknowledged this ranking of priorities in its opening text: "Some of these marriages didn't stand the test of time, but the weddings remain in our memories. These weddings set trends for brides around the world." On this Web site, even brides whose grandiose weddings ushered in famously failed marriages—such as the Princess of Wales and actress Jennifer Aniston—remained worthy role models. In a society where noncelebrity brides were themselves increasingly "obsess[ed] with the ceremony, the cake, the dress, everything but the relationship," celebrity brides seemed yet again to be high-profile advertisements for the latest trend in weddings and marriage.[46]

At a time when people casually referred to the *"InStyle* Curse"—the high divorce rate for couples whose weddings appeared in the popular celebrity magazine *InStyle* or its spin-off publication *InStyle Weddings*— consumers understood that a perfectly choreographed celebrity wedding did not necessarily launch a perfect marriage. Since the magazine's founding in the mid-1990s, a number of *InStyle* couples had even broken up before the issues publicizing their weddings hit the newsstands. But none of that mattered if their wedding cake was eye-catching enough for Web surfers and magazine browsers to want one just like it. Unlike the days of Princess Grace and Prince Rainier, consumers no longer needed to believe that their heroines and heroes lived happily ever after in suburban-style domestic bliss. In this era of upscale consumer tastes, fans did not want their own wedding stories—much less those of their idols— to appear too "middle class" anyway. As a commentator on the *"InStyle* Curse" noted, celebrity wedding watchers cared primarily about a famous bride's lavish wedding day—not the day after.[47]

In the decades following World War II, the most highly publicized brides communicated a consistent message to their audience: the most significant day in a woman's life was when she stood "all dressed in white" as the centerpiece of an expensive wedding celebration. Whether she emerged in 1956 or 1996, the superstar bride perpetuated the idea that a woman's wedding day marked her best and most justified opportunity to consume conspicuously. From their designer gowns to their abundant floral displays and towering wedding cakes, the princess brides spent lavishly to produce the beautiful wedding pageants that the American public viewed in popular periodicals, television programs, coffee table books, and eventually on the Internet. In 2000, etiquette advisor Letitia Baldrige published a guide entitled *Legendary Brides*, in which she told "brides-to-be, their mothers, and friends" how to reproduce the weddings that Grace Kelly, Tricia Nixon, Diana Spencer, Carolyn Bessette, and other celebrities enjoyed. While most readers lacked the means to reproduce such extravaganzas precisely, they nevertheless saw elements that they could afford for themselves—from a certain brand of champagne to a particular style of wedding gown. According to Baldrige, bringing a celebrity's "sense of style, ceremony, and tradition to a wedding" was something "every bride" could do with "a little imagination and the willingness to learn from the triumphs and disasters of the famous brides who have gone up the aisle before her." Long after their wedding days ended, the princess brides and their glamorous weddings remained highly effective advertisements for wedding industry wares.[48]

CHAPTER 4

WATCHING *CINDERELLA* ON VIDEO

The Movie Wedding

In 2002 a cinematic Cinderella story entitled *My Big Fat Greek Wedding* took the nation by storm. The movie broke all existing box office records for an independent film and inspired a short-lived television series by presenting the ultimate female success story for a new millennium: the heroine finds personal identity, career advancement, and a handsome prince.[1]

The film centers on Toula (Nia Vardalos), the 30-year-old daughter of Greek immigrants who works as a hostess in her family's Chicago restaurant, a self-described "frump girl" whose family controls every aspect of her life. Tired of her drab existence and inspired by a chance meeting with a handsome restaurant patron (John Corbett), Toula takes action and plays fairy godmother for herself. She enrolls in college to study computers, buys the right products to give herself a makeover, and ends up running a travel agency almost single-handedly. Now that she is a success, she accidentally meets the handsome stranger again, and the rest of the fairy tale falls into place. In a final blow for independence, Toula defies family tradition by making plans to marry her dream man—even though he is not Greek. All conflicts are resolved, however, when she and her fiancé agree to hold a big, fat Greek wedding. Wearing an enormous white gown and surrounded by cousins in outrageous bridesmaid costumes, Toula develops a new appreciation for her family. The elaborate wedding represents the love and stability they provide, and the heartwarming occasion even melts the reserve of her uptight WASP in-laws.[2]

Wondering in the *New York Times* how a film based on the hackneyed ugly duckling story could become such a big hit, journalist Lori Leibovich reasoned that it must be the payoff scene at the end of the picture. Whether weddings take place on the movie screen or in real life, Americans look to them for crowd-pleasing entertainment. After checking her wristwatch and rolling her eyes through most of the movie, even Leibovich teared up during the wedding scene. But along with their love of big weddings, audiences embraced the film because Toula is the perfect Cinderella for the early twenty-first century. She uses her own brains, spunk, effort, and consumer power to secure a better job, a new appearance, and a dashing groom. And at her lavish wedding, the former wallflower shows off these achievements and basks in the attention and gifts her loved ones bestow. Her parents even present the bride and groom with a new house. The movie is both an escapist fantasy and a guide to success for the American woman of the 2000s.[3]

My Big Fat Greek Wedding was just the latest in a long line of motion pictures—going back at least as far as Disney's 1950 *Cinderella*—that familiarized audiences with the appropriate components of a formal white wedding and sometimes even explicitly tutored them in how to go about purchasing wedding industry products. Scholars, social critics, and moviegoers themselves may debate the extent to which audiences deliberately pattern their lives on what they see at the movies, but all agree that films have an influence on viewers' real-life thinking and behavior. This impact has become particularly noticeable since the 1980s, when the home-video industry began renting and selling fans their favorite films for repeated viewings. But long before the arrival of VCRs and DVD players, fans absorbed—and often emulated—the lessons they learned in the movies. Given the ubiquity of motion pictures, film industry publicity, and fans' conversations about the movies they have seen during the past 100 years, "it is hard to see how anyone could escape the influence of the movies, unless they simply stayed home and talked to no one until they were past being influenced by anything."[4]

Before the ascendancy of television in the 1950s, motion pictures held an especially strong grasp on the American imagination. In 1940, when the country's total population was 132 million, U.S. movie theaters sold

75 million tickets each week. In the decade before Pearl Harbor, 40 percent of American adults attended movie theaters on at least a weekly basis, and their favorite genre was the romance picture. Love stories comprised approximately 30 percent of all Hollywood releases, were especially popular among female viewers, and often included wedding scenes. Between 1930 and 1940, filmmakers produced a total of forty-nine English-language pictures that even included the words "wedding" or "bride" in the title. Movies that portrayed elaborate formal weddings usually centered on wealthy brides—like the heroines in *It Happened One Night* (1934) and *The Philadelphia Story* (1940)—who enjoyed designer gowns and extravagant gifts that most real-life brides and wedding guests could not afford.[5]

These films provided movie patrons with a "tangible model" for molding or measuring their own life goals, deeds, expectations, and acquisitions. In an influential examination of American advertising entitled *Our Master's Voice* (1934), James Rorty theorized that films depicting elaborate weddings or otherwise having "a high content of 'romance,' 'beauty' and conspicuous expenditure" represented the "movie product of maximum salability" because society's dominant values were "material and acquisitive." Since Depression-era audiences were "economically debarred from the attainment of these values in real life," they enjoyed them "vicariously in the dream world of the silver screen," where their frustrations with reality were "both alleviated and sharpened by the pictures." Motion pictures and consumer culture thus complemented one another perfectly. Movies inspired material desires that advertisers could exploit, and advertisements inspired wants that movies could satisfy vicariously.[6]

This symbiosis continued during the war years, even as production for the American war machine replaced production for the consumer market. Manufacturers now producing bombers and torpedoes rather than cooking ranges and toasters still advertised to the home-front consumer, telling her their products would be back bigger and better at war's end. After all, one advertisement reminded female consumers, it was "*American* . . . to want something better" after the war. And the American cinema, whose function was to educate about the nation's war aims in documentaries and raise wartime morale in entertainment films, continued to inspire consumer desires that would be satiated with the return to a peacetime economy. Escapist costume pictures and cinematic fairy tales continued to present the opulent sets, clothing, and props that were typical of prewar Hollywood while pictures set on the contemporary American home front featured situations and characters that reflected the consumer frustrations of the audience—but always with the message that postwar abundance was just around the corner.[7]

After years of viewing glamorous weddings on the movie screen and hoping they might be better able to afford such luxuries once the Great Depression ended, female moviegoers now faced consumer shortages, rationing restrictions, and other obstacles that prevented them from enjoying white weddings during wartime. And the movies addressed this frustrating dilemma. As the U.S. marriage rate reached new heights and women expressed an increasing desire for the white wedding, Hollywood encouraged these longings in films that portrayed the indignities of rushed wartime civil ceremonies. Even films that did not centrally focus on weddings, such as *Arsenic and Old Lace* (1944), frequently included scenes showing hoards of people—including men in uniform and their mates—lining up to face the cold bureaucracy of a simple courthouse or city hall ceremony. The entire plot of one film, 1945's *The Clock*, revolved around a whirlwind wartime romance and the negative consequences of failing to hold a white wedding.

Having played teenagers in MGM musicals for a number of years, 23-year-old Judy Garland now made the transition to dramatic adult roles by portraying a timely character—the American war bride—in *The Clock*. Directed by future husband Vincente Minnelli, Garland plays an office worker named Alice who meets, falls in love with, and marries a soldier named Joe (Robert Walker)—all during the course of his two-day New York furlough. The couple's rushed civil ceremony—witnessed only by an office cleaning woman—leaves Garland's character noting wistfully, "I didn't have any flowers." Later, as the couple half-heartedly eats a meal in a greasy spoon, she breaks down entirely, pronouncing their wedding "ugly" and admitting, "I guess I don't feel very married." Her dissatisfaction is magnified when she and Joe see a white-gowned bride and officer bridegroom triumphantly exit a church with elegant bridesmaids and cheering guests in tow. But it is this scene of another couple's wedding-day happiness that provides Alice with a solution. She leads Joe into the empty church, and as an altar boy slowly extinguishes the candles, the couple read the wedding service aloud to one another from a prayer book. Illuminated by another bride's candles and with the right words and setting, Alice now feels truly married.[8]

The Clock, which was both a critical and box-office hit, reflected the real-life experiences of many audience members. Its rushed, bouquet-less civil ceremony was typical of the times. The movie told its audience, however, that such weddings were not good enough. A real wedding was like the atypical wartime celebration that the film's protagonists witness and then attempt to replicate in their own mock ceremony. Once the war ended, that was the kind of wedding everyone should have.[9]

A year after *The Clock*'s release and the war's end, Hollywood indeed began depicting the white wedding as the new American norm. One movie that audiences flocked to see in 1946–1947 was *The Best Years of Our Lives*, a film that won the Best Picture Oscar and sold more first-run tickets than any motion picture since 1939's *Gone with the Wind*. Inspired by a *Time* magazine article about real-life World War II veterans, the film follows three returning servicemen as they reintegrate themselves into the American family and adjust to postwar gender roles. Al (Fredric March), a middle-aged infantry sergeant, returns to a wife and children who have grown independent of his influence and authority. Fred (Dana Andrews), a heroic pilot, comes home to a lowly soda fountain job and an unfaithful war bride who is only attracted to his uniform and medals. Homer (Harold Russell), a sailor who lost his hands in a torpedo attack, worries that he will no longer be an adequate husband to his loyal fiancée Wilma (Cathy O'Donnell). The men's gender anxieties are only resolved at the end of the three-hour movie, when all the major characters gather for Homer and Wilma's wedding.[10]

In the picture's closing minutes, an entire wedding ceremony plays out for the audience, from Wilma's entrance to the strains of "Here Comes the Bride" to the couple's closing kiss and the cheers of the wedding guests. The wedding's living-room setting is humble, but it is appropriately festooned with hothouse greenery and crepe-paper wedding bells, and Wilma is exquisitely dressed in flowing white gown and veil. Having weathered alcoholism and a disillusioning banking career, Al has now reestablished a close relationship with his wife (Myrna Loy), and the couple looks on approvingly as Homer overcomes his fears and takes his vows as a husband. Fred, who has left behind his demeaning job and hasty wartime marriage to pursue a romance with Al's daughter Peggy (Teresa Wright), proudly serves as best man and watches as Homer uses his prosthetic hooks to place a ring on Wilma's finger (Figure 4.1). The spectacle of his friend's wedding is so impressive that it inspires Fred to rush across the room, embrace Peggy, and promise that they too will live happily ever after in postwar America, where he will support them by transforming junked war planes into prefab metal houses for the nation's growing number of new families.[11]

By ending the picture with this scene, screenwriter Robert E. Sherwood and director William Wyler successfully captured the optimistic mood of 1946 America. Americans had fought a war and emerged victorious as the world's only atomic power. The GI Bill was easing concerns about postwar recession and unemployment by providing veterans with jobs, education, and housing, and the Cold War with the Soviet Union had not yet begun. The moviegoing audience, like the fictional characters in *The Best Years of Our Lives*, had faced war-induced sacrifice and disappointment, but they were now ready to reclaim traditional gender roles and face a prosperous new future. They were also in the mood to celebrate that future—like the bride and groom in the movie—with some greenery, crepe paper, and pretty clothes.

At a time when young Americans viewed weddings and marriage as perhaps the ultimate expression of postwar normalcy, the closing scene of *The Best Years of Our Lives* decisively championed that way of thinking. In the readjustment to peacetime living standards and reconversion to a consumer economy, many real-life Americans who staged white weddings in this first postwar year—like the characters in the film—necessarily availed themselves of only the most basic formal wedding props. This cinematic portrayal of love and marriage in the early postwar period thus both echoed and encouraged a vision of the formal white wedding that was realistically achievable for middle-class members of the nation's moviegoing audience. Ordinary people could now celebrate weddings that looked like those in Hollywood movies.

In *The Best Years of Our Lives*, Wilma is Cinderella as the girl next door. She marries her long-time love and is on her way to comfortable

FIGURE 4.1. *As Fred (Dana Andrews), Peggy (Teresa Wright), and Peggy's parents (Myrna Loy and Fredric March) look on, Homer and Wilma (Harold Russell and Cathy O'Donnell) exchange vows in the inspiring final scene of* The Best Years of Our Lives. *(RKO/Samuel Goldwyn/Photofest)*

domesticity. Although the picture does not indicate that she and Homer will ever rise above their lower-middle-class origins, they are enjoying a level of prosperity that people on that rung of the ladder had not previously known. Her snowy wedding gown is the first of many one-time luxuries that consumers in their circumstances can now afford.

For the movie's other young female character, the future looks even brighter. Like Wilma, Peggy has found her true love. But unlike Homer, Fred is able-bodied, a former officer, and a war hero. And the movie has already established his strong work ethic in scenes at the dead-end soda fountain job. Now that he has found an opportunity in the prefab housing industry, Fred will be an excellent provider. As the picture ends, he tells Peggy, "It may take us years to get anywhere. We'll have no money, no decent place to live. We'll have to work—get kicked around." But as Peggy smiles broadly and kisses him, the audience knows they will eventually achieve their American dream. In the meantime, they can always borrow money from Peggy's banker father to put a down payment on one of Fred's inexpensive metal houses. With a little imagination, the era's moviegoers could even envision Fred and Peggy as the tuxedoed groom and white-gowned bride who advertised "Modern, Attractive, Well-Built Homes" for the real-life Stran-Steel company. Like the bride in the Stran-Steel brochures, Peggy's Prince Charming is poised to carry her over the threshold of their postwar castle—even if it is only a modified Quonset hut.[12]

On the heels of the triumphant wedding scene in *The Best Years of Our Lives*, the Cinderella myth received another major boost in 1950 when Walt Disney released an animated version of the story of the girl with the glass slipper. In *Cinderella*, Disney presented a thoroughly Americanized depiction of the European fairytale heroine to a broad audience of consumers for the first time. Not only does Disney's Cinderella speak with an American accent, but she neatly conforms to the nation's postwar domestic ideal—even going so far as to adopt a batch of mice as her surrogate children.[13]

From beginning to end, *Cinderella* instructs its viewers in the appropriate gender roles, courtship rituals, and consumer practices of 1950s America. Doted on by her father when she was a child, Cinderella once enjoyed every material advantage. After her father's death, however, Cinderella's stepmother pitches her into a consumer hell. While the stepmother lavishes her own two daughters with jewelry, beautiful clothing, musical instruments, and a fat pet cat, Cinderella wears cast-off rags and settles for making pets of the trembling mice who somehow escape the household's ravenous feline. When the prince of the kingdom hosts a debutante ball for the land's "eligible maidens," Cinderella at first attempts to go in a homemade gown that the mice and some friendly birds construct for her. Seeing that her ensemble includes some of their own discarded clothing, Cinderella's stepsisters tear it to shreds before making their own way to the ball and leaving Cinderella in tears. But the arrival of her fairy godmother—a sort of one-woman department store—saves the day. She provides Cinderella with a coach, horses, driver, and footman to travel to the ball and with the appropriate attire for dancing with a prince. Along with a pair of glass slippers, Cinderella now has the ideal garment for a debutante ball—a dazzling white gown far superior to the homemade dress her stepsisters destroyed. Her new dress even turns a romantic ice blue when the moonlight hits it from just the right angle.[14]

Once at the ball, Cinderella captivates both the prince and his father. The king's goals for his son mirror those of the 1950s domestic ideal. He is in search of a woman who will be a "suitable wife" for his son and, more important, a "suitable mother" for his grandchildren. The demure and beautiful Cinderella seems to fit the bill—until the fairy godmother's spell ends at midnight and Cinderella's dress, coach, and other glamorous accessories dissolve into thin air. Only one glass slipper is left behind on the palace stairway. Without the appropriate accouterments, Cinderella can no longer attract a suitor who outranks her, and she gives up her dream of life with Prince Charming. But when the prince's retainer comes looking for the maiden who fits the lost slipper, Cinderella reveals that she still possesses its mate and was indeed the beautiful mystery woman who looked good enough to marry a prince. And in the movie's closing wedding scene, she emerges wearing a perfect 1950s bridal ensemble—complete with bouffant skirt, sweetheart neckline, and a delicate veil held aloft by two fluttering birds who serve as bridesmaids (Figure 4.2).

Disney's *Cinderella* was the sixth-highest grossing movie of 1950 and spawned an endless series of children's books, toys, and other merchandise that ensured Disney's adaptation would become the best-known rendering of the fable. Frequently re-released in movie theaters, and eventually broadly distributed as a home video and DVD, Disney's *Cinderella* further familiarized Americans with a fairytale wedding story that advertisers could exploit.[15]

But Disney's *Cinderella* set a high standard for consumers and wedding professionals to match. Animation artists ensured that every strand of Cinderella's blonde hair was in place and that her wedding gown was a perfect fit. Real life was messier. One bride remembered the devastating effect of "watching *Cinderella* on video" immediately prior to her autumn 2000 wedding. After viewing Cinderella's magical transformation, the bride slipped into her gown hoping for similar results. She was sorely disappointed. While the saleswoman had assured her the fit was

FIGURE 4.2. *When Disney's animated* Cinderella *(1950) emerged from her wedding wearing a stylish bouffant gown, she created an image of bridal perfection that was difficult for real-life brides to duplicate. (Walt Disney Pictures/Photofest)*

"fine," the mirror now revealed that her shoulders were too "slopey" for the dress. Realizing she would never look as lovely as her cartoon heroine, the real-life bride broke into bitter tears and had to be comforted by her confused brother.[16]

Cinderella was not the only Hollywood bride whose appearance was difficult to replicate. The year 1950 also found legendary beauty Elizabeth Taylor donning a wedding gown for MGM's *Father of the Bride*, a film that *New York Times* critic Bosley Crowther hailed as "grandly funny . . . a honey of a picture of American family life!" As Crowther's review implied, unlike *Cinderella*, *Father of the Bride* was intended as an accurate albeit slightly exaggerated vision of real family life—at least for members of the white upper middle class. Subsequent film critics have even characterized it as "one of the first Hollywood productions to use the wedding celebration as a plot device that helped the audience to identify characteristics" of WASP suburbia. Directed by Vincente

Minnelli, the film stars Spencer Tracy in the title role as Elizabeth Taylor's befuddled father (Figure 4.3). A critical and popular success, *Father of the Bride* earned Academy Award nominations for Best Actor, Best Picture, and Best Screenplay; tied with Disney's *Cinderella* as the sixth-highest-grossing film of 1950; and spawned a 1951 sequel and 1960s television series.[17]

Based on a popular 1949 novel of the same name, the film accurately reflects the gender politics and the social and economic concerns of the upper middle class during the postwar era, and the class status of the family in the movie is clearly established in the early moments of the film. The father, Stanley Banks, introduces himself to the audience as a partner in a New York City law firm. In conformity with postwar residence patterns, he has moved his family to a Connecticut suburb, where his wife Ellie—a full-time homemaker—can afford to employ an African American maid as household help. Stanley and Ellie have two teenage sons and a 20-year-old daughter named Kay, who apparently does not have a job or go to school but instead largely spends her time pursuing leisure and consumer activities. The audience does not meet her fiancé, Buckley Dunstan (Don Taylor), until several minutes into the film but learns early on from Kay that he has great faith in the postwar economy and believes that "everyone should marry young"—a philosophy that many other Americans held in 1950. In that year, one in three American women married by the age of 19, and in real life, Elizabeth Taylor herself married for the first time at the age of only 18.[18]

The father of the bride begins to get an inkling of the financial investment required to marry off his young daughter in a scene that takes place at her engagement party. One of the male guests tells Stanley Banks, "From now on the gals take over. You think they can't add two and two, but when it comes to weddings, they're giants of industry. And they put it on like a big theatrical production too; the bigger the better. From now on your only function is to pay the bills. . . . Weddings are either confined to the bosom of the family or held in Madison Square Garden."

Its sexism aside, the party guest's statement is rather insightful. While women certainly remained in charge of planning and executing weddings in the post–World War II era, economic realities and gender customs dictated that the male breadwinner foot the bill for the festivities. *Father*

FIGURE 4.3. *The 1950 film* Father of the Bride *starred Spencer Tracy in the title role and Elizabeth Taylor as his consumer-oriented daughter. (MGM/Photofest)*

of the Bride reflects this real-life situation by consistently portraying men as providers and women as consumers. And as the engagement party guest notes, there seemed to be no middle ground for the providers and consumers of an upper-middle-class wedding; they could either ignore the expensive wedding ideal altogether or buy into it entirely. Purchasing certain professional goods and services seemed to lead inevitably to procuring others, and soon the wedding became, in Stanley Banks's words, "a show, a big flashy show" that was difficult to afford.[19]

The social pressures for conforming to the commercialized wedding were enormous for members of the postwar upper middle class. At one point in the film, Stanley Banks reminds his wife, Ellie (played by Joan Bennett), that she was married in the family parlor in a blue suit, apparently sometime in the late 1920s. Ellie Banks insists, however, that that kind of wedding is not good enough for their daughter. Kay deserves an elegant, professionally produced wedding because, as Ellie notes, "All her friends have given weddings like that." Ellie makes the case that a young woman of Kay's socioeconomic status must have a "wedding with all the trimmings" if she is to remain in sync with her peers and prevailing standards. In Ellie's words, "A wedding, a church wedding—well it's what every girl dreams of. A bridal dress, orange blossoms, the music. It's something lovely for her to remember all her life." Such reasoning ultimately causes Stanley to relent and allow his wife and daughter to make purchases for an elaborate wedding and honeymoon, prompting a scene in which Kay's female friends rush into the Banks home to look approvingly at the expensive new clothes the bride has acquired for her trousseau. The daughter conforms to the standards of her peers but in the process places a financial strain on her father.

Friends and neighbors were not the only ones who pressured postwar families to conform to the commercialized wedding ideal; members of the growing wedding industry also worked diligently to urge middle-class Americans to subscribe to all aspects of the professionally produced wedding. In one of the film's pivotal scenes, Stanley and Ellie Banks attempt to procure the services of a caterer (played by character actor Leo G. Carroll). Try as they might to purchase a bare-bones wedding reception, the caterer has other ideas and is not above employing snob appeal and exploiting the Bankses' own class-status concerns to sell them a more ostentatious version. From telling them that their original idea for a simple reception reminds him of a children's birthday party to suggesting that a country club is a better reception location than their suburban home, the caterer succeeds in making the Banks parents feel inadequate in their attempts to organize a successful nuptial celebration.

In the scene with the caterer and throughout the film, the audience is urged to identify with the picture's first-person narrator—the level-headed father of the bride. As played by screen hero Spencer Tracy—whose patented role was the beleaguered but highly principled American male—the character is an island of sanity amid a sea of impractical and pretentious people. Although manipulative caterers and spendthrift female relatives may pressure him into compromising his standards now and again, Stanley Banks firmly resists the more absurd excesses of the lavish wedding in practice and remains in opposition to the entire concept in principle. Nevertheless, even Stanley Banks, the sensible Everyman, ultimately relents and ends up providing his daughter with many of the recognized accouterments of the commercialized white wedding.

To the movie audience of 1950, *Father of the Bride*'s vision of youthful marriage in a setting of material abundance was an increasingly familiar concept. Its portrayal of domestic-oriented spending as a means to secure and celebrate familial relationships certainly rang true at a time when family-centered spending was on the rise. The 1950 audience could also relate to the film's representation of the growing list of consumer items that a family now had to display in order to define itself as appropriately middle-class. As American hero Spencer Tracy demonstrates so effectively in the movie, the bar had been raised for proving achievement of the American Dream and playing the role of generous family provider. While the film tells its wedding story from the perspective of the paternal provider and therefore focuses less on the duress its female consumers experienced in planning and executing the ideal upper-middle-class wedding, *Father of the Bride* also indicates that these characters expend significant time and concern creating an appropriate nuptial pageant. The film portrays the bride's mother as being particularly worried that the wedding celebration accurately reflect her daughter's membership in a happy and prosperous nuclear family. An increasing number of the movie's female viewers could empathize with this character's insistence that the capital-intensive wedding communicate to its guests some very important ideas about a family's emotional and fiscal health.

Father of the Bride did not limit its message of conspicuous consumption strictly to the nation's movie screens. Product tie-ins ensured that the film's vision of the perfect upper-middle-class wedding reached even those consumers who never bought a movie ticket. Lux facial soap ads featured a clearly identified photograph of Elizabeth Taylor and co-star Don Taylor in their *Father of the Bride* wedding costumes. The ad portrays Don Taylor, in character as Buckley Dunstan, exclaiming to his bride, "You're adorable!" Elizabeth Taylor, a much-better-known performer than her co-star, answers the compliment as herself: "I'm a Lux Girl." The fact that Taylor was famous as a real-life bride in 1950 also allows her to speak in her own voice, implying that her renowned beauty both on and off screen owed a debt to Lux soap. Perhaps her use of the product made her attractive enough to capture the heart of millionaire bridegroom Nicky Hilton in her off-screen life. In a similar vein, Artcarved engagement and wedding rings ran a print ad in 1950 that touted the company's wares as beautiful enough for the year's "loveliest bride" and illustrated the ad's copy—in a move that promoted both the rings and the Hollywood picture—with another clearly captioned photograph of Elizabeth Taylor and Don Taylor in their *Father of the Bride* wedding costumes (Figure 4.4). In towns where the movie was already playing, MGM publicized the film and promoted the wedding industry by distributing souvenir photos of Taylor in her wedding costume. Each photo was captioned with the name of a local theater showing the picture as well as the name of a local gift store or women's apparel shop.[20]

As a result of this kind of exposure in the popular media, by the mid-1950s the commercialized wedding had become a familiar concept to a significant cross-section of the American public. One outcome of this development was that Hollywood could now realistically present a working-class version of *Father of the Bride* to a national big-screen audience. Only six years after it released the upper-middle-class story of the Banks family, MGM studios presented the working-class saga of the Hurley family in *The Catered Affair*.

Based on a Paddy Chayefsky teleplay that aired live on NBC the previous year, the 1956 film stars Bette Davis as Aggie, a woman who long ago

FIGURE 4.4. *In a promotional strategy that publicized both the MGM picture and Artcarved engagement and wedding rings, a 1950 advertisement featured a clearly identified photograph of movie actress Elizabeth Taylor in her* Father of the Bride *wedding costume. (Life, 5 June 1950, p. 62)*

entered into an arranged marriage with a gruff taxi driver named Tom Hurley (Ernest Borgnine). In a cramped Bronx apartment devoid of any consumer luxuries, Aggie faithfully cares for her husband, children, and older brother and quietly makes peace with her drab existence. When her daughter, Jane (Debbie Reynolds), suddenly announces her engagement, Aggie takes stock of her own broken dreams and determines that her daughter will enjoy a different kind of life. Like the Spencer Tracy character in the earlier MGM film, Bette Davis's character now faces the prospect of financial strain in order to launch her daughter's marriage with a formal church wedding.[21]

Throughout *The Catered Affair*, Aggie's actions and words echo those of characters in *Father of the Bride*. Like the middle-class mother in the earlier film, this working-class heroine keenly feels peer-group pressure to give her daughter a wedding "with all the trimmings." The women who shop with Aggie at the neighborhood fish market argue that the Hurleys should make the event an elaborate affair because a wedding is "a big thing in a girl's life." They even suggest that the neighborhood will believe Jane is pregnant out-of-wedlock if her family holds the small, rushed wedding that the bride envisions. To make matters worse, in a scene very similar to one in *Father of the Bride*, Aggie and Tom's first meeting with the groom's well-to-do parents makes the Hurleys realize that they will inevitably lose any parental competition to "help out" the newlyweds financially. These challenges to her family's pride and standing in the community finally cause Aggie to issue her husband an ultimatum: "We've got to have a real wedding. . . . [Otherwise] people will think we're on relief or something."

Telling her daughter, "You're going to have a big wedding whether you like it or not," Aggie sets off with her husband and brother to purchase a "catered affair" at a luxury hotel. Here the Hurleys encounter another scene directly reminiscent of *Father of the Bride*. As the caterer's plans become more extravagant, the bride's father becomes more outraged, and he wonders why his wife and brother-in-law do not share his concerns. He ultimately informs his wife that a breakfast for 200 wedding guests will wipe out his $4,000 life savings and thus his dream of buying his own cab and driver's medallion. Aggie, however, remains un-

deterred in her plan to provide their daughter with a professionally produced wedding celebration.

In the meantime, the Debbie Reynolds character takes time off from
her job to shop for a gown similar to the one the actress herself had worn
for her recent marriage to singer Eddie Fisher. Unlike the real-life Debbie Reynolds, however, her character is not used to such luxury. After
trying on the $120 dress, she exclaims to her matron of honor, "Wouldn't
it be wonderful if we could dress up this way all the time?!" Shopping
together for the wedding dress also allows the bride and her mother an
intimacy that has heretofore eluded them (Figure 4.5). Aggie views buying her daughter's wedding dress as a way to make up for the previous
distance in their relationship, and it is at this point that she tells Jane
that her own marriage was not a love match. Impressed by the elegance
of her gown and touched by the new level of closeness with her mother,
Jane Hurley enthusiastically embraces her role as a white-clad bride. Although she initially balked at the idea of a formal wedding, this working-
class bride is now perhaps even more eager to play queen-for-a-day than
her upper-middle-class counterpart in *Father of the Bride*.[22]

But in the end, Jane Hurley and her mother relinquish their Cinderella fantasy. The distraught matron of honor reports that she cannot afford the organdy dress and accessories required for a formal wedding,
and Aggie finally decides that she cannot foil her husband's plan for
self-employment. As the picture ends, the audience understands that the
Hurley women have sacrificed an important goal in giving up their plans
for a white wedding.

The picture's realistic sets, Davis's deliberately dowdy costumes and
makeup, Reynolds's naturalistic performance as the bride at the center
of the story, and Chayefsky's reputation as an author whose dramas were
slice-of-life depictions of modern America all contribute to the sense that
this story of working-class aspirations reflects the experience of many
real-life households. This is a family teetering on the brink of middle-
class status. The father is on the verge of owning his own business, and
both his daughter and live-in brother-in-law are laying plans to marry up
the socioeconomic ladder. In his wife's mind, however, a key marker of
middle-class status lies just beyond their grasp. When purchasing one

FIGURE 4.5. *As her mother, Aggie (Bette Davis), looks on approvingly, Jane Hurley (Debbie Reynolds) tries on a wedding gown in* The Catered Affair *(1956).* *(MGM/Photofest)*

status symbol (the white wedding) jeopardizes accomplishment of another (her husband's self-employment), Aggie Hurley has to drop her plans for a catered affair.

With its focus on a female rather than a male protagonist, *The Catered Affair* emphasizes gender issues that are more peripheral in *Father of the Bride*. While family finances are a significant subject of discussion in *The Catered Affair*, the mother's emotional investment in the white wedding, rather than the father's financial investment in the event, stands at the center of the story. In the tear-jerking "women's pictures" in which Bette Davis specialized in the 1930s and 1940s, the stories usually revolve around her participation in a doomed romance. Typically, these pictures feature Davis as a social misfit or unfulfilled neurotic whose life transforms when she enters into a love affair with the film's male lead. Eventually, however, some insurmountable obstacle—illness, death, her lover's marriage to another—thwarts the Davis character's desire for eternal happiness, and she ends the picture a wiser, braver, but sadder young woman. As a middle-aged actress in *The Catered Affair*, Davis portrays a character whose hopes focus not on a man but on her family. Playing a venerable Hollywood archetype, the heroic mother, Davis's character now suffers and endures not for the sake of romantic love but for her husband and children. Like the supporting character that Joan Bennett plays in *Father of the Bride*, Aggie Hurley in *The Catered Affair* worries that her daughter will not achieve appropriate social standing if the young woman does not have a white wedding, and she is willing to make almost any sacrifice to achieve that goal. Aggie only draws the line when her dream for her daughter conflicts with her husband's dream for himself. Whether concerned about her daughter or her husband, the mother of the bride serves the needs of the nuclear family.[23]

The motivations behind the Hurleys' desire for a formal wedding generally parallel those of the Banks family. For both mothers, it means the opportunity to achieve their own unrealized wishes and strengthen the mother-daughter bond. For both fathers, the ceremony has the power to demonstrate—especially to their more prosperous future in-laws—that they can adequately play the role of paternal provider. For the daughters, it helps them conform to peer standards. One key difference, however, separates the situations of the Banks and Hurley families. For the

Bankses, a formal white wedding merely affirms the socioeconomic standing they long ago achieved. For the Hurleys, such a celebration serves as a high-profile means to demonstrate socioeconomic improvement. Like a growing number of real-life families, though, the Hurleys can only host a white wedding if they sacrifice other important material goals. For the fictional Hurleys, those sacrifices are simply too great, and the white wedding remains an unrealized dream. For the already financially secure Bankses, the dream can become a reality.

Unlike the movie audience of twenty years earlier, cinema patrons of 1956 did not find it absurd that a taxi driver's frowsy wife almost purchases her daughter an elegant church wedding and hotel banquet. In real life, many working-class families—especially those with middle-class aspirations—now mortgaged homes, spent life savings, and employed other heroic measures to help their daughters conform to the standards of the day and enjoy commercially produced wedding celebrations. The presentation of such values and goals on the big screen simply reinforced the notion that these ideas and ambitions were increasingly central to a widening segment of American society. Media campaigns and product tie-ins even encouraged consumers to adopt the modestly situated Hurley family as their role models. *Modern Bride* pictured Debbie Reynolds's *Catered Affair* wedding gown. *Seventeen*, a consumer-oriented magazine for future brides, named the movie its June 1956 picture of the month. And MGM planned for extra ground space in front of drive-in movie screens showing *The Catered Affair* so that real weddings could be performed there before projectionists rolled the Hurleys' story.[24]

In the years following *The Catered Affair*'s release, the novelty of ordinary Americans attempting to host an elaborate white wedding diminished, and Hollywood pictures less frequently focused on the ritual as central subject matter. Films that reflect the values of the 1960s counterculture are an exception. In their explorations of American materialism, alienated youth, and bourgeois marriage, such films take on the commercialized wedding as a natural target. In the Oscar-winning box-office hit *The Graduate* (1967), traditional gender roles and middle-class marriage take their blows from the minute protagonist meets ingénue. As Benjamin Braddock (Dustin Hoffman) waits in the Robinsons' TV room for his first date with Elaine (Katharine Ross), her father laughingly watches a *Newlywed Game* contestant scold his wife about her lax leg-shaving habits. But the film's most damning indictment of middle-class marriage occurs in the famous final scene. When Benjamin interrupts her marriage to another man, Elaine Robinson literally runs away from her groom and expensive white wedding to jump aboard a passing city bus with the disheveled hero.[25]

In *Goodbye, Columbus* (1969), the white wedding comes in for similar irreverent treatment. Ali MacGraw plays a bridesmaid who falls on the floor in a drunken heap while dancing at her brother's extravagant wedding reception. The mountain of blossoms that features prominently in the film's indictment of over-the-top wedding celebrations even contributed to a brief fashion for simpler wedding bouquets. According to florist Mel Atlas, the artiste responsible for the wedding scene props, his success in creating outlandish bouquets for the cinematic celebration ultimately harmed his real-life wedding business. Wishing to avoid the cartoonish excess displayed in the movie's wedding scene, Atlas's customers scaled back on their own wedding flower budgets. For several years following the film's release, brides and their mothers issued Atlas a straightforward directive: "Don't give me a *Goodbye, Columbus* wedding."[26]

Goodbye, Columbus, The Graduate, and other films that demonstrate an affinity with the decade's counterculture and youth movements examine a variety of middle-class customs and conventions, including prohibitions against premarital sex, deference to parental authority, and the sanctity of monogamous marriage itself. This direct criticism of the institution of marriage and its surrounding rituals and practices only emerged on film in the 1960s because movies were by that time no longer the nation's main means of visual entertainment. Having been decisively supplanted by television as the country's favorite type of mass entertainment, American movies no longer had to strive to entertain everyone and offend no one. Television now assumed those functions. The American movie industry stayed in business by producing products that appealed to distinct marketing niches. And the youth market, in an era when the large Baby Boom audience enjoyed a significant amount of discretionary income, was a particularly profitable niche. Films that present a critique of middle-class, middle-aged values and feature young players in the central roles thus often appealed to a youthful audience and made money. As sociological data indicated, however, most young people of the 1960s were not directly modeling themselves on the rebellious heroes and heroines they viewed on the silver screen. Instead of rejecting marriage and white weddings, young Americans continued to flock to both institutions in large numbers throughout the decade. If the reactions of Mel Atlas's bride-customers are to be taken seriously, young viewers of the 1960s apparently did not so much absorb the substance of movie-land critiques of marriage and consumerism as they did the movies' comments on the style in which people should organize tasteful wedding celebrations.[27]

Numerous films released in subsequent years include key scenes or entire plot lines that use the formal wedding as a backdrop for dramatic or humorous interactions among characters. Reflecting a growing real-life trend, the young couple whose marriage draws together the multiple characters in *Lovers and Other Strangers* (1970) stage a large white wedding even though they have been (semi-covertly) cohabiting. Another ensemble film, Robert Altman's *A Wedding* (1978), comments on the sexual mores of various of its characters and even provides brief insight into the inner workings of the wedding industry in its portrait of a harried wedding coordinator (Geraldine Chaplin). And several critical and box-office successes of the 1970s and 1980s—including Francis Ford Coppola's *The Godfather* (1972), Michael Cimino's *The Deer Hunter* (1978), and John Huston's *Prizzi's Honor* (1985)—use lengthy opening wedding scenes to introduce the characters, relationships, and key plot points that drive the remainder of the films. But films that directly address the conspicuous consumption of the modern white wedding did not appear again until the recession period of the early 1990s.[28]

In an era when many American families were experiencing financial strain, the struggle to purchase all the elements of a formal wedding was once again a topic that resonated with movie audiences. Even in the midst of a recession, industry sources reported that the average American wedding ceremony and reception of the early 1990s cost $16,144 ($23,290 in current dollars)—a questionable investment given the popular prediction that half those marriages would end in divorce. Just in time to capitalize on recession-weary Americans' mixed feelings about the white wedding, Hollywood released a remake of *Father of the Bride*. Starring comedian Steve Martin in the old Spencer Tracy role, the film reflects the increased size and acceptance of commercially produced weddings in the four decades that had passed since the original version played in movie theaters[29] (Figure 4.6).

Appropriately enough, since the film stars a professional comedian, the 1991 version of *Father of the Bride* plays as broad rather than subtle comedy. But there are other changes as well. Updating the film for the 1990s, the setting is now Southern California rather than Connecticut, reflecting America's increasing population shift to the Sun Belt since 1950, and the Banks family now has only two children, reflecting the smaller family size of the 1990s. Although still firmly ensconced in the upper middle class, the father of the bride now has a trendier job for the 1990s—he is the hands-on owner of a small athletic shoe company—and his first name is now George rather than Stanley.[30]

The most significant changes between the two versions of the film concern the gender politics of the Banks family and the economic roles of the household's women. Mrs. Banks, now named Nina and played by Diane Keaton, is the owner/manager of her own business and—unlike the wife in the previous version of the film—apparently does not employ any household help. In true 1990s superwoman fashion, Nina Banks is both a successful businesswoman and the keeper of an immaculate home. Mrs. Banks has evolved into the era's dominant media image of the woman in a dual-career marriage. As sociologist Rosanna Hertz describes this media archetype, "She knows how to dress, how to act in the board room, how to compete, and also how to be a team player with her colleagues. Not only is she accomplished in her chosen field, but she is also the perfect wife and mother. In her home dinner is served on time every night, the house is clean, her children receive 'quality time,' and she and her husband are mutually supportive of their respective careers." Rather than providing a critical look at the superwoman media stereotype, however, the 1991 version of *Father of the Bride* presents her in unproblematic fashion.[31]

Like her mother, the bride-to-be in the remake of *Father of the Bride* is also an ideal woman of the 1990s. Now named Annie and played by Kimberly Williams, the Bankses' daughter is studying for her master's degree

FIGURE 4.6. *Wearing a gown that designer Susan Becker based on Grace Kelly's wedding dress, Kimberly Williams plays the happy bride and Steve Martin her beleaguered father in the 1991 remake of* Father of the Bride. *(Buena Vista Pictures/Photofest)*

in architecture. At age 22, she is older than the bride in the original film, a reflection of the fact that women's median first-time marriage age had risen to 23.9 years. And in a major departure from the 1950 version, the daughter now frequently demonstrates a feminist consciousness. When her father protests that Annie is too young to marry, she assures him that her career plans and personal identity are not at risk. After all, she indignantly informs him, "I'm not going to marry some ape who wants me to wear go-go boots and an apron!" And when her fiancé gives her a blender, Annie's distress over the gift's gender-role implications nearly causes her to cancel the wedding.[32]

As the wedding plans unfold, the more assertive bride of the 1990s relegates her father to an even smaller role than the father of 1950. His marginalized position is best demonstrated in what is again a pivotal scene—the Bankses' visit to the caterer. Reflecting the greater level of consumer decision-making power that brides had acquired since the 1950s, the daughter now accompanies her parents to this appointment. In this scene between the Banks family and the wedding industry professional, the audience sees that the commercialized wedding is alive and well in the 1990s. The stakes have even been raised. Demonstrating the increased level of specialization within the wedding industry, the wedding caterer, a flamboyant character named Franck, is now referred to as the "wedding coordinator." Played by comedian Martin Short, the character was reportedly based on a real-life Los Angeles wedding planner whose prices—exclusive of his own personal fee—started at $150 per wedding guest. Whereas in the original film the caterer's grandiose plans extend only to ice sculptures and giant platters of seafood, Franck goes so far as to suggest decorating for the reception by planting color-coordinated tulips in the Bankses' yard and renting live swans. Perhaps reflecting the increased opportunities for upward mobility in the wedding industry since 1950, Franck speaks in an indecipherable foreign accent—in contrast to the upper-crust dialect used by Leo G. Carroll in the original film—and he employs an Asian American assistant named Howard Weinstein. As well as being an awkward attempt at ethnic humor, the improbable Jewish surname helps to emphasize the assistant's outsider status and further the implication that he and Franck are in the lucrative wedding business to make a fast buck and elevate their station in life. The fact that both Franck and his assistant are played as stereo-typical gay characters furthers their status as "Other" in the world of George Banks. Once in the wedding coordinator's domain, however, it is the father of the bride who becomes the outsider. When George Banks protests that the wedding cake Franck proposes costs more than his first car, he is summarily put in his place. "Welcome to the '90s, Mr. Banks," Franck laughs derisively. Realizing that he is out of touch with appropriate social standards, George Banks slinks into the background and leaves negotiations with Franck to his wife and daughter. From now on his only role is to pay the bills and let the women in the family make all the plans. As the scene ends, George tells the audience, "Old Dad was history."[33]

The scene between the Banks family and Franck demonstrates the staying power of the commercialized white wedding, even during the less financially secure, feminist-influenced years of the early 1990s. Americans continued to embrace this ideal, and it had now expanded beyond the white middle class of the suburbs and cities into rural areas and the nonwhite population. Films such as *Father of the Bride* reflected this reality but also perpetuated it with the movie's message that there is no escape from the tentacles of the wedding industry and that a commer-cialized wedding is the only appropriate way to be married in American society. This blanket acceptance of the commercialized wedding is best voiced by the mother of the bride in the second version of the film when she tells the father that he is the last resister: "A wedding is a big deal. Everybody seems to understand this but you." The filmmakers present this story based on the premise that the audience already knows a wedding is a "big deal" and thus considers George Banks an unreasonable character—all because he does not want to spend more on his daughter's wedding than he had once paid for a house. The character's attempts to resist the conspicuous consumption of a formal wedding appear par-ticularly ludicrous given his embrace of the consumer ethos in all other aspects of his life. In contrast to Spencer Tracy's buttoned-down style in the original film, the Steve Martin character wears stylish clothing, drives a fancy sports car, and surrounds himself with expensive brand-name products.[34]

The audience of 1950 was intended to sympathize with the father of the bride as a sensible Everyman; the audience of 1991 was intended to view the father as an eccentric, an object of ridicule because he does not want to spend several thousand dollars on his daughter's wedding. In one of the film's most outrageous scenes, the stress of planning his daughter's wedding causes Martin's character to go on a rampage in the neighborhood grocery store. Wearing an ill-fitting tuxedo, he runs through the store tearing hotdog buns off the shelf, and lands in jail. Such buffoonish behavior contrasts with Spencer Tracy's low-key portrayal of Stanley Banks forty years earlier and forcefully drives the point home to the audience of the 1990s: anyone who resists the commercialized wedding is tilting at windmills.

The shift in tone from the 1950s, when the audience was expected to sympathize with the father of the bride in his attempts to resist the commercialized wedding, to the early 1990s, when the audience was intended to view such resistance as futile and illogical, raises the question of how this transformation in the public's perception of the expensive white wedding occurred. The answer lies in part in the success the American wedding industry had achieved in making itself indispensable in the years between 1950 and 1990. Playing on the status anxiety of members of the middle class—such as the fictional Banks family—wedding professionals were able in the second half of the twentieth century to market their services as necessities rather than luxuries to persons of a certain socioeconomic standing. The elaborate marketing schemes and product tie-ins that had sustained the industry since the 1940s continued to do so during the economic downturn of the early 1990s. The actors portraying the bride and groom in the 1991 version of *Father of the Bride* soon showed up playing a young couple in a series of television commercials for a major greeting card company that sold cards, wrapping paper, and decorations for bridal showers, weddings, and wedding anniversaries.[35]

Styles in costumes, hairdos, and soundtrack music might change from decade to decade, but the American myths that the movies absorbed and purveyed remained the same. In a postwar society where more and more Americans could reasonably afford to host such celebrations, the white wedding became a staple in movie depictions of Middle American family life. According to Hollywood, weddings featured white gowns, elaborate banquets, and excessive bills. These rituals also demonstrated a family's material success and the affection its members felt for one another. Whether it was the traditional bride of the 1950s who voices the notion that "everyone should marry young" or the feminist bride of the 1990s who refuses to marry a sexist "ape" who wants her in apron and go-go boots, the movie bride receives her fabulous white wedding as a symbol of her family's emotional and financial health. The Banks family—in both its midcentury and late-century versions—demonstrates material prosperity and affection among its members by organizing a successful wedding celebration. The Hurley family, headed by a financially strapped couple whose own marriage was not a love match, fails in their noble attempt to provide their daughter with a white wedding. The dysfunctional Robinson family in *The Graduate* buys their daughter an expensive wedding, but she ultimately runs away from it and leaves her alcoholic, adulterous mother screaming in the aisles of the church.

At the time that the *Father of the Bride* remake was released, an increasing number of real-life white weddings served a dual purpose. They demonstrated the financial and emotional security the participating families enjoyed and also illustrated the bride's own personal level of success. *Father of the Bride* avoids this second potential meaning of a late twentieth-century wedding by portraying its bride as younger than the median-aged bride of the era. At age 22, Annie Banks has not yet fully developed a professional identity or even permanently moved her belongings out of her girlhood bedroom. By portraying a very youthful bride, the film is able to explain away her continued dependence on parental support. The film thus remains true to the premises of the original 1949 novel and 1950 film while updating it for the 1990s by including a businesswoman wife and a daughter who quotes feminist rhetoric.

The conservative values at the center of the film make it a movie that transcended niche marketing to be presented as a film appropriate "for the whole family." Released by the Disney company's Touchstone division, it is a throwback to the traditional Hollywood film that sought to please everyone and offend no one. *Father of the Bride*'s success at the box office proved that with the right movie, this old-fashioned strategy could still work in 1991. In contrast, when a year earlier writer-director Alan Alda cast a more critical and cynical eye on the capital-intensive wedding in a film entitled *Betsy's Wedding*, the film failed miserably. Alda's film includes several familiar, crowd-pleasing plot devices—such as a mother who regrets her own civil ceremony and a doting father who competes with his daughter's wealthy in-laws by throwing a lavish wedding—but it also tackles more controversial situations. The bride and groom openly cohabitate before marriage, criticize the sexist and religious language of the typical wedding ceremony, and discuss the complications of representing divergent ethnic traditions in the wedding celebration. And at the last minute, the bride rejects the conventional white lace gown and veil to make an avant garde fashion statement. Like the PG-rated *Father of the Bride*, *Betsy's Wedding* was a Touchstone release, but its rough language, R rating, and examination of contemporary controversies limited its audience appeal.[36]

From 1945 through the early 1990s, no matter what changes occurred in the practice and perceived meaning of real-life white weddings, on the silver screen they largely celebrated traditional middle-class notions about the nuclear family and material success. In that respect, they communicated to their audiences only a portion of the ritual's evolving meaning and purpose. With a few exceptions, movie weddings presented a happy, escapist fantasy where love between parents and children as well as between brides and grooms could still prevail.

The success of 1991's *Father of the Bride* and the impressive ticket sales three years later of the British film *Four Weddings and a Funeral* prompted Hollywood to release an unprecedented number of big-budget wedding films throughout the remainder of the decade. Films such as *My Best Friend's Wedding* (1997), *The Wedding Singer* (1998), *Runaway Bride* (1999), and *The Wedding Planner* (2000) made impressive profits with the same general formula: casting Hollywood stars in romantic comedies set against the backdrop of a lavish wedding or weddings. None of the wedding-themed hits of this period questions the concept of the capital-intensive wedding, regardless of whether the movie bride is a waitress, a hardware store clerk, or the daughter of a multimillionaire. The class issues so prevalent in *The Catered Affair* were now invisible forty years later. Whereas Debbie Reynolds frets over the cost of one $120 gown in 1956, Julia Roberts dons no less than six elaborate and expensive creations in *Runaway Bride*. In the latter half of the 1990s, movies suggested that women from a variety of economic circumstances should not only aspire to but achieve spectacular wedding celebrations.

And whether she played the bride, the groom's best friend, or the wedding planner, the title character was more likely than ever to be someone whom young female fans might wish to emulate. Whereas Elizabeth Taylor, Debbie Reynolds, and Kimberly Williams once played supporting roles as financially dependent brides in their early twenties, Julia Roberts and Jennifer Lopez now starred as characters who were several years older and financially independent. These more mature characters better reflected the real-life women who spent freely on weddings in the late twentieth century. For the most part, the over-the-top weddings these screen characters create, attend, or marry in are exaggerated versions of the real thing. They represent escapist fantasy rather than mirror reality. Nevertheless, as in previous years, the film and wedding industries suggested that moviegoers might borrow selected aspects of these Hollywood extravaganzas for their own real-life events. For instance, the Wedding Guide 2001 Web site advised brides to rent *The Wedding Planner* and learn why investing in both a professional wedding coordinator and dance lessons could ensure a successful and stress-free nuptial celebration.[37]

But the bride of the twenty-first century does not limit herself only to films of her own era. With easy access to the products of Hollywood's Golden Age on DVD or one of the classic movie TV channels, she often takes inspiration from films produced long before she was born. In 2003, when an attorney in her late twenties spent thousands of dollars on a wedding dress with a "crinoline so wide it would have been sufficient to support a parachute jump," a companion thought the gown "looked as if it might have been designed by a cartoonist for Disney." The bride herself, however, reported that 1950's Cinderella was not her fashion role model. Instead, she looked to a bride who first hit movie screens in 1939: "This is going to sound gay, but when I was a kid I loved the dresses on *Gone with the Wind* so much." As a bride, the young lawyer could finally indulge in the flamboyant attire favored by Scarlett O'Hara (and apparently by drag queens). And like Scarlett in the 1939 film, she was willing to go to great lengths to acquire just the right gown. But rather than create a head-turning gown from the velvet window drapes as Scarlett did, the twenty-first-century bride bought one with her own paycheck.[38]

Whether the modern bride models her appearance and behavior on movie-screen characters from her own time or from a bygone era, matching their glamour is often difficult. When a real-life bride attempts to replicate the seeming perfection that a Disney artist or an MGM costume designer created, she is bound to be disappointed. Nevertheless, brides continue to strive for screenland glamour in their own wedding productions, and, like the young *Gone with the Wind* fan, are often willing to spend freely in the hopes of achieving it.

When in the 1960s a bridal consultant noted that at a wedding a bride was "the whole works: producer, director, and star," her movie-making metaphor was apt. This is particularly true for brides of the 2000s. As one of them noted, members of her "extremely media-savvy" generation readily absorbed the message that "weddings are mini-movies starring themselves." After years of viewing films that portray the white wedding as the ultimate symbol of family love and material security, real women want to create some of that Hollywood magic for themselves. And the wedding industry continues to stand ready to serve a bride's desire to be the "whole works" at her wedding show.[39]

Riding the coattails of popular films and arranging elaborate product tie-ins, the wedding business profited from the symbiosis between the film and advertising industries as they nurtured consumer longings. From the end of World War II through the early twenty-first century, the movie brides who enjoyed both a successful white wedding and a box-office triumph shared some common characteristics. They hailed from loving, stable, financially secure families and accepted the major conventions of the formal wedding—from the white gown to the paternal escort down the aisle—without question. And like the majority of wedding magazine brides, they were Caucasians. Movie brides who deviated from this script were usually doomed to failure. Near the end of director Robert DeNiro's *The Good Shepherd* (2006), a pregnant African woman is thrown from an airplane on her way to marry into an alcoholic and adulterous family of white CIA operatives. As her body tumbles above the African continent, the wedding gown she was carrying floats after her like a white angel. Most movie brides did not pay such a heavy price for mixed marriage, out-of-wedlock pregnancy, dysfunctional in-laws, or other deviations from the standard happy family storyline. But they rarely enjoyed successful weddings.[40]

The big-screen brides who achieved a happy ending were still those who largely hewed to convention. In order for movie brides to hold their influence over those in real life, however, they necessarily changed with the times in some key ways. A bride without educational and career ambitions could sell movie tickets and wedding rings in the 1950s, but a bride who was a budding architect could better ensure box-office success and sell greeting cards in the 1990s. Like the other institutions that nurtured the white wedding ideal and aided its adaptation to changing cultural standards and gender roles, motion pictures entered the postwar era championing the bride who only wanted a groom and a beautiful wedding. Sixty years later, most white wedding brides on the movie screen longed for those same goals, but they also wanted personal fulfillment and workplace success. Their dreams thus both mirrored and encouraged the desires of women in the movie theater audience.

CHAPTER

ADDICTED TO THE SHOW

The Reality Wedding

On February 15, 2000, a phenomenal 22.8 million Americans watched some portion of a two-hour Fox Network television broadcast entitled *Who Wants to Marry a Multimillionaire?* The program featured fifty single women who strutted across a Las Vegas stage in what *Philadelphia Daily News* columnist Ellen Gray called a cross "between Spin the Bottle and a cattle auction." In the shadows, unseen by the fifty contestants or the television audience, sat the reputed multimillionaire. After viewing all fifty women, most of whom were white and under 40, the mystery bachelor chose ten semifinalists to parade around in swimming suits. Based on how the women looked in their beachwear and how they answered questions about their personal tastes and goals, the man chose five finalists to appear near the end of the program wearing white wedding gowns and veils. In her formal finery, each finalist took the microphone to tell the still-unseen bachelor the kind of wife she would be if he chose her as a bride. In the opinion of the show's mystery man, the woman who looked and talked like his best match was Darva Conger, a 34-year-old platinum blonde emergency room nurse and former Air Force medic. At the show's end, the groom, who turned out to be a real estate developer in his early forties named Rick Rockwell, gave Conger a $35,000, three-carat wedding ring provided by the Fox Network. He immediately made her his wife in an on-stage ceremony presided over by a Nevada judge.[1]

Public outrage was instantaneous. Patricia Ireland, president of the National Organization for Women, denounced the show as worse than the Miss America pageant, charging that it perpetuated "some very lim-ited stereotypes" of men as "success objects" and women as "sex ob-jects." *Los Angeles Times* television critic Howard Rosenberg called *Who Wants to Marry a Multimillionaire?* televised prostitution. Commenta-tors around the country complained that the show demeaned Ameri-can women and the institution of marriage, portraying it as a mercenary proposition and a commercialized spectator sport. Nevertheless, within twenty-four hours it became apparent that the program had intrigued many of the nation's young women. One-third of all women under the age of thirty-five who tuned into prime-time television on February 15 watched *Who Wants to Marry a Multimillionaire?* And on the day fol-lowing the broadcast, a Fox Web site soliciting future bridal contestants received so many hits that it crashed within hours.[2]

Even with its ratings success and appeal to young female viewers—ad-vertisers' most coveted consumers—a proposed second version of the program never materialized. Controversy surrounding the program's bride and groom, as well as its format, derailed plans for a sequel. Con-ger quickly decided that Rockwell was not the man of her dreams and refused to consummate their marriage on the Caribbean honeymoon provided by Fox. Conger herself soon bore the brunt of intense media criticism for allegedly padding her resume with inflated claims about her service in the Gulf War and capitalizing on her *Who Wants to Marry a Multimillionaire?* notoriety by posing nude for *Playboy.* The media ex-posed Rockwell, in turn, as a failed stand-up comedian and long-time self-promoter whose history included a restraining order issued by a for-mer girlfriend and "only" $750,000 in liquid assets. Noting that Rock-well was not the Prince Charming promised by the Fox Network, one of Conger's friends commented, "I always pictured her with someone like JFK Jr."[3]

In the weeks and months of discussion following the February 2000 broadcast of *Who Wants to Marry a Multimillionaire?* one issue re-mained at the center of debate: observers continued to wonder why the program struck such a chord with young female viewers. Some reasoned that women watched the program out of a combination of curiosity and revulsion; they tuned in to see what kind of women would participate in the bizarre spectacle. Noting not only the program's ratings but the popularity of the Web site soliciting future contestants, others argued that women perceived the program as the enactment of a Cinderella fantasy. These commentators argued that if Rick Rockwell had indeed had the looks, charm, and money of "someone like JFK Jr.," Darva Conger, the Fox Network, and millions of female viewers would have had their happy ending. The program would have spawned numerous sequels, and the network simply would have ignored the outrage of feminists, moralists, and television critics.

Placed in a larger historical context, the outcry and debate over *Who Wants to Marry a Multimillionaire?* were both naive and excessive. Since the late 1940s, when a greater portion of the U.S. population began to celebrate formal weddings, the media had devoted significant attention to ordinary Americans whose rites now included white bridal gowns, multiple attendants, and elaborate receptions. In 2000, Darva Conger was just the latest in a long line of ordinary brides to gain national media attention. Indeed, a major reason for female viewers' attraction to *Who Wants to Marry a Multimillionaire?* was its exploitation of conventions and fantasies that the media had been popularizing for decades. The show admittedly presented an exaggerated version of these wedding themes, but it was merely the most recent media presentation to glorify conspicuous consumption, portray seemingly narrow gender roles, elevate pageantry above human relationships, and celebrate an ordinary woman's transformation into a figure of glamour and envy.

Long before *Who Wants to Marry a Multimillionaire?* aired, periodicals and early television broadcasts created the images and storylines that sixty years later still intrigued women and instructed them in the ways of the white wedding and American marriage. The media established these themes and conventions while documenting the white wedding's mid-twentieth-century transformation into a widespread popular practice. While most brides played queen for a day before an audience of friends and family, those plucked from obscurity by a magazine or television program attracted a much larger viewership for their triumphant walk down the aisle. And from the beginning their most enthusiastic fans were other women, who vicariously enjoyed a chosen bride's temporary celebrity and her achievement of the postwar domestic ideal. Viewers frequently copied elements of the lucky bride's wedding for their own celebrations, but they could never achieve the perfection of her big day. Although these magazine and television treatments purported to show the wedding next door, it was a carefully orchestrated and edited "reality."

Americans had long acknowledged the pure entertainment value of white weddings. Even before the development of mass media, ordinary people had performed weddings for the amusement of their peers. In the late nineteenth century and early twentieth century, mock wedding participants entertained their friends and neighbors in churches, schools, and community centers throughout the country. These skits usually played as comedy, with small children taking all the parts or women playing best man and groom as well as bride and bridesmaid (Figure 5.1). But the most popular motif was the "Womanless Wedding," in which men borrowed cast-off clothing and jewelry to play what are arguably society's most exaggerated female roles: bride, bridesmaid, and flower girl. Reaching the height of their popularity in the years between World War I and World War II, these burlesques presented audience members with a glimpse of faux wedding glamour at a time when many of them could not yet afford the real thing[4] (Figure 5.2). With the development of modern photojournalism and the arrival of popular photo magazines in the mid-1930s, the idea of weddings as entertainment entered a new phase. Readers from coast to coast could now view the same set of visually pleasing images. They did not have to rely on friends and neighbors to enact elaborate wedding scenes; they could see celebrities and persons of wealth performing the real thing. The leader in national coverage of real-life weddings was *Life* magazine, and it was in its pages that the standard media portrayals of the white-wedding next door first appeared.

As *Time* magazine cofounder Henry R. Luce noted when he launched his new large-format picture magazine in 1936, *Life* allowed its readers "to see life; to see the world; to eyewitness great events; to watch the faces of the poor and the gestures of the proud; to see . . . the women that men love and many children; to see and be amazed; to see and be instructed." As creator in the early 1930s of the *March of Time* movie-house newsreels, Luce recognized the power of visual images to inform twentieth-century audiences about the world around them, and he hoped the high-quality photographs in his new magazine would "instruct" readers in the values that he and his conservative editorial staff endorsed. In the fa-

FIGURE 5.1. *Women played all the roles in this 1917 mock wedding. (State Historical Society of Iowa)*

FIGURE 5.2. *Intended for comic effect, the cast member playing bride towers over his groom in this highly elaborate all-male mock wedding of the 1920s. (State Historical Society of Iowa)*

mous February 1941 essay in which he informed *Life*'s readers that they lived in the "American Century," Luce enunciated those values as a belief in nationalism, capitalism, classlessness, and American exceptionalism; a sense of confidence and optimism; and a resolve to export the American way of life around the world. Whereas his earlier publishing ventures *Time* and *Fortune* focused on an elite readership, Luce intended *Life* to have a more popular appeal. Luce and his staff helped ensure this broader readership by locating the people and situations pictured in *Life*'s "classless" America primarily in the homes, schools, workplaces, and recreational spaces of Middle America. When images of "the poor" or "the proud" appeared in *Life*, the accompanying captions and texts indicated that these photographs were there to educate middle-class readers about people who were not like them. As Luce explicitly acknowledged in a 1939 address, *Life*'s journalism was "concerned mainly with the middle and upper-middle classes."[5]

The magazine for Middle Americans was an unprecedented success. A dozen years after its creation, Luce's picture magazine enjoyed three times the circulation of *Time*, his company's flagship publication. By 1940 it attracted almost 20 million readers a week. Survey data of the late 1930s indicated that between fourteen and seventeen people read each copy of *Life*, whether they purchased it themselves, borrowed it from a friend, or read it in a library or waiting room. Studies that separated casual from committed readers estimated that one-fourth of the American population read *Life* on a regular basis and that those readers were predominantly members of the urban middle class. But *Life*'s photographic images often had an impact on the lives of Americans who never directly scanned its pages. Other publications frequently reproduced its most dramatic or entertaining photos, and the middle-class community and business leaders who regularly read *Life* and were influenced by its visual images implemented policies that affected millions. Repeated study of a single photograph in *Life* could potentially influence its viewer in ways that staid newspaper and newsmagazine stories or fleeting newsreel and radio reports did not. As veteran journalist Charles Peters notes, by the end of the 1930s *Life*'s "impact . . . could only be compared to that of a combination of several of today's television networks."[6]

Among the images that *Life* regularly presented to its middle-class audience were countless pictures of the "women men love." The bathing beauty, the mother, and the girl next door all figured prominently in *Life*'s pages. Another female archetype that frequently appeared was the bride in white gown and veil. The white-swathed bride—the most widely recognized visual symbol of the formal wedding—graced myriad ads and photo essays throughout *Life*'s thirty-six-year history as a weekly periodical. The photographers who composed images of brides and other female figures, as well as the editors who chose which ones to publish, based their decisions on the visual preferences of heterosexual males. Even the few female photographers on *Life*'s staff, such as Margaret Bourke-White and later Nina Leen, assumed the dominant "male gaze" by employing camera angles, lighting, props, and subject groupings that emphasized women's sexuality, domestic orientation, or deference to men. Along with their gender-role messages, *Life*'s wedding photographs—and the accompanying captions and texts—communicated important ideas about race and class. Unlike the fictional brides in Hollywood films, the professional models in bridal magazines, or the well-to-do brides who appeared in newspaper society pages, the white-gowned women in *Life*'s wedding features ostensibly provided a more accurate representation of the nation's brides. In *Life*'s wedding coverage, readers supposedly saw a cross-section of people who celebrated white weddings and gained some insight into their class and cultural backgrounds.[7]

From *Life*'s first issue in late November 1936 to the attack on Pearl Harbor five years later, a score of pictorials featured contemporary brides, but only a handful of those focused on noncelebrities: a working-class Jewish woman marrying under a chuppah in Brooklyn; Chinese Christians wedding in Western-style clothing at the Tientsin YMCA; a Nebraska farm woman marrying in her local Lutheran church; a Polish American bride tying the knot in Cicero, Illinois; a coal miner's daughter marrying in Kentucky. Highlighting the novelty of these photographs, the accompanying texts and captions usually noted the subjects' limited finances. The text accompanying photos of the Jewish wedding noted that it resulted from photographer William Finley's boredom with "photographs of smart socialite weddings" and his decision to focus instead on a bride who earned fifteen dollars a week in a sweater factory. The story on the Chinese brides explained that with the assistance of YMCA personnel, the mass wedding of twenty-six young couples cost a mere $4 apiece. The text describing the photos of the Nebraska wedding explained that the bride's female relatives cooked all the food for the wedding reception and served it in her parents' humble farm home. The 23-year-old bridegroom in Cicero spent seven and one-half months of his modest annual salary to give his bride a 300-guest wedding. The Kentucky bride wore a $2.50 veil and a dress made by her mother from $9 worth of Sears and Roebuck fabric. As these examples indicate, *Life*'s portrayal of the white-wedding next door emphasized themes of struggle, sacrifice, thrift, pluck, and ingenuity. The message was obvious: only carefully laid plans and a high level of determination and commitment allowed average Americans to mount such celebrations.[8]

During American participation in World War II, *Life*, like the rest of American society, focused on the war and thus provided fewer images of weddings of any kind. The dearth of wedding pictures, however, did not deter *Life* from glorifying marriage and family as it reported the war news. In ads and feature stories, *Life* typically portrayed military service within a family context, publishing pictures of soldiers saying goodbye to their children, printing servicemen's letters to their parents, and presenting American civilian life as a domestic ideal where wives waited patiently for husbands at home rather than on a defense plant assembly line. Ads for consumer products that would be available after the war portrayed soldiers returning to wives and children in single-family houses that contained the latest appliances. And now and then, references to the white wedding still surfaced. A June 1942 story noted that wedding bells were "ringing more frequently than ever before in U.S. history" and acknowledged that since "so many of their bridegrooms [were] servicemen, most brides [were marrying] in haste." Photos showed busy New York–area bridal shops where saleswomen helped brides, their mothers, and their bridesmaids put together formal weddings "on a day's notice." According to the story's text, 70 percent of the nation's "furlough brides" wanted formal weddings, but most would not be as fortunate as the women pictured. A 1944 Jergens ad gave *Life* readers a more realistic picture of wartime marriage when it portrayed a woman with "soft and smooth" hands who receives a sudden proposal from a soldier on a ten-day furlough: "White satin, a bride's veil? There simply wasn't time. We wanted our whole 10 days for our honeymoon."[9]

Hoping that their widely read magazine could help sustain wartime America's unity and national consensus, Luce and his editorial staff continued their focus on middle-class domestic themes once the fighting ceased. *Life* photographers easily found appropriate subject matter in a postwar nation experiencing record marriage and birth rates, a 60 percent rise in average income, and 64 percent of its population growth in the suburbs. Not satisfied simply to document the expanding middle-class experience, however, Luce and his staff also hoped to shape it, hosting a series of *Life* round tables in the late 1940s that focused on postwar "Housing," "Movies," "Modern Art," and "The Pursuit of Happiness." *Life* articles summarizing these two-day discussions among historians, authors, artists, museum directors, business leaders, union officials, and politicians emphasized the themes of moral uplift, community responsibility, and other traditional middle-class values. Expanding the proportion of white-wedding stories devoted to middle-class couples was one way to both reflect and influence the experiences and values of postwar Middle Americans.[10]

Concerns about gender and race, as well as class, influenced *Life*'s coverage of postwar weddings. Luce and his staff used the pages of *Life* to shore up gender roles battered by an economic depression that had undermined men's bread-winning opportunities and a war that had attracted women to defense plants and other new places of employment. *Life* editors were particularly concerned that the number of working wives continued to grow, doubling from only 15 percent of all married women in 1940 to 30 percent by 1960. Adding more pictures of the white wedding, with its clearly defined roles for men and women, thus furthered *Life*'s postwar domestic agenda. Another reason for *Life*'s expanded coverage of weddings in the postwar years was the editorial staff's penchant for presenting controversial news stories—such as the emergence of the modern civil rights movement—through the comfortable lens of domesticity. Picturing nonwhites enjoying a popular family ritual, such as a wedding, was one way to illustrate their common ground with white citizens.[11]

The quality as well as the quantity of *Life*'s wedding stories changed following the war. Now, whether the bride and groom were millionaires or folks who punched a time clock, America's favorite picture magazine presented white weddings as effortless, easily achievable celebrations. *Life*'s coverage of weddings still favored members of the military, business, political, and entertainment elite, but the magazine's preference for celebrity weddings was less pronounced than in previous years. From 1946 to 1949 *Life* devoted an average of seven pictorials a year to white weddings among the world's rich and famous, but the magazine also published wedding photographs of ordinary citizens an average of five times a year. And while the prewar emphasis on brides and grooms of northern European ancestry continued, *Life* photo essays for the first time now occasionally included African American and Hispanic couples—albeit famous ones.

Although Luce and his editors toed the conservative line on a variety of postwar issues—from the Cold War with the Soviet Union to the role of American women—they staunchly supported the civil rights movement and sought to persuade their largely white readership of its merits, often doing so by presenting persons of color enjoying family rituals familiar to white Americans. Photos of nonwhite couples enjoying the delights of a formal wedding neatly served this purpose. In the first few years after the war, *Life* devoted multiple pages not only to the nuptials of Britain's Princess Elizabeth and Philip Mountbatten but to the Harlem wedding of singer Nat "King" Cole and to the Washington marriage of Maria Gloria Chavez—daughter of New Mexico's junior senator—to the son of a Puerto Rican sugar grower. Rivaling Elizabeth's marriage in Westminster Abbey, Cole's wedding to singer Maria Ellington cost nearly $25,000, was attended by 3,000 guests, and was presided over by Congressman Adam Clayton Powell, an ordained Baptist minister. The Chavez wedding took place in St. Matthew's Cathedral, included President Harry Truman's daughter Margaret as a bridesmaid, and featured among the 500 wedding presents a new apartment for the happy couple. The celebrity status of the participants and the opulence of the ceremonies obviously set them apart from the typical African American and Hispanic marriage celebrations of the period, but their coverage put Americans on notice that extravagant weddings were not the exclusive prerogative of white brides and grooms.[12]

While *Life* occasionally featured nonwhites in its celebrity wedding stories, coverage of noncelebrity weddings continued to focus on white brides and grooms who closely conformed to the postwar domestic ideal of young, role-based marriage. A November 1948 story entitled "Career Girl Marries" emphasized both highly differentiated gender roles and youthful marriage by portraying its heroine as a Cinderella figure rescued from her harried work life by a timely proposal. The essay was a sequel to a cover story of the previous May entitled "Career Girl: Her Life and Problems," which had profiled a New York ad agency employee named Gwyned Filling. Intended as a photographic exposé of the life of a typical career woman, the earlier story pictured its subject literally crying on her roommate's shoulder and included other downbeat images of Filling's struggle for success in the big city. In contrast, the magazine's update six months later opened with a photograph of Filling in a frilly wedding gown, beaming into the face of her groom as they prepared to drive away from a New York church. According to the picture's caption, both the bride and the groom—who played a supporting role as Filling's "favorite beau" in the earlier photo essay—now looked "far happier than they did when she was intent on her career." The photo essay pictured them in romantic and domestic pursuits: embarking on a Caribbean honeymoon and diagramming the furniture arrangement for their new apartment. While the follow-up essay's brief text never identified the job that Filling abandoned, the story encouraged *Life* readers to applaud the fact that she escaped it:

> Six months ago . . . Gwyned Filling was so busy with her career in New York that she thought marriage was many years away. As Miss Filling struggled to get along she made a wan picture which deeply disturbed hundreds of kindly readers who wrote letters imploring her to take it easy. The letter writers can now relax. On Nov. 3, after quitting her job, Miss Filling was married to Charles Straus Jr., the young advertising copywriter with whom she was pictured in *Life*'s essay. This gave a happy ending to her story.[13]

By highlighting her groom's career but neglecting to mention that Filling had held an identical position with the same ad agency, the narrative clearly privileged his professional identity over hers. The essay's text also suggested that Filling's life as a wage earner, which had merited a dozen-page photo spread six months earlier, was in reality a mere prelude to her saga's main event: becoming a white-gowned bride. And since Filling's wedding day marked the "happy ending" of her tale, the many decades that presumably stretched ahead of the 23-year-old woman were at best an anticlimax. The story's primary message was clear: the highlight of a woman's life was her wedding day.

In molding Filling's story to fit *Life*'s usual wedding saga conventions, its author necessarily manipulated a few of the facts. The text of "Career Girl Marries" noted that after the magazine's original profile of Filling, *Life* readers had "implored her to take it easy"—presumably by marrying her "favorite beau" and leaving her advertising career behind. But published reader responses to the first essay told a different story. Only one letter writer blatantly criticized Filling's big-city career ambitions, telling *Life*'s editors that she should return to her native Missouri where she "would look much more appealing ironing diapers." Several other letter writers actually complained that *Life* had painted its portrait of single life too negatively. Numerous unmarried working women wrote in to argue that they were nothing like the apparently unhappy and nervous Filling and instead enjoyed fulfilling and comfortable lives. A small item of information appeared in the November wedding story, however, suggesting that Filling's life as a wage earner had not been entirely unsatisfying. While the essay largely emphasized middle-class domestic and gender values, it also included a slight O. Henry twist. The caption beneath one honeymoon photo noted that although marriage had saved Gwyned Filling from her "wan" fate as a "career girl," she reported that she still might "look for a job when she returned" home from her wedding trip.[14]

Life's acknowledgment in 1948 that Gwyned Filling might continue to harbor career ambitions as a married woman marked a departure from its standard portrait of postwar marriage. A more typical *Life* treatment of love and marriage appeared the previous year when the magazine's editors chose the nuptials of a Kansas City contractor's daughter and an Army Air Force veteran to illustrate the nation's ongoing "boom in weddings, which was set off at the end of the war." As *Life* photographer Nina Leen followed the 23-year-old University of Kansas graduates through the major events surrounding their marriage, everyone conformed to expected type.[15]

The text of the *Life* photo essay noted that blonde, blue-eyed Barbara Winn took on the planning of her June 1947 wedding as "a full-time job" requiring maternal assistance. The camera captured Winn's enthusiastic mother, who "had eloped herself and had missed the excitement of a big church ceremony," accompanying her daughter to a wedding gown fitting at a local department store and helping the bride select $1,500 worth of flowers. The caption beneath a photo of the mother and daughter visiting a bakery noted that the bride chose a five-layer, $100 cake: "a marvelous thing, adorned with candy gardenias and bowknots." While the story portrayed the bride and her mother as central players in this tale, it devoted only two pictures in the eight-page photo spread to the bride's father—a distant image of him escorting his daughter to the altar and a medium shot of him paying $5,000 in wedding bills (a whopping $45,000 in current dollars). The essay's text, however, indicated that the father of the bride did not resent playing the provider; instead, he "was anxious to make the wedding a resounding success" for his only daughter.[16]

Like the bride's father, the groom played only a supporting role. Leen's camera captured Tom Bailey as he accompanied Barbara Winn to book the church, receive their marriage license, and dine at various prenuptial parties. Only one photograph in the eight-page spread focused on Bailey exclusively, and it was the singular image suggesting that he too was an active participant in the consumer frenzy accompanying a modern wedding. The picture showed Bailey shelling out $48 to buy gloves for his ushers, and its caption assured readers that the groom would also purchase a boutonniere for each of his eight attendants.[17]

As portrayed in the pages of *Life*, the capital-intensive wedding was largely a female-centered endeavor that paved the way for a young woman's entrance into full-time housekeeping. Coverage of Barbara Winn's festivities included a picture of the bride at a kitchen shower that provided her with "unglamorous but useful things like mops and mouse traps." The caption accompanying a large photograph of fancier wedding gifts on display at the Winn home noted that the bride's father had insured the presents for $5,000 and that their purpose was to help the bride "start a home of her own." Unfortunately for the bride, wedding guests did not coordinate their gift-giving, and the bride ended up with too many inkwells, candlesticks, and silver bowls but no cocktail shaker or vacuum cleaner. This meant exchanging a fourth of her presents in order to end up with all the necessities for upper-middle-class housekeeping. *Life*'s profile of the Winn-Bailey nuptials ended by noting that after the two-week honeymoon in Colorado Springs, the couple "would move to Oklahoma City, where Tom expected to work for the Almareda Oil company and Barbara would start to hunt for a home."[18]

Even when a man served as the main character in a *Life* wedding story, the essay made it clear that women were the central players in a wedding celebration. A 1949 essay that coincided with novelist Edward Streeter's publication of *Father of the Bride* recounted the real-life experiences of a California steel tank manufacturer named Peter Saracco. Throughout the seven-page spread, Michael Rougier's photographs depicted Saracco's central involvement in his daughter Joanne's wedding. But the words that accompanied Rougier's pictures fell back on the venerable hen-pecked husband stereotype to tell a different story. The caption beneath a photo of Saracco and his daughter having breakfast reported that Joanne dominated the conversation with talk of her impending nuptials, as her father "meekly" sipped his coffee. Another caption described Joanne monopolizing the telephone with wedding plans, while her father missed an important business call. Other captions described images of the Saraccos organizing their home for the reception. The bride "ordered" her father to move furniture to the second floor, while her mother "scolded" him for tracking mud on the carpet and "shanghaied" him into hanging new drapes. Saracco's older daughter, Pat, "vanquished" him in an argument about the placement of a sofa. When he suggested a particular arrangement of garden furniture, his wife dismissed him: "Your decisions don't go." Under these circumstances, Saracco eventually surrendered. In discussions with the reception's florist, he simply told his wife, "Do it your own way." The father of the bride was merely a supporting player in the family he reputedly headed.[19]

Commentary on the pictures of Saracco interacting with vendors indicated that he fared no better with them than he did with his female relatives. The reception's "cateress" organized the event "like a general," quickly demoting the bride's father to a mere foot soldier. At the church, a professional wedding consultant barked orders on how to escort his daughter down the aisle. And when he accompanied his wife and daughter to buy appliances for the newlyweds' new home, Peter Saracco found himself "at the mercy of [a] salesman who beglamour[ed] them with [the] costliest refrigerators and stoves," urging him to spend money with joy and abandon: "You want the best for them. Why don't you look happy instead of miserable?" The author of the essay's text observed, "Father acted the role of errand boy, moving man and signer of checks. Curiously, his presence was needed always, his advice never."[20]

By picturing the father of the bride as a fish out of water in the women's world of a modern wedding, the photo essay drove home the point that his proper role lay elsewhere. *Life*'s profile of Peter Saracco was one of several postwar pictorials that portrayed male incompetence in the domestic sphere. The lesson of these features was clear: a man's chief obligation to the smooth running of a household was to finance its operation. Women were the ones who organized and implemented the fine details of weddings and other family events, but it was the "signer of checks" who made it all possible. A husband and father could best ensure domestic tranquility by earning a solid wage and spending it generously on goods and services that brought pleasure to the family.[21]

A final way in which *Life*'s profile of Peter Saracco reinforced conventional gender roles was the piece's relative neglect of his future son-in-law. As a female reader noted in a letter to the editor, the photo essay "showed everything about the wedding but only one tiny picture of the man the bride married." The groom's comparative absence from the story indicated yet again that women were the ones appropriately located in the world of weddings. In casting the groom as something less than a supporting character at his own wedding, the story also suggested that a bride's most important relationship with a male was not with her future husband but with the father who financed her wedding purchases.[22]

In the late 1940s, *Life* entertained and instructed its audience with images and words that reflected and perpetuated middle-class values. Pictures of the wedding next door showed families new to the middle class how to use their recently acquired consumer power: members could demonstrate responsibility or affection for one another, group cohesion, and faith in their future by throwing a white wedding. *Life*'s wedding photos apprised nonwhites of what they should aspire to in postwar America, and the magazine encouraged these aspirations by occasionally picturing people of color in formal wedding dress. Families already firmly ensconced in the middle class could view these images and be assured that their material values, gender-role arrangements, and rituals represented the postwar American norm. Young women could receive vicarious enjoyment of someone else's rescue fairy tale and consumer acquisitions and keep alive their own hopes for such opportunities. Young men could look at *Life* and remain confident that their futures included wives willing and eager to make the marital home comfortable for them. Women who had married under austere prewar or wartime conditions could achieve a fantasy wedding of their own through the pages of *Life* and perhaps escape the tensions and disappointments of their own marriages by musing about the magazine's portrayal of young love. Those who were mothers could look at the pictures and maintain hope that their daughters faced a happier and more financially secure young womanhood than they themselves had known. Fathers could look at *Life*'s portrayal of the wedding next door and rest assured that the stresses and strains of providing for the household resulted in the family's emotional as well as economic stability. They could also see that an elaborate wedding was a way to celebrate their own success as family breadwinner.

The themes established in the years immediately following World War II continued to dominate *Life*'s coverage of weddings in the 1950s, as the magazine's popularity reached its peak. By the mid-1950s, 36 percent of the nation's households read *Life* magazine each week and found the middle-class family prominently celebrated in its pages. Between 1950 and 1957, while the magazine devoted significant attention to celebrity brides such as Jacqueline Bouvier Kennedy, Grace Kelly, and Margaret Truman, it also covered the white weddings of many ordinary, ostensibly middle-class Americans. During these eight years, the gap between coverage of elite and nonelite weddings narrowed even further than it had in the late 1940s. *Life* annually featured 4.6 white weddings among the rich and famous and 3.5 celebrations among the ordinary. And although brides of color remained relatively rare, an increasing proportion of *Life*'s brides were clearly identified as Italian Americans, Polish Americans, and Jewish Americans. In an extensive 1952 cover story, *Life* acknowledged that the expensive white wedding was now enjoyed by such a broad cross-section of Americans that it was the new national norm[23] (Figure 5.3).

Regardless of the race, ethnicity, or class of the free-spending brides and grooms featured in *Life*'s portrayal of the white wedding, they always conformed to middle-class gender roles and values. In this respect they mirrored the characters in the advertisements that the magazine published—with a notable exception. Although only whites appeared in advertisements, *Life* feature stories continued their occasional portrayal of persons of color in formal wedding attire. At a time of rising expectations among nonwhites, *Life* thus suggested that even those Americans comparatively new to the middle class—or those still merely pursuing middle-class status—should aspire to capital-intensive commemorations that celebrated sharply contrasting male and female gender roles.[24]

Life's reliance on the white wedding as a mechanism for discussing postwar gender issues even extended to its examination of those who on

FIGURE 5.3. *In the six months prior to posing here for* Life's *cover story on the wedding industry, 21-year-old Martha Boss appeared on the cover of* Bride's *magazine three times. Less than a week after appearing on the cover of* Life, *the nation's "most photographed bridal model" donned a white gown to marry in real life. (Leonard McCombe/Time Life Pictures/Getty Images)*

the surface challenged gender role prescriptions. When *Life* published a special double issue at the end of 1956 entitled "The American Woman: Her Achievements and Troubles," its cover featured the photograph of a "Working Mother" who managed the bridal service at a Carson Pirie Scott department store in suburban Chicago. In choosing a member of the wedding industry to represent the wage-earning mother, *Life*'s editors found a safe way to deal with a troublesome reality: at a time when *Life* and other American institutions assiduously promoted a home-centered role for women, female employment continued to rise.

In the mid-1950s, women made up one-third of the American work-force—up from less than a quarter in 1940—and the bulk of female employment gains occurred among married women. By the end of the 1950s more than 18 percent of wives with children younger than age 6, nearly 35 percent of wives without children, and 39 percent of wives with children ages 6 to 18 years old were employed on at least a part-time basis. In the "Working Mother" cover story, *Life* reconciled the era's domestic ideology with increasing female wage work by representing women's employment as an extension of their domestic role.[25]

The cover photo privileged 27-year-old Jennie Magill's domestic guise by picturing her in a tender moment with her young daughter rather than on the job at Carson Pirie Scott. Inside the magazine, *Life*'s profile of Jennie Magill further emphasized the working mother's domestic identity by telling her story in her husband's words rather than her own. Under the title "'My Wife Works and I Like It,'" Jim Magill extolled the virtues of an employed spouse, noting that his wife's income furthered his steel executive's salary and now allowed them to buy a new piece of furniture whenever they wanted it. Photographer Grey Villet's illustrations of the working mother's daily routine also highlighted domestic and consumer themes. In a photo illustrating the couple's reunion at the end of the workday, Villet pictured Jim and Jennie Magill riding an escalator through the consumer paradise of Carson Pirie Scott. A picture portraying her arrival home from the department store showed Jennie Magill greeting her 2-year-old son and taking "over the family reins" from the housekeeper who had managed the household in her absence. Another photo emphasized the working mother's contribution to the family budget by showing Jim and Jennie Magill at home together paying household bills. The only image that actually showed the working mother as she labored in the workplace portrayed her starting another young woman on the path toward her primary role as housewife-consumer: Jennie Magill helped a customer try on a wedding gown[26] (Figure 5.4).

With its profile of Jennie Magill as the archetypal working mother, *Life* effectively portrayed married women's employment as a middle-class quest for pin money. In doing so, America's favorite magazine ignored the hundreds of thousands of single and working-class mothers who labored of necessity. *Life*'s portrait of the bridal service manager, however, was consistent with its usual stance in essays that included images of the white wedding. The overriding message was that middle-class gender values and customs were the American way. And conforming to dominant ideology, most middle-class wives and mothers in the nation's workforce reported viewing their employment as an extension of their domestic duties. Studies showed that they characterized themselves primarily as housewives who earned their paychecks mainly to increase their families' access to consumer pleasures.[27]

As a sort of national family photo album, *Life* helped establish the formal white wedding as the American way to wed at a time when a sizeable number of Americans looked to the magazine for their cultural cues. As long-time *Life* staffer Loudon Wainwright noted, the magazine's visual depiction of American life continued as both a major influence on and reflection of national trends for "a surprisingly long time—even as television began to make its real strength felt":

> Somehow, in a time of increasing affluence and great change from wartime austerity (and an accompanying need for reaffirmation of traditional stabilizing values), *Life* was playing back to these readers images of their country and of themselves that seemed both authentic and reassuring. One could, figuratively speaking, find himself or herself in the magazine's pages, or recognize one's hopes, or stoke one's indignation, or appease one's need for self-improvement . . .
>
> The magazine of the 1950s was a place where millions of people could discover modern American life, be stimulated by it and feel part of it.[28]

FIGURE 5.4. *In its 1956 special issue on the American woman,* Life *pictured a wife and mother who performed acceptable women's work as the bridal service manager at a suburban department store. Here she helps another young woman try on a wedding gown. (Grey Villet/Time Life Pictures/Getty Images)*

At the time of *Life*'s founding, Henry R. Luce expressed his desire that a hundred years hence "the historian should be able to rely largely on [*Life*] instead of having to fumble through dozens of newspapers and magazines." The king of the Time, Inc., empire envisioned his company's picture magazine as the one location where future generations could learn everything they needed to know about the period he dubbed the "American Century." The view of twentieth-century America that *Life* presented, however, was one that reflected the perspective of the majority of its readers and staff members. Like most midcentury media outlets, it primarily showcased the values and desires of the white male middle class and presented them as the American norm. Images of poverty and racial injustice usually appeared in *Life* only because these were problems the middle class needed to solve or control, and female subjects appeared in the magazine mainly because they were "the women men love[d.]" Scholars of the magazine have argued that a major reason for its demise as a weekly publication in 1972 was the failure of its homogenous perspective on American life to appeal any longer to an audience fragmented by the class, race, gender, and generational divisions of the 1960s. Nevertheless, during the height of its popularity, *Life*'s extensive audience, nearly half of whom were women, came back week after week to a diet of images they obviously felt comfortable with and responded to in some fashion. And in the dozen years following World War II, that menu included regular offerings of the white-clad bride and conservative gender messages.[29]

In the mid-1950s *Life* ceded to the growing television industry its role as the nation's major visual conduit for gender messages. Whereas only 11 percent of American households owned televisions in 1950, 85 percent of homes had sets by the 1956–1957 broadcast season, and viewers watched an average of five hours of television daily. The audience that broadcasters most wanted to attract to their programs and advertisements were the nation's chief household consumers—adult women. By the time television ownership and viewing became a mass phenomenon in the mid-1950s, producers were explicitly tailoring programs to bolster women's identification with the role of housewife-consumer. In the first half of the decade, network schedules included situation comedies like *Beulah*, *The Goldbergs*, and *The Honeymooners*, which portrayed urban,

working-class, and minority women. But in the late 1950s, sitcoms featured only well-dressed women who presided over beautiful homes in
fictional towns and suburbs populated entirely by white Gentiles. And
this television version of the middle-class housewife became the dominant media image of the American woman for the next decade and a
half. As scholar Carolyn Kitch notes, in the 1950s and 1960s "magazines
were still a site for conveying ideals about womanhood. But such notions
were even more broadly distributed on television, which had usurped
magazines' role as the most influential and pervasive national medium in
America."[30]

Kitch and others have recognized the power of scripted programs like
Leave It to Beaver and *Father Knows Best* to idealize role-based postwar
domesticity, but early reality shows also strongly promoted the idea of
male breadwinners and female housewives as the American norm. Although it is a genre largely associated with the early twenty-first century,
reality programs existed from the beginning of broadcast television, and
several of these shows specifically targeted a female audience. The most
popular program of this type was the long-running and highly rated
Queen for a Day, which every weekday featured several women—predominantly white and working-class—who competed for studio audience sympathy with stories of personal misfortune. The woman whose
widowed status, unemployed husband, frail child, or personal injury
inspired the most enthusiastic audience reaction on an applause meter
won prizes that moved her one step away from working-class drudgery
and a stride closer to middle-class domesticity. At least a third of each
daily episode featured display of the prizes at stake, with washers and
dryers the most coveted items. At the height of its popularity, the broadcast expanded from a half hour to forty-five minutes to sell additional advertising time and display a greater array of desirable goods to the female
viewer at home.[31]

A similar but less frequently remembered series was the *Bride and
Groom* television show, a fifteen-minute New York–based program that
aired live on weekdays from 1951 to 1953 on CBS and from 1953 to 1958
on NBC. Each daily episode featured one couple, chosen from hundreds
of applicants on the basis of enclosed photographs and letters outlin-
ing the stories of their meeting, romance, and future plans. Couples who

appeared on the show received rings, the officiant's fee, flowers, wedding photos, home movies of the ceremony, and a honeymoon trip. Appliance, silverware, carpet, and cosmetics companies sponsored the show and presented their products to featured couples as gifts, thereby advertising these wares to a daytime viewing audience who, in the words of one observer, "ate it up like wedding cake." Like *Queen for a Day*, the program allowed viewers to hear some compelling personal stories and see a variety of products that enhanced the efficiency of housekeeping and the appearance of both the home and homemaker. And like *Queen for a Day*, it provided viewers with the pleasure of seeing people receive items that brought them closer to the middle-class ideal touted as the postwar norm. Whereas poverty or tragedy caused the *Queen for a Day* contestant to seek her chance for a better life on national television, the decision to marry early on a modest income was the usual reason behind a couple's choice to marry on reality TV.[32]

Participants on the program represented a range of middle-class and lower-middle-class Americans. Twenty-year-old Earl Stiles and his 19-year-old fiancée, Claudine Smith, traveled by train from their Arkansas farm homes to hold their wedding on-camera in NBC's Radio City Chapel on St. Patrick's Day, 1954 (Figure 5.5). For the Stileses, as for many other featured couples, marriage on *Bride and Groom* was the only way they could afford an elaborate white wedding. Wearing a wedding dress borrowed from a New York City store, the bride exchanged vows with her groom under the watchful gaze of a Methodist minister, the show's master of ceremonies, its house vocalist and musicians, the show's studio audience, and TV viewers across the country. Back in Lee County, Arkansas, friends and family gathered around the community's few local television sets to watch. When the Stileses returned to Arkansas from their honeymoon at a New York luxury hotel, their neighbors were most interested in hearing about the prizes that would start the young couple on the road to middle-class domesticity.[33]

The show's producers made sure that local Lee County newspapers heavily publicized the delivery of the Stileses' prizes: a kitchen range, a sewing machine, a silverware set, cosmetics, carpeting, a toaster, a waffle iron, and a refrigerator. In contrast to the small, simple ceremony the couple would have had if they had married in their neighborhood

FIGURE 5.5. *Arkansas residents Claudine and Earl Stiles married on the 1954 St. Patrick's Day episode of* Bride and Groom. *Claudine's only regret about marrying on television was having to return the stylish gown she borrowed from a New York department store. (Courtesy of Claudine and Earl Stiles)*

church, the Stileses instead tied the knot in a prize-filled extravaganza that their friends and family around the country could "attend" from their own living rooms. According to Claudine Stiles, the couple's loved ones were "thrilled to death" about their televised wedding because it "was really something special." Looking back on the experience decades later, she noted, "It was an adventure and gave us a chance to go to New York." She did, however, harbor one regret: that she had to return her borrowed gown and thus could not pass it down to her daughter and granddaughters.[34]

Nineteen-year-old Shirlee Peck of Jamaica, Queens, and 21-year-old Long Island resident Harry Schwedock traveled a considerably shorter distance than the Stileses when they too married on *Bride and Groom* in March 1954. During the couple's fifteen minutes of network fame, the house vocalist crooned "My Funny Valentine" and a rabbi performed an abbreviated ceremony that lacked a chuppah but ended with the traditional breaking of a wine glass. At the show's conclusion, the master of ceremonies and the vocalist advertised the Canadian resort where the young couple would honeymoon and then presented them with the sponsors' "wedding gifts"—Jergens toiletries, silverware, a vacuum cleaner, a washing machine, an electric blanket, and a cooking range. As the credits rolled, the florist who provided the wedding bouquet and the manufacturer of the bridal gown took the opportunity to promote their products.[35]

Both the Stiles and Schwedock nuptials served to educate Americans in the correct way to wed in the postwar era. *Bride and Groom* clearly relayed the message that expensive household wares were appropriate wedding gifts. Its dignified staging of the wedding music suggested that professional musicians were preferable to homemade musical accompaniment. The program established a stylish white gown and expertly arranged flowers as necessities for the American wedding (although television brides received these items for free from wedding industry members eager to advertise their goods). And although producers of *Bride and Groom* allowed couples to name their preferred religious service and clergy member, the fifteen-minute broadcast best lent itself to the rites of denominations that had very brief marriage services. Because each program included the wedding ceremony itself plus an interview with the couple, a musical number, and presentation of the sponsors' wares, some couples obviously had to modify traditional religious rituals to accommodate the program's format and limited time frame. The weddings broadcast on *Bride and Groom* thus largely followed a homogenized blueprint, much like nontelevised celebrations that increasingly relied on the "one size fits all" services of professional musicians, caterers, and clothiers.[36]

Watching *Bride and Groom* with her mother in Tupelo, Mississippi, African American teenager Betty Norwood learned the "proper" way to marry. She had never attended such a wedding and had never even seen pictures of black people in formal wedding clothing because the Tupelo newspaper did not publish African American wedding announcements. Norwood's exposure to *Bride and Groom* nevertheless convinced her that she would one day have a formal wedding of her own. And although her mother was a poor woman with seven other children, she shared the teenager's ambition and vowed that she would help her youngest child achieve her white-wedding dream.[37]

For families like the Norwoods, exposure to the commercialized wedding ideal created aspirations that were difficult—if not impossible—to achieve during the period when *Bride and Groom* was on the air. They were among the 20 percent of families, many of them nonwhite, who did not share in the prosperity of 1950s America and continued to earn less than $3,000 a year. In 1952, median nonwhite family income was $2,338. In that same year, Hecht's department store in predominantly black Washington, D.C., advertised a package of bargain wedding supplies and services for $300. Purchasing this relatively inexpensive white wedding, however, would place most African American families in financial distress. Under these circumstances, the chief participants in the commercialized white wedding remained—literally—white. For many residents of the black community, such as Betty Norwood and her mother, the ritual was one they knew only through television and other popular media.[38] As the Norwoods' experience illustrates, the mass media's frequent presentation of the commercialized white wedding convinced many viewers that it was the American norm. For a young woman to marry in any other way was simply not "a proper kind of wedding." Such media messages demonstrated to families like the Norwoods that they

were missing out on the nation's celebrated postwar abundance and reminded them of other ways in which their lives fell far short of the American dream. As scholars have noted, one factor behind development of
a mass movement for African American civil rights was participants'
recognition of the gap between their own experience and the image of
American life projected in the media. Televised images of the freedoms
and material goods that white citizens enjoyed were particularly potent
cues for black action. Down the road from the Norwoods, in Jackson,
Mississippi, another black woman—activist Myrlie Evers—explicitly
made the connection between media images and the heightened ambitions and expectations of African Americans in the 1950s and 1960s. As
she noted in a 1967 memoir,

> Nearly any movie, almost any page of *Life* magazine, the advertising
> on the billboards and in the newspapers, most of what we see each
> day on television—all of these constitute a kind of torture to many Ne-
> groes. For they know that this—or something like it, is what awaits the
> American who is willing to work for it—unless he is a Negro. Amer-
> ican advertising is responsible for much of the Negro's current de-
> mand that he, too, be allowed to participate in the fulfillment of the
> American dream.[39]

As essentially a daily fifteen-minute commercial for both the white
wedding and household appliances and furnishings, *Bride and Groom*
showcased one piece of a dream potentially available to African Americans if they worked toward political and economic change. And a decade
and a half after Betty Norwood watched the program with her mother,
a larger portion of the American dream was indeed available to the nation's black citizens. The civil rights struggle had brought an end to legal segregation and voter discrimination in the South and had inspired
affirmative action programs throughout the nation that permitted African Americans greater access to higher education and middle-class employment. The civil rights crusade had also given birth to a women's
movement that opened new educational and employment doors for the
nation's female citizens. As a result of such changes, by the early 1970s
Betty Norwood—the poor black girl from Mississippi—was a successful 28-year-old journalist living in New York and engaged to a Madison

Avenue ad man. And like many other young blacks who came of age during the civil rights revolution, Norwood and her fiancé, Bob Chaney, proudly embraced their African roots.[40]

With her circumstances so dramatically changed, Betty Norwood forgot her one-time pledge to marry in church with white gown and veil. She had by this time actually attended a white wedding and found it a disappointing experience. She had watched her niece's ceremony in annoyance as the "white ladies from the floral shop downtown [made sure] that the flowers were pinned on right" and the bridal party posed endlessly for the hired photographer who acted "as if the whole thing had been staged for his benefit." Norwood's mother, however, continued to cherish her daughter's girlhood promise. While Norwood and her fiancé busily wrote their own vows and designed African-inspired dashikis for their wedding attendants, her elderly, ailing, and widowed mother promoted a different vision of her daughter's wedding day and vowed that she would not attend the event if the couple insisted on a self-styled ceremony.[41]

Acceding to the threat, Norwood and her groom pooled resources with her mother to produce a wedding that demonstrated to family and friends that the couple were firmly ensconced in the middle class. As Norwood came to realize, for her mother, the "proper kind of wedding for a daughter who had been living and working in New York would be one to top even the weddings [they] had watched on TV." Norwood's description of her mother's desired scenario reflected the older woman's adherence to the white-wedding ideal: "Like most mothers, I guess, and maybe more especially Black mothers who have not had the opportunity themselves, my mother was really impressed with church weddings. . . . My dress should be the most beautiful white possible and my veil should be long and flowing. The bridesmaids should be dressed in pastels or in deep-colored velvets and the men should be in tuxedos with bow ties and stiff collars." In the end, to please her mother, that was the kind of wedding that Betty Norwood and Bob Chaney had.[42]

As the experiences of the Norwoods, Stileses, and Schwedocks suggest, Americans who accepted *Bride and Groom*'s version of the perfect 1950s wedding learned some basic lessons. Weddings that incorporated the principle of consumption served to demonstrate that a young man and woman were living up to the material standards of the postwar middle class. Whether they hailed from the cotton fields of Arkansas, the immigrant enclaves of greater New York, or the black community of the Deep South, persons who participated in the commercially produced white wedding showed that they had now joined mainstream American society. *Bride and Groom* also promoted the idea that the white wedding should provide youthful brides and grooms with gifts that immediately allowed them to set up independent households furnished with appropriate middle-class appointments.

The program's ideological content and visual cues regarding a "proper kind of wedding" had such a profound influence on some viewers that *Bride and Groom* became their permanent blueprint for the American wedding. Nearly twenty years after viewing the program on a daily basis, Betty Norwood's mother still insisted on imitating its conventions at her daughter's wedding. She desired such a ceremony even though it held little personal meaning for her racially conscious daughter and son-in-law and provided them with domestic-oriented gifts that they could easily afford to purchase for themselves with their middle-class salaries.

As the experiences of Betty Norwood and her mother suggest, the conventions established for the American white wedding in the 1940s and 1950s continued into the later decades of the twentieth century, even as cultural trends—such as older, self-supporting brides and greater black cultural awareness—transformed the national landscape. In this regard, the democratized white wedding of the postwar years was a conservative institution. A greater cross-section of Americans adopted the ritual as their own, but its main characteristics still seemingly reflected the gender roles and cultural values of the white urban/suburban upper middle class.

As the *Bride and Groom* series and the 1950s came to an end, the popularity of marriage and the penchant for family-oriented consumer spending continued unabated. And the conventions of wedding reporting remained much as they were in the 1940s and 1950s. The bride's attire continued to receive significant attention, both in terms of visual display and in written or oral descriptions. This focus on the bride's distinctive clothing reinforced the notion that the woman's chief identity lay in simply being a bride. In contrast, media treatments typically granted at least some attention to the groom's employment aspirations or status. Even when, in a nod toward second-wave feminism, such profiles began in the 1970s to expand their coverage of the bride's educational or employment background, they continued to devote a greater number of words and visual cues to her one-day status as bride. Whether the woman was a Hollywood star, a president's daughter, a royal bride, or the noncelebrity next door, the media focused more on a woman's *being* a bride than on her necessarily *doing* anything else with the rest of her life. In this respect, the feminist revolution had little impact on media treatments of the American wedding. And like mid-twentieth-century coverage of real-life weddings, latter-day presentations emphasized the theme of consumption and often included images or descriptions of lavish wedding cakes, gifts, floral displays, or honeymoons.

A popular treatment of real-life weddings that continued conventional media themes into the twenty-first century was a weekday cable television program entitled *A Wedding Story*. The huge viewership attracted to the 1986 wedding of Sarah Ferguson and Britain's Prince Andrew had convinced *Wedding Story* creator Chuck Gingold that the audience existed for a daily dose of televised weddings. Debuting on The Learning Channel (TLC) in 1996, *A Wedding Story* was an immediate hit. By 1999, 200 episodes of the show had aired, and its success with women between the ages of 18 and 34—advertisers' most coveted audience—resulted in several TLC spin-offs, including *A Baby Story*, *A Dating Story*, and *A Makeover Story*. The series also eventually inspired other cable and broadcast networks to develop their own wedding reality programs, with titles such as *Weddings of a Lifetime* and *Will You Marry Me?* (It even led to a reality program entitled *Bridezillas*, which focused on the dark side of the "my day" phenomenon by featuring ill-tempered, hard-to-please brides whose wedding micro-management made everyone around them miserable.) Each episode of *A Wedding Story* was recorded in vérité style on videotape rather than film, which provided its audience with the illusion that they were watching the bride and groom's home video. The series was so successful in presenting its featured ceremonies as the way all "real weddings . . . are supposed to look," that many viewers reported watching it primarily as a "how-to" guide for their own celebrations.[43]

At first glance, the couples featured on *A Wedding Story* were largely interchangeable. Most brides and grooms who appeared on the

Philadelphia-based program resided on the East Coast, and they were heterosexual and predominantly white. Another common characteristic was their apparent economic security. In her examination of fifty episodes of the program broadcast in 1998, communication scholar Erika Engstrom found that each episode was an endorsement of unbridled consumption and "an extended advertisement for the wedding industry." Forty-seven of the fifty brides wore stylish white gowns, and among the three who did not, their wedding costumes still entailed substantial expense. One bride wore a reproduction of a Civil War–era wedding dress, another wore a reproduction of a Revolutionary War–era wedding gown, and the third bride wore a traditional German wedding costume. Sixty-six percent of the weddings took place in a house of worship, but several of the alternative wedding sites—including a horse show and a yacht—were locations that communicated notions of wealth and prestige. Forty-eight percent of the brides had four or more bridesmaids, 48 percent of the weddings included a hundred or more guests, 58 percent of the weddings featured limousine transportation for the bridal couple, and 74 percent of the wedding receptions occurred in a hotel, country club, or other hired location.[44]

On *A Wedding Story* as elsewhere on television in the late twentieth century, everybody married in style. A viewer was no longer likely to see a TV program built around the daughter of an Arkansas cotton farmer in a borrowed wedding dress. For most Americans who came of age in the 1970s, 1980s, and 1990s, middle-class status, white weddings, and the nonchalant purchase of goods once deemed luxury items were the American norm. And television both reflected and perpetuated such attitudes. Even by the general standards of post–1970 America, however, the celebrations on *A Wedding Story* and its imitators looked lavish. In part, this upscaling of reality weddings was a response to consumer tastes that developed during the economic good times of the late 1990s, when a growing number of Americans no longer viewed middle-class status as a worthy final goal and instead saw it as merely a springboard toward eventual placement in the upper class. This "mainstreaming of affluent attitudes" enabled coverage of even the flashiest noncelebrity weddings to maintain the "just plain folks" tone employed in earlier treatments of the wedding next door. While the people who married on *A Wedding Story* appeared to enjoy above-average incomes, the program presented them as simply average Americans.[45]

In addition to its endorsement of conspicuous consumption, *A Wedding Story* also seemingly condoned a traditional, circumscribed role for women. Most of the show's brides explicitly voiced their desire to look like "princesses" and typically referred to their fiancés as "Prince Charming." The program's dominant portrait of the American bride was someone who exchanged her primary identity as one man's daughter for a new one as another man's wife. Engstrom's research, for example, found that 68 percent of the featured brides were "given away" by their fathers, and investigation of episodes aired in 2001 found that "the bride and groom [were never] announced to their assembled guests as anything but 'Mr. And Mrs. Insert Male First and Last Name Here.'" The program also portrayed its female participants ignoring other activities and facets of their personalities to concentrate entirely on playing the role of bride. While the program showed grooms engaging in a variety of activities in the hours leading up to the ceremony, it simply portrayed brides in the act of being brides. Engstrom's study found 46 percent of grooms dressing, visiting the barber shop, or otherwise preparing for the wedding ceremony. But the TV cameras also recorded 42 percent of grooms enjoying golf or some other outdoor sport, 7 percent going out to eat with friends, one man participating in a Civil War battle reenactment, and one groom buying a present for his bride. In contrast, the show exhibited all the women at home, hotels, or beauty salons as they donned the appropriate clothing, cosmetics, or hairstyles to play the role of bride.[46]

Amidst all their white-gowned sameness, the Everybrides of *A Wedding Story* were nevertheless able to assert some degree of individuality. In her choice of flowers, bridesmaids' dresses, bridal gown style, wedding and reception locations, and musical accompaniment, a featured bride communicated information about her own personal tastes and sometimes announced her ethnic background, hobbies, and interests. These individualized touches also frequently provided insight into some unique aspect of her relationship with the groom. A bride might be playing the same basic role as every other woman on *A Wedding Story*, but playing it in a German costume or at a horse show allowed her an element of self-expression.

Poll results of the late 1990s indicated that many brides responded positively to the type of weddings they saw showcased on *A Wedding Story* and other media versions of the wedding next door. Survey evidence also suggested that these brides—although planning old-fashioned white weddings—were beneficiaries of numerous post-1970 reforms inspired by second-wave feminism. With an average age of 26 and 65 percent of them college graduates, most white-wedding brides at the end of the twentieth century were women who had delayed marriage to concentrate on their education, career development, or wage earning. With school bills largely behind them and mortgage payments and child-rearing expenses still in the future, these were women who could afford to spend money on themselves. In adopting this mindset, these bride-consumers were responding to a message that advertisers in the wedding industry and elsewhere had been promoting since the early 1980s: that women who possessed sufficient leisure time and resources could take control of their lives by buying the appropriate clothing, cosmetics, and other products of self-presentation. Or as media critic Susan J. Douglas explained the equation, "the ability to indulge oneself, pamper oneself, and focus at length on oneself . . . [had become] the mark of upscale female achievement" in the late twentieth century. And with etiquette books now advising brides and grooms that it was acceptable to pay for their own weddings rather than rely on the bride's family, many financially secure women chose to purchase their own fairytale weddings that approximated the ones on TV.[47]

While reality TV focused on brides with significant consumer power, and American media in general tended toward portrayals of young women who enjoyed upper-middle-class career success and significant disposable income, not every woman conformed to that model. At the time *A Wedding Story* premiered on national television, more than 60 percent of the nation's adult females were wage earners. But although affirmative action policies and other post-1970 reforms had allowed women major gains in the professions, most women workers remained in lower paid, predominantly female jobs, such as clerical work, nursing, and teaching on the elementary or secondary level. As a result, in the mid-1990s the average female worker still made only 77 cents for each dollar a man earned. Nevertheless, the working-class or lower-middle-class bride still aspired to the media's version of the American wedding.[48]

For brides, grooms, and parents of modest means, approximating the televised fairy tale could entail significant debt. The stories were legion. In 1998 a young Florida couple used two credit cards and built up $12,000 in debt paying for a wedding that included a $4,200 bridal gown, live doves released after their vows, and a horse-drawn carriage that transported them to their 340-guest reception. Three years later, after struggling with the debt and bouts of unemployment, the couple separated, leaving the bride to comment, "I hope everyone had a good time, because I'm still paying, really paying in a big way—not only financially, but with my marriage." A Bellevue, Washington, father reported that the debt from his daughter's 2001 wedding imperiled both his finances and his marriage when his wife's employer reduced her work hours and the couple had difficulty even paying for their own groceries. Nevertheless, at the time of his daughter's marriage he felt that it was a "matter of pride" to spend beyond the family's means for an upscale wedding: "We did not want to appear cheap, or that we were incapable of giving her the wedding she wanted. And that's just part of the illusion." A 26-year-old office manager from Houston reported that repayment of the loan for her wedding meant scrimping and saving for more than three years, periodic suspension of her phone service, and ultimately a divorce from her husband. Yet, for every person who bitterly complained that the costs of a marriage ceremony had translated into high costs to the health of a marriage, there was someone else who believed the sacrifice was worth it. Two months after one couple's 2001 celebration racked up $20,000 in credit card debt, the groom lost his job and they had to move in with the bride's aunt. Still, the young wife had no regrets about purchasing an elaborate white wedding: "It was such a fun day, I didn't care how much we put on our credit cards."[49]

Regardless of the time and energy expended—and the possible debt incurred—in the final analysis, an off-camera wedding could never look as good as those on television. On TLC, an American wedding was an efficiently organized, richly costumed romantic fantasy. Any shots of disgruntled in-laws, lopsided cakes, reluctant flower girls, and torn dress hems remained on the cutting-room floor. As one observer noted, this image of visual perfection risked communicating that the ultimate purpose of a wedding was "not a declaration of commitment but a presentation of a spectacle." Nevertheless, escapist spectacle was what viewers wanted. While TLC promoted *A Wedding Story* as a primer for future brides—and indeed many women who posted on the program's Internet forum reported watching it to glean ideas for their own upcoming celebrations—the majority of fans who logged on were already married. As they enthusiastically commented on the color schemes and settings of the televised weddings, and speculated on the personal lives of the featured brides and grooms, many of these women undoubtedly escaped the flawed reality of their own lives and relationships to bask in the romance and pageantry of *A Wedding Story*. Other, happier married viewers perhaps tuned in to relive the pleasures and excitement of their own wedding days and early married lives.[50]

At the heart of the white wedding's continuing appeal lay the elements of fantasy and performance. Regardless of the groom's identity and the marriage's chance for success, the opulent celebration itself served a key purpose in allowing women a vacation from their everyday existence. The comments a teenage viewer posted on *A Wedding Story*'s on-line forum in December 2000 summarized the sentiments many women expressed when explaining their attraction to media versions of the white-wedding next door:

> I've been addicted to the show for about three years now. I watch it faithfully and can't bear to miss an episode! I'm quite infatuated . . . with weddings and have been since my sister and I first started purchasing bridal magazines at the young age of thirteen. . . . I think I love weddings because of the excitement and joy they bring to people! It's usually one of the happiest days of someone's life, apart from the birth of a child. . . . I'm planning my wedding right now, though I have yet to find my soulmate! It's many girls' dreams to live out that Cinderella fantasy! Watching it gets people like me sooo excited about my future, even though I'm only just starting in college. The show is an excellent way to keep your hopes up, and get some great ideas for weddings![51]

This young woman's fascination with the elaborate white wedding did not center on its power to celebrate a lifelong commitment to any particular man. After all, she did not yet even have a "soulmate." Instead, the bridal magazines she perused—and especially the reality weddings she watched on television—seemingly served another important purpose: they provided escapist fantasies and romantic goals to distract her from her present life, which inevitably included stressful, humdrum, and difficult-to-control situations—such as making the transition from high school to college. With their simple plot lines and prescribed roles, their love-conquers-all philosophy, and their promise of material bounty, these televised weddings made an elaborate wedding look like the perfect, readily available antidote to the complications of everyday life. And one did not even really have to be there to enjoy the comfort and joy of the occasion. The viewer could achieve these feelings vicariously via the magazine page or TV screen.

Enjoyment of someone else's big day was nice, but many viewers also looked to the reality wedding for guidance in how to organize their own celebration or help a daughter, sister, or friend plan hers. The teenager "infatuated" with weddings was just one of many female viewers who looked to media presentations of the wedding next door to learn how weddings should ideally proceed. The exaggerated gender roles, expensive clothing, and giddy emotions displayed in these presentations conveyed a particular set of messages to the viewer. Media treatment of the wedding next door suggested that the white wedding provided brides with a sense of personal comfort and a chance for public display of their popularity, their romantic desirability, their personal tastes, their acceptance of dominant social standards, and their—or their families'—apparent material success.

As a new millennium began, American women remained enamored with the vision of a romantic white wedding, even as they recognized the difficulty of sustaining a life-long marriage. Most marriages lasted longer than the Darva Conger–Rick Rockwell union, but a high percentage of them nevertheless ended in divorce. That fact, however, did not deter the majority of women from pursuing the goal of a formal wedding. Throughout the nation, women, their family members, and their grooms celebrated weddings by investing large amounts of money in showy rings, gowns, receptions, and honeymoon trips. White weddings were more popular than ever, regardless of the ritual's apparent implications of heterosexual and class privilege and its seeming endorsement of old-fashioned gender roles.

In the early twenty-first century, dozens of new series and prime-time specials joined *A Wedding Story* in purporting to portray a slice of real life on the nation's TV screens. The escalating production cost of conventional scripted programming and the intense competition among the proliferating cable and broadcast networks caused the television industry to rely more than ever on reality shows. Among the most successful programs were ones such as *Survivor*, *Fear Factor*, and *American Idol*, which achieved high viewer ratings by pitting ordinary citizens against one another in contests of skill, endurance, talent, bravery, or just plain chutzpah. Unlike programs such as *A Wedding Story* that placed ordinary people in ordinary (albeit televised) circumstances, these programs placed ordinary people in extraordinary circumstances. In the process, some of these ordinary people inevitably became household names. And in doing so, they blurred the line between professional celebrities (such as movie stars or national office holders whose jobs automatically make them famous) and accidental celebrities (people who unexpectedly achieve a high profile by involvement in a well-publicized scandal or other newsworthy event). The most popular reality show competitors often went on to lucrative modeling, show business, and product endorsement contracts. Noting these success stories, and validating radio comedian Fred Allen's famous quip that imitation "is the sincerest form of television," creators of reality programming inevitably returned to the combination of competition and romance that in 2000 had made *Who Wants to Marry a Multimillionaire?* a ratings winner.[52]

Only two years after Darva Conger and Rick Rockwell captured both millions of viewers and endless scorn, ABC premiered *The Bachelor*, a sort of higher-stakes, more dramatic version of the network's *Dating Game* of the 1960s. On *The Bachelor*, twenty-five photogenic and professionally successful young women competed for the attention of an attractive single man, but unlike *Who Wants to Marry a Multimillionaire?* it was a multiepisode competition and did not end with a televised wedding. Instead of becoming a bride, the woman whom the bachelor chose as his most compatible companion simply won the chance to continue a relationship with him off-camera. The series was not an overnight hit but ultimately became a ratings winner and helped fuel the proliferation of courtship and wedding-related reality shows all over the television dial. Intriguing titles such as *My Big, Wild, You're-Not-Going-to-Believe-This Wedding* (ABC); *Race to the Altar* (NBC); and *Who Wants to Marry My Dad?* (NBC) drew viewers to the broadcast networks, while the Bravo channel broke new ground on cable TV with *Gay Weddings*. *The Bachelor* also spawned a spinoff series entitled *The Bachelorette*, in which a woman chose a companion from among twenty-five eligible men.[53]

The bachelorette who kicked off the new series in January 2003 was a 29-year-old blonde named Trista Rehn, whose resume included a career as a pediatric physical therapist, a stint as a Miami Heat cheerleader, and a failed attempt at winning the competition on *The Bachelor* months earlier. In promotional statements before the program's premiere, Rehn speculated that *The Bachelorette's* portrayal of a woman as the romantic initiator would cause viewers to question the sexual double standard. As she told her audience on ABC's *Good Morning America*, "I think that women have a lot of power these days. Why shouldn't a woman be in this position?" By allowing both men and women to choose potential mates and enabling them to make their decisions and build relationships over an extended period of time, the *Bachelor/Bachelorette* programs avoided the massive outcry that met *Who Wants to Marry a Multimillionaire?*[54]

Eleven months after *The Bachelorette's* debut, ABC attracted 17 million viewers to an event the network billed as "the wedding of the decade"—*Trista and Ryan's Wedding*. The prime-time broadcast captured every detail of Trista Rehn's marriage to Ryan Sutter, the dashing firefighter she had chosen as her "soul mate" on *The Bachelorette*. The wedding marked the first time that a relationship begun on the *Bachelor/Bachelorette* actually culminated in marriage, and ABC and the wedding industry made the most of the occasion. The network built up drama and suspense in the weeks leading up to the two-hour wedding broadcast by airing two one-hour programs that examined the couple's lives and the history of their relationship. In addition to the ceremony itself, the wedding broadcast featured interviews with key participants and footage of events leading up to what the show's host called the "most anticipated wedding" since that of Prince Charles and Lady Diana. As preparations for the wedding proceeded at a Southern California resort, the professional wedding planner assured television viewers that Rehn's favorite color appeared wherever possible—from the pink frosting on the cake to the pink dresses on the bridesmaids to the pink slipcovers on the guests' chairs. The audience glimpsed backstage as the bride and her female entourage donned pink towels and blush-colored robes emblazoned with the words "Think Pink" to receive professional manicures and tension-relieving massages. Meanwhile, viewers watched as the groom, who complained that the wedding's color scheme was "too feminine," joined his male companions in a rousing game of basketball.[55]

As on *A Wedding Story*, traditional gender roles were obviously highlighted on *Trista and Ryan's Wedding*. Although she had touted women's power and challenged conventional gender relations in her January appearance on *Good Morning America*, Rehn now told her December audience that all she ever really wanted was the "fairy tale ending": marriage and family. In an interview segment that preceded the ceremony, Rehn confided to the wedding's presiding pastor that her "one dream" was to become a mother. And when she and the groom later exchanged their self-penned vows, she explicitly promised to take his last name.[56]

Conspicuous consumption also loomed as a major theme of *Trista and Ryan's Wedding*. Throughout the evening, the program's host informed viewers of each item's cost while the dollar figures flashed across the screen: $15,000 for the cake, $100,000 for the bridal gown, $500,000 for the flowers. The designer of Rehn's footwear described his creation as "the most expensive bridal shoe ever made," and the audience watched as an armored Brinks truck delivered the $50,000 diamond-and-platinum sandals to the waiting bride. In total, ABC spent $3,778,000 on the goods and services for the "wedding of the decade." The network paid an additional $1 million salary to Rehn and Sutter for participating in the televised pageant. For ABC, these investments translated into coveted prizes: big ratings and happy sponsors. For the jewelry company, cosmetics manufacturer, evening wear designer, and other wedding-related businesses that aired commercials during the broadcast or publicized their products directly on the program, *Trista and Ryan's Wed-*

ding celebrated a match made in heaven. When real-life romance joined hands with over-the-top show business, everybody profited.[57]

In an era when pop music stars and TV actresses routinely used television broadcasts, photo magazines, and Web sites to share their weddings with the world, Trista Rehn proved that the girl next door could do it too. By the time ABC aired her December 2003 wedding, however, Rehn was no longer really just another bride. Both she and her groom had become famous on reality TV, given up their day jobs, relocated to Los Angeles, hired an agent, and embarked on new careers in show business. *Trista and Ryan's Wedding* was not so much the launching of their marriage as it was the launching of their first media coproduction. In that sense, though, they differed only in degree from thousands of other couples who spent enormous sums of money and energy on extravagant weddings that never aired on national television but instead showed up in family photo albums and local newspapers. In a scathing review of the program the day after it aired, cultural critic Dana Stevens noted the event's similarity to numerous untelevised weddings but pronounced that its high point was a detail that only television could produce: "the sublimely crass moment in which the cost of every item was literally tallied up onscreen." Stevens drew the review to a close by asking a question at the heart of many a costly wedding: "Is this event important because it's expensive or expensive because it's important?"[58]

At a time when the cost of an American wedding averaged over $22,000, Stevens's question was difficult to answer. Since the end of World War II, the popular media had prescribed conspicuous consumption for middle-class family occasions—from weddings to bar mitzvahs to Christmas celebrations—and had thus closely identified significant cost with the innate significance of the event being celebrated. These occasions were simply not worth recognizing as special events unless they entailed obvious expense. Perhaps it was only a matter of time before the perceived need for spectacle eclipsed all other meanings of these red-letter days on the family calendar. With members of the general public spending sizeable sums on weddings and the media devoting extensive attention to lavish celebrity ceremonies, reality TV reflected these trends. Unlike earlier noncelebrity weddings that received media attention, those of the early 2000s more frequently featured brides and grooms who had hefty bank accounts or weddings heavily financed by the media itself. But the "mainstreaming of affluent attitudes" contributed to the public perception that these were just average Americans. When Trista Rehn and Ryan Sutter made a post-wedding appearance on *Good Morning America*, interviewer Diane Sawyer never mentioned the nearly $4 million spent on their wedding or the $1 million salary they received for participating in it. Instead, she portrayed them "as a perfectly normal all-American couple."[59]

Excessive material display may have been the most obvious characteristic of *Trista and Ryan's Wedding*, but celebration of traditional gender ideology did not lag far behind. Like the real-life weddings that once appeared in *Life* magazine or on the *Bride and Groom* television show, latter-day media depictions of the wedding next door continued to promote the idea that a woman's most important role lay in playing queen for a day at her wedding. As in earlier media presentations, a woman's previous identity in the workplace or elsewhere received little attention on the day she became the star of a wedding show. At a time of high divorce and remarriage rates, even the possibility that the televised wedding might not be her first trip down the aisle received no mention on these programs. The media portrayed each bride as Cinderella in a love-conquers-all, once-in-a-lifetime, happily-ever-after fairy tale. And in an increasingly segmented media world, where cable television networks, Internet Web sites, and popular magazines marketed themselves to particular age, gender, and interest groups, the creators of these media wedding stories specifically targeted and attracted a young female audience.

While many veteran feminists puzzled over the white wedding's continuing popularity on reality television and elsewhere, their younger counterparts clearly understood its appeal. In the June/July 2000 *Ms.* cover story on marriage, one of the magazine's interns voiced the point of view that earlier that year had made *Who Wants to Marry a Multimillionaire?* such a success with youthful female viewers and would do the same for *Trista and Ryan's Wedding* in 2003:

Maybe because the norm growing up was for people's parents, including my own, to be separated, or because I get bored easily and have never learned to share my space. . . . but the funny thing is, there was never a time when marriage seemed ideal. I do, however, want the ceremony. I've been planning a ghost wedding for the longest time, complete with gown, 12 of my girlfriends, and 200 guests. The groom is ???, but that doesn't matter because I never go home with him after the honeymoon. The ceremony is the exciting part. The ceremony is the part people talk about. And the ceremony gets you in *Jet* magazine.[60]

To the young *Ms.* intern and many other members of her generation, the scorn that middle-aged television critics and feminists directed at *Who Wants to Marry a Multimillionaire?* and other versions of the white wedding was a distinct overreaction. Darva Conger's televised wedding had simply enveloped the familiar ritual within a game-show format. As in many untelevised weddings, the game-show bride launched her marital gamble while holding center stage in a glamorous pageant that relegated her groom to the sidelines. In Conger's televised wedding, the groom even literally stood in the shadows. And in another familiar scenario, when her new husband did not live up to her expectations after the ceremony, the take-control television bride dissolved the union. For the *Ms.* intern, a feminist movement that taught her women did not have to conform to any one gender model had convinced her it was all right to choose a white wedding if she so desired. If she chose to be the center of attention in a dramatic white gown for one day out of her life, that did not mean she had thrown away all her other life goals and ambitions. And in a media-saturated age when reality programs continually blurred the lines between real life and media-made life, what really counted was the event that captured a person her fifteen minutes of fame—and that experience was the marriage ceremony, not the marriage. It was the wedding pageant, after all, that could potentially show up in *Jet* magazine as the latest nationally publicized wedding next door (Figures 5.6 and 5.7).

The white wedding the *Ms.* intern fantasized about while perusing *Jet* looked very much like the one her grandmother had perhaps dreamed of fifty years earlier when peering at *Life.* Like their mid-twentieth-century counterparts, most media brides next door of the twenty-first century

FIGURES 5.6–5.7. *Playing celebrities for a day, a bride and her groom stop traffic on the streets of Washington, D.C., to pose for the wedding photographer. (Courtesy of Michael DiBari Jr.)*

created the appearance of at least upper-middle-class status. And viewers who lacked that financial footing were often willing to scrimp, save, and even go into debt to achieve a celebration that looked like the media's version of a "real wedding." Brides of color now appeared more often, whether in media products focused on a nonwhite audience—such as *Jet*—or in more broadly targeted venues. But most media brides were still Caucasians, their whiteness often further emphasized by their blondeness. The central props of the media's version of the wedding next door also remained largely the same, even though their symbolic meaning had sometimes altered. (This was particularly true of the white gown, which no longer necessarily communicated information about the bride's sexual history.) And in addition to the white dress, multitiered cake, and multiple attendants of the mid-twentieth-century white wedding, a variety of other props—from live doves to horse-drawn carriages—had been added to marriage celebrations in the new century.

In the early twenty-first century, women's infatuation with the glamorous white wedding remains intact. Even Darva Conger, the woman who had failed as a bride as the 2000s dawned, later confided to interviewers that she looked forward to the time when she could reprise her role as white-clad bride. Someday, in an off-screen ceremony, she would indeed marry the real man of her dreams, and she assured the American public he would be nothing like Rick Rockwell. In that respect, for all the negative publicity her first trip to the altar garnered, Conger remains the archetypal 2000s bride. Like many other women at the turn of the twenty-first century, Conger believed that the Cinderella story could be successfully rerun—but with a different supporting actor in the groom's part. The next time around, Conger and her loved ones, rather than the Fox Network, would purchase the elaborate items necessary to display her personal tastes, showcase her professional success, and allow her to play queen for a day. Women's continuing desire to portray the white-clad bride—again and again, if necessary, in order to "get it right"—ensures that the expensive formal wedding will continue to thrive as the twenty-first century progresses (Figures 5.8–5.14).

FIGURE 5.8. *Even if her wedding does not create a media sensation, the twenty-first-century bride carefully enacts each scene of the wedding performance, from a final adjustment of her veil . . .*

FIGURE 5.9. *. . . to her walk down the aisle with Dad . . .*

FIGURES 5.10–5.11. . . . *the tender scenes at the altar* . . .

FIGURE 5.12. . . . *her emergence as a new wife on her husband's arm . . .*

FIGURES 5.13–5.14. . . . *and the wedding reception's first dance and cake-cutting rituals. (Photos courtesy of Michael DiBari Jr.)*

Epilogue

In late summer 2005, Hurricane Katrina devastated large swathes of Louisiana, Mississippi, and Alabama, leaving many thousands of people homeless, jobless, and hungry. The tragedy provided people around the world the opportunity to see, hear, and read about events that reflected America's most salient characteristics. The inordinate number of dispossessed Gulf residents who were poor and black exposed America's class and racial divisions, while the unprecedented outpouring of assistance from around the country displayed the nation's generous spirit. From coast to coast, schools volunteered to educate displaced children, households invited strangers into their guest rooms, and animal lovers adopted pets made homeless by the storm. A lesser-known appeal, from a church worker in Madisonville, Louisiana, called on Americans to assist "brides whose dresses were carried away in the flooding and now have nothing (but a fiancé.)" Characterized as a "ministry to those brides, to help bring wedding 'supplies' together for them so that they can still have a wedding," the "Hurricane Brides" project sought used wedding gowns, bridesmaid dresses, and silk flower arrangements from women throughout the nation.[1]

That hurricane survivors would think of formal wedding paraphernalia when they had lost homes, livelihoods, and even loved ones is testament to the centrality of elaborate weddings in contemporary American culture. In the minds of those who organized, publicized, contributed to, and benefited from Hurricane Brides, a woman simply could not "still have a wedding" if all she had was a fiancé. The act of marrying was not a wedding. Sixty years of media images and wedding-industry publicity had convinced most Americans that a wedding was about wearing the right clothing, in the correct setting, surrounded by the appropriate objects. And women who had lost just about everything near and dear to them might particularly desire the comfort of these familiar trappings. Like couples who held elaborate ceremonies in the immediate aftermath of the September 11, 2001, terrorist attacks, participants in the Hurricane

Brides project viewed the white wedding as an "affirmation of life in the face of death." And at a time when they had lost control of all other aspects of their lives, following the white-wedding script helped restore some sense of order. This impulse was echoed several weeks after the hurricane when a television reality program entitled *Katrina Brides* engaged wedding professionals to help beleaguered storm survivors organize dream weddings.[2]

In 2005, young women on the Gulf Coast and elsewhere continued to wed in lavish style—no matter what—because they assumed that launching a marriage automatically meant being a white-wedding bride. Raised in the 1980s with images of Princess Diana and her famous wedding gown on TV screens and magazine covers and entering young adulthood in the 1990s under a deluge of bridal magazines, wedding movies, wedding reality shows, and advertisements for Vera Wang gowns, most brides knew no other way to marry. Unlike their grandmothers, these brides did not view white weddings in terms of early marriage, young motherhood, and full-time homemaking. Women's average first-marriage age was 25, and their median remarriage age was 34.2. Regardless of the white dress, paternal escort, and ceremonial introduction as "Mrs. So-and-So," most brides wanted to maintain the independent identities they developed in the years prior to marriage. Marrying on a delayed schedule allowed women to save money for mega-weddings that eclipsed those of their mothers and grandmothers and made a dramatic statement about the personal success they had achieved before marriage. These ceremonies also announced women's determination to beat the odds and succeed in marriage at a time when the institution seemed in some peril. Census data for 2005 showed that for the first time in U.S. history fewer than half the nation's households—49.7 percent—now contained a legally wed couple.[3]

Although media and advertising images, peers, and etiquette advisors all played a role in convincing twenty-first-century brides that a lavish formal wedding was mandatory, the most significant influence remained family. Just as the experiences and values of the World War II generation induced most Baby Boomers to have white weddings, the boomers now prompted their children to host such celebrations. The ways in which Baby Boomers inspired their children's allegiance to the ritual, however, differed from the World War II generation. With 27 percent of couples now paying their own wedding expenses and 30 percent paying at least a portion of the bill, parental funding was no longer the primary inducement for having a formal wedding. And with their generation's high divorce rate, boomers were not their children's best role models for marriage. By the turn of the twenty-first century, 41 percent of the men and 39 percent of the women born in the first five years after World War II had divorced at least once, and their children often viewed a high-profile white wedding as a rebuke of their parents' failures. But while some divorced boomers were the unintentional catalysts for their off-springs' white weddings, other Baby Boomers consciously encouraged their children to have formal ceremonies. In the woman-centered world of weddings, mothers particularly contributed to the fashion for large weddings in the early 2000s. Second-wave feminism enriched the lives of many women born in the 1940s, 1950s, and early 1960s, but they had arrived on the scene too late to reap all its benefits. They now hoped their daughters would be able to do so. Studies showed that mothers were a key factor in raising women's average age at first marriage to 25 years. By delaying marriage, daughters could take the time to choose a compatible spouse, establish a career, and save up funds for a wedding that showed the world they were new-millennium Cinderellas who had achieved "the best of everything."[4]

Just as their grandmothers once strove for the postwar domestic ideal, brides in the twenty-first century now reach for an ideal that includes both personal and professional success. The author of a study of American wives since World War II describes the twenty-first-century wife as engaged in a "dance of perfection with the desire for a life rich in choices." Feminists of the 1970s characterized their agenda as one of choice: the choice of whether or not to marry, reproduce, or hold a job historically performed by a man. And women of the next generation—even those who deny that they themselves are feminists—embrace this legacy of the second wave in their daily vocabulary. But in their consumer- and media-driven world, young women of the twenty-first century often cling so tightly to one particular image of American womanhood that it negates all others. Most success-oriented Cinderellas of the new millennium attempt to follow the same basic road map: finish college, launch a career, choose a soul mate (male or female), hold a big-budget wedding, and become a mother (by birth or adoption). Upwardly mobile post-boomers talk about the variety of options open to them but typically aspire to only one: the consumer-oriented have-it-all ideal.[5]

Striving for a life that matches the impossible perfection of the have-it-all media image—including the opulent white wedding—can be an overwhelming proposition. In the months before her 2000 wedding, Kamy Wicoff's life in some ways resembled a TV reality show: while her fiancé continued his usual wide range of activities, she became a full-time bride who endlessly planned, shopped, and primped. She came to realize that just as organizing a wedding in 1945 had trained her grandmother to be a postwar housewife, such activities now introduced Wicoff to the classic role of the upper-middle-class wife of the 2000s: a woman who has both a full-time career and primary responsibility for supervising social events and other domestic tasks. Looking back on the strain of organizing her wedding, another new-millennium bride complained, "Sometimes I felt like I had so much to do in so little time, on top of a full-time job, that my head would explode." And in spring 2005, a 32-year-old Georgia woman made headlines as the "Runaway Bride" when she caught a bus to Albuquerque rather than continue preparations for her 600-guest, fourteen-bridesmaid wedding. The "choice" to hold an elaborate wedding when society deems any other kind of wedding a "failure" is frequently perceived as no choice at all for women determined to live up to the have-it-all ideal. With the pressure on, Kamy Wicoff married in a Vera Wang gown surrounded by nine bridesmaids and later unburdened herself in a postwedding memoir. In contrast, Georgia's "Runaway Bride" hopped a west-bound bus.[6]

Most women nevertheless continue their pursuit of the Cinderella fantasy. It is undeniably a story of gender desires, but it is primarily a fable of class. White weddings project an image of family stability and financial and personal-life success to wedding guests and the people who read newspaper or Internet wedding announcements. Spending money, time, and effort to create a scripted event that approximates the flawless weddings on the magazine page or movie or TV screen frequently allows a woman to feel that she is in control of at least one day of her life, and she can spend that day enjoying the glamour and excitement usually reserved for movie stars, royalty, and other rich and famous women. (Unfortunately, however, when the wedding is over and she returns to real life, she risks suffering the postwedding blues.) The occasional clergy person, feminist, or environmentalist still criticizes what she or he sees as the spiritual emptiness, sexism, or wastefulness of the mega-wedding. And Web sites such as Indiebride and Conscious Weddings counsel brides who wish to avoid the stress, excess, and often troubling sexual politics of the conventional big-budget white wedding. But these voices remain largely unheard amid the advertising, media events, and peer and family influences that advise in the other direction. The typical bride wants to spend thousands of dollars on a "perfect" wedding that commemorates a "perfect" relationship on which she will build a "perfect" life as a wife, mother, and successful career woman.[7]

Striving to have it all, including the mega-wedding, is expensive and often physically and emotionally exhausting for twenty-first-century brides. But a white wedding also provides numerous pleasures, including the opportunity for a bride to spend meaningful time with her mother, sisters, and best female friends while planning and shopping for the event. The twenty-first-century wedding ideally celebrates a woman's success in both the employment and personal life arenas. In doing so, it provides a bride with comfort and joy—but it can also lead to significant stress and strain. Most women remain convinced that the messages they receive from the media, the wedding industry, their family members, and their peers are correct. They believe that the rewards of the white wedding outweigh its drawbacks and enthusiastically continue their love affair with the elaborate ritual. In a world where both the perfect wedding and the perfect marriage are impossible to achieve, the continuing popularity of the white wedding truly represents the triumph of hope over experience.[8]

Notes

INTRODUCTION

1. The Editors, "I Do! I Do?" *Ms.*, June/July 2000, pp. 54–55, front and back covers.

2. Elizabeth H. Pleck, *Celebrating the Family: Ethnicity, Consumer Culture, and Family Rituals* (Cambridge, Mass.: Harvard University Press, 2000), pp. 222–223.

3. Sheelah Kolhatkar, "Gloria Steinem, Power Geezer," *New York Observer*, 11 January 2006. Accessed at http://www.alternet.org/story/30494. Susan Weidman Schneider, "Isn't It Ironic . . . Retro Weddings in a Feminist Age," *Lilith*, Spring 2000, p. 16.

4. Carroll Smith-Rosenberg, "The Female World of Love and Ritual: Relations between Women in Nineteenth-Century America," *Signs* 1 (Autumn 1975): 22; Julie Flaherty, "Freedom to Marry, and to Spend on It," *New York Times*, 16 May 2004, Section 9, p. 2; Jeremy Caplan, "Metrosexual Matrimony," *Time*, 3 October 2005, p. 67.

5. Marcia Seligson, *The Eternal Bliss Machine: America's Way of Wedding* (New York: William Morrow, 1973), p. 2. For evidence of the long-term and continuing influence of Queen Victoria's ceremony, see Satenig St. Marie and Carolyn Flaherty, *Romantic Victorian Weddings: Then and Now* (New York: Dutton Studio, 1992), and chapter 1 of Letitia Baldrige, *Legendary Brides* (New York: HarperCollins, 2000). For a meticulously researched history of the use of "tradition" to sell wedding goods and services, see Vicki Howard, *Brides, Inc.: American Weddings and the Business of Tradition* (Philadelphia: University of Pennsylvania Press, 2006).

6. Jessica Weiss, *To Have and To Hold: Marriage, the Baby Boom, and Social Change* (Chicago: University of Chicago Press, 2000), p. 31; Paul W. Kingston, *The Classless Society* (Stanford, Calif.: Stanford University Press, 2000), p. 222.

7. Sociologist Chrys Ingraham has coined the term "wedding-industrial complex" to refer to "the close association among weddings, the . . . wedding industry, marriage, the state, religion, media, and popular culture." See Ingraham, *White Weddings: Romancing Heterosexuality in Popular Culture* (New York: Routledge, 1999), p. 26.

8. Cele C. Otnes and Elizabeth H. Pleck, *Cinderella Dreams: The Allure of the Lavish Wedding* (Berkeley: University of California Press, 2003), p. 2; Howard, *Brides, Inc.*, p. 1; Cate Doty, "Along with 'I Do' Comes a Chance to Say 'We Care,'"

New York Times, 14 November 2005, p. E3; Jennifer Bayot, "For Richer or Poorer, to Our Credit Limit," *New York Times*, 13 July 2003, pp. 1, 17. Statistics regarding wedding costs derive from wedding industry surveys and include engagement and honeymoon expenses as well as the cost of ceremonies and receptions.

9. Barbara Ehrenreich, *Fear of Falling: The Inner Life of the Middle Class* (New York: Pantheon, 1989), p. 35. Previous works that critically examine the history of the American wedding industry and the democratization of the white wedding include Kitty Hanson, *For Richer, For Poorer* (New York: Abelard-Schuman, 1967); Seligson, *The Eternal Bliss Machine*; Ingraham, *White Weddings*; Otnes and Pleck, *Cinderella Dreams*; and Howard, *Brides, Inc.*

10. On the rarity of cross-dressing and other ironic, transgressive acts in formal same-sex celebrations, see Howard, *Brides, Inc.*, p. 234.

CHAPTER 1. THE BEST OF EVERYTHING:
THE WHITE WEDDING IN AMERICAN CULTURE, 1945–2005

1. Erica Jong, "From Fear of Flying to No Fear of Tying the Knot," *Sunday Times* (London), 9 November 2003, Section 5, p. 7.

2. Ibid.

3. Emily Post, *Etiquette: The Blue Book of Social Usage* (New York: Funk and Wagnalls, 1937), pp. 434, 436. For discussion of the elite's development of the white-wedding ritual in the nineteenth century, see chapter 7 of Ann Monsarrat, *And the Bride Wore . . . : The Story of the White Wedding* (London: Gentry, 1973), and Ellen K. Rothman, *Hands and Hearts: A History of Courtship in America* (Cambridge, Mass.: Harvard University Press, 1987), pp. 80, 167–172, 273–277. For discussion of prewar wedding practices in the twentieth century, including those of immigrant families, see Elizabeth H. Pleck, *Celebrating the Family: Ethnicity, Consumer Culture, and Family Rituals* (Cambridge, Mass.: Harvard University Press, 2000), pp. 216–218, 224–227, and Katherine Jellison, "From the Farmhouse Parlor to the Pink Barn: The Commercialization of Weddings in the Rural Midwest," *Iowa Heritage Illustrated* 77 (Summer 1996): 52–57, 65. Discussion of the establishment of wedding services in urban department stores is included in Vicki Howard, *Brides, Inc.: American Weddings and the Business of Tradition* (Philadelphia: University of Pennsylvania Press, 2006), pp. 121–122.

4. Nancy F. Cott, *Public Vows: A History of Marriage and the Nation* (Cambridge, Mass.: Harvard University Press, 2000), p. 187; Judy Barrett Litoff, David C. Smith, Barbara Wooddall Taylor, and Charles E. Taylor, *Miss You: The World War II Letters of Barbara Wooddall Taylor and Charles E. Taylor* (Athens: University of Georgia Press, 1990), pp. 10–12; Jessica Weiss, *To Have and To Hold: Mar-*

riage, the Baby Boom, and Social Change (Chicago: University of Chicago Press, 2000), p. 22; Donald Katz, *Home Fires: An Intimate Portrait of One Middle-Class Family in Postwar America* (New York: HarperCollins, 1992), pp. 5–6; Beth L. Bailey, *From Front Porch to Back Seat: Courtship in Twentieth-Century America* (Baltimore: Johns Hopkins University Press, 1988), p. 42; U.S. Bureau of the Census, *Statistical Abstracts of the United States: 1942* (Washington, D.C.: Government Printing Office, 1943), p. 27; Howard, *Brides, Inc.*, p. 170. Thirty-six percent of Oakland, California, couples who responded to a postwar study noted that World War II had "accelerated their desire to marry and start a family." See Weiss, *To Have and To Hold*, p. 22.

5. Cott, *Public Vows*, pp. 187–188; Maria Mcbride-Mellinger, *The Wedding Dress* (New York: Random House, 1993), pp. 34, 37; Community silverplate advertisement, *Life*, 27 April 1942, p. 43; Trushay advertisement, *Life*, 16 April 1945, p. 75; Shuron advertisement, *Life*, 11 October 1943, p. 15; Woodbury advertisement, *Life*, 5 July 1943, p. 55; Woodbury advertisement, *Life*, 4 September 1944, p. 43; Woodbury advertisement, *Life*, 11 February 1946, p. 5; Woodbury advertisement, *Life*, 4 March 1946, p. 23. For discussion of wartime advertising strategies in general, see Juliann Sivulka, *Soap, Sex, and Cigarettes: A Cultural History of American Advertising* (Belmont, Calif.: Wadsworth, 1998), pp. 230–236. For discussion of wartime advertising aimed at female *Life* readers, see Sue Hart, "Madison Avenue Goes to War: Patriotism in Advertising during World War II," in M. Paul Holsinger and Mary Anne Schofield, eds., *Visions of War: World War II in Popular Literature and Culture* (Bowling Green, Ohio: Bowling Green State University Popular Press, 1992), pp. 114–126.

6. John H. Mariano, *The Veteran and His Marriage* (New York: J. J. Little and Ives, 1945), p. 142; Cott, *Public Vows*, p. 188; Litoff et al., *Miss You*, p. 280.

7. Bailey, *From Front Porch to Back Seat*, pp. 41–42; Loren Baritz, *The Good Life: The Meaning of Success for the American Middle Class* (New York: Harper & Row, 1990), p. 193; William M. Tuttle Jr., *"Daddy's Gone to War": The Second World War in the Lives of America's Children* (New York: Oxford University Press, 1993), p. 27; Maxwell Droke, *Good-by to G.I.: How to Be a Successful Civilian* (New York: Abingdon-Cokesbury, 1945), p. 68; Katz, *Home Fires*, p. 14. For further information on women's wartime and immediate postwar employment, see Susan M. Hartmann, *The Home Front and Beyond: American Women in the 1940s* (Boston: Twayne, 1982), pp. 31–32, 67–68, 77, 92–93.

8. Elaine Tyler May, *Homeward Bound: American Families in the Cold War Era* (New York: Basic, 1988), p. 165.

9. "Speaking of Pictures: Master Baker Builds Cake 'Spectaculars,'" *Life*, 24

June 1946, p. 12; "*Life* Visits Palumbo's: In Philadelphia Nearly Everybody Has His Wedding Party in an Italian Restaurant on Catherine Street," *Life*, 27 June 1949, pp. 113–115; "Spring Weddings and Our Bridal Service," *Strawbridge and Clothier Store Chat*, March 1949, p. 2; "The Curtain Lifts on Our New Bride's Shop: Glimpses of the Shop and Its Personalities," *Strawbridge and Clothier Store Chat*, April-May 1949, pp. 10–11. *Store Chat* was Strawbridge and Clothier's in-house publication for its employees. The magazine is available to researchers at the Imprints Department, Hagley Museum and Library, Wilmington, Delaware.

10. McBride-Mellinger, *The Wedding Dress*, p. 123; printed advertisement, Edith N. McConnell Papers, Accession 1119, Business Records, Vol. 3, 1955–1956, Manuscripts and Archives Department, Hagley Museum and Library, Wilmington, Delaware. For extended discussion of female entrepreneurship, including the careers of Kidder and McConnell, see chapter 5 of Howard, *Brides, Inc.*

11. Willie Dolnick, sales representative since 1947 for the Bridal Originals wedding gown company, interview with the author, Chicago, 14 October 1995; "The Wedding Business: It Profits from the U.S. Sentiment for Brides at the Unsentimental Rate of $3 Billion a Year," *Life*, 9 June 1952, p. 124; "Capture and Train Your Maid," *Bride's*, Winter 1936–37, pp. 62, 104, 106; "What Shall I Wear?" *Bride's*, Autumn 1940, p. 53.

12. "How Much of a Wedding," *Bride's*, Winter 1946–47, pp. 108–109, 153–154. All cost conversions are determined using the American Institute for Economic Research Cost-of-Living Calculator at http://www.aier.org/research/col.php.

13. Brett Harvey, *The Fifties: A Women's Oral History* (New York: Harper Perennial, 1994), p. 74; Martin King Whyte, *Dating, Mating, and Marriage* (New York: Aldine de Gruyter, 1990), p. 89. As children's author Jane Yolen notes, the story of Cinderella remains America's favorite marriage fable—even though it does not conform neatly with the national "rags to riches" myth. Instead, it is a story of "riches recovered; *not* poor girl into princess but rather rich girl (or princess) rescued from improper or wicked enslavement." According to Yolen, "We Americans have it all wrong. 'Rumpelstiltskin,' in which a miller tells a whopping lie and his docile daughter acquiesces in it to become queen, would be more to the point." See Jane Yolen, "America's Cinderella," in Alan Dundes, ed., *Cinderella: A Casebook* (Madison: University of Wisconsin Press, 1988), p. 296.

14. De Beers advertisement, *Life*, 18 February 1946, p. 92; De Beers advertisement, *Life*, 15 April 1946, p. 55; Artcarved ring advertisement, *Life*, 7 January 1946, p. 99; Artcarved ring advertisement, *Life*, 22 April 1946, p. 47; Keepsake ring advertisement, *Life*, 25 February 1946, p. 69; Keepsake ring advertisement, *Life*, 25 March 1946, p. 101; Community silverplate advertisement, *Life*, 4 March 1946,

p. 49; Community silverplate advertisement, *Life*, 6 May 1946, inside front cover; Lane hope chest advertisement, *Life*, 27 May 1946, p. 22; Barbasol shaving cream advertisement, *Life*, 28 January 1946, p. 113; Barbasol advertisement, *Life*, 2 September 1946, p. 68; Chesterfield cigarette advertisement, *Life*, 27 May 1946, p. 45; Budweiser advertisement, *Life*, 20 May 1946, p. 30; Golden Wedding whiskey advertisement, *Life*, 4 March 1946, p. 125; Rittenhouse door chimes advertisement, *Life*, 27 May 1946, p. 126; Listerine advertisement (little girl in bride's costume), *Life*, 17 June 1946, p. 1; Sal Hepatica laxative advertisement, *Life*, 4 February 1946, p. 12; Colgate toothpaste advertisement, *Life*, 17 June 1946, p. 15; Prolon toothbrush advertisement (cartoon pig wearing bridal costume), *Life*, 24 June 1946, p. 4.

15. RCA radio advertisement, *Life*, 24 February 1947, p. 47; GE radio advertisement, *Life*, 4 June 1951, p. 5; Hoover vacuum cleaner advertisement, *Life*, 26 May 1947, p. 24; Wurlitzer jukebox advertisement, *Life*, 16 June 1947, p. 56; Kelvinator range advertisement, *Life*, 4 June 1951, inside front cover; Swiss watch advertisement, *Life*, 7 April 1952, p. 123; U.S. Royal tires advertisement, *Life*, 2 June 1952, p. 55; Prudential Life Insurance advertisement, *Life*, 22 September 1947, p. 32; New York Life Insurance advertisement, *Life*, 2 June 1952, p. 113. For general discussion of advertising trends of the 1946–1953 period, see Sivulka, *Soap, Sex, and Cigarettes*, pp. 240–241.

16. Nancy A. Walker, "Introduction: Women's Magazines and Women's Roles," in Walker, ed., *Women's Magazines 1940–1960: Gender Roles and the Popular Press* (Boston: Bedford/St. Martin's, 1998), pp. 12–13; Harvey, *The Fifties*, p. 52; Hartmann, *The Home Front and Beyond*, p. 165; Baritz, *The Good Life*, p. 194.

17. May, *Homeward Bound*, pp. 165–166, 181; Wendy Kozol, Life's *America: Family and Nation in Postwar Journalism* (Philadelphia: Temple University Press, 1994), p. 53; Bailey, *From Front Porch to Back Seat*, pp. 41–42; Baritz, *The Good Life*, p. 193; Walker, "Introduction," in Walker, ed., *Women's Magazines 1940–1960*, pp. 12–13; Karal Ann Marling, *As Seen on TV: The Visual Culture of Everyday Life in the 1950s* (Cambridge, Mass.: Harvard University Press, 1994), pp. 96, 132, 134–135; Nancy A. Walker, *Shaping Our Mothers' World: American Women's Magazines* (Jackson: University Press of Mississippi, 2000), p. 151.

18. Harvey, *The Fifties*, p. 191.

19. "The Wedding Business," p. 119; Harvey, *The Fifties*, p. 110.

20. "The Wedding Business," p. 124.

21. Sivulka, *Soap, Sex, and Cigarettes*, p. 241; Chevrolet advertisement, *Life*, 13 June 1955, p. 73; Metropolitan Life Insurance advertisement, *Life*, 21 May 1956, p. 21; Postum advertisement, *Life*, 18 March 1957, p. 167.

22. International Sterling advertisement, *Life*, 22 April 1957, p. 87; International Sterling advertisement, *Life*, 27 May 1957, p. 107.

23. Wini Breines, *Young, White, and Miserable: Growing Up Female in the Fifties* (Boston: Beacon, 1992), pp. 53–54.

24. Benita Eisler, *Private Lives: Men and Women of the Fifties* (New York: Franklin Watts, 1986), pp. 265–266.

25. Baritz, *The Good Life*, p. 194; Walker, "Introduction: Women's Magazines and Women's Roles," p. 12; Lizabeth Cohen, *A Consumers' Republic: The Politics of Mass Consumption in Postwar America* (New York: Vintage, 2004), pp. 122–123, 164, 261; May, *Homeward Bound*, p. 166; Denise Mann, "The Spectacularization of Everyday Life: Recycling Hollywood Stars and Fans in Early Television Variety Shows," in Lynn Spigel and Denise Mann, eds., *Private Screenings: Television and the Female Consumer* (Minneapolis: University of Minnesota Press, 1992), p. 48. For in-depth discussion of how television programs of the period portrayed white middle-class values and practices as the universal norm, see chapter 2 of Ella Taylor, *Prime-Time Families: Television Culture in Postwar America* (Berkeley: University of California Press, 1989), and material throughout Nina C. Leibman, *Living Room Lectures: The Fifties Family in Film and Television* (Austin: University of Texas Press, 1995).

26. Bailey, *From Front Porch to Back Seat*, pp. 75–76. Cost of a new car in 1960 comes from U.S. Bureau of the Census, *Statistical Abstract of the United States: 1970* (Washington, D.C.: Government Printing Office, 1970), p. 546.

27. Eisler, *Private Lives*, pp. 174–175.

28. "Here Comes the Bride . . . Presenting Some S & C Brides of 1964," *Strawbridge and Clothier Store Chat*, March 1965, p. 8; Kitty Hanson, *For Richer, For Poorer* (New York: Abelard-Schuman, 1967), pp. 15, 21, 26.

29. Statistics on teenage consumer practices derive from Hanson, *For Richer, For Poorer*, p. 28. For further discussion of teenage consumerism and marketing campaigns of the era that focused on young female Baby Boomers, see Joan Jacobs Brumberg, *The Body Project: An Intimate History of American Girls* (New York: Vintage, 1998), pp. 85–90, 113–116.

30. Hanson, *For Richer, For Poorer*, p. 65; Pleck, *Celebrating the Family*, p. 218; Marcia Seligson, *The Eternal Bliss Machine: America's Way of Wedding* (New York: William Morrow, 1973), p. 263; "Redstockings Manifesto" and Pat Mainardi, "The Politics of Housework," in Alexander Bloom and Wini Breines, eds., *"Takin' It to the Streets": A Sixties Reader* (New York: Oxford University Press, 1995), pp. 485–487, 491–495. For an in-depth discussion of how American business and advertising co-opted counterculture style, see Thomas Frank, *The*

Conquest of Cool: Business Culture, Counterculture, and the Rise of Hip Consumerism (Chicago: University of Chicago Press, 1997).

31. Seligson, *Eternal Bliss Machine*, pp. 1–2.

32. "Afro: A Beauty Happening," *Bride's*, November 1969, pp. 138–139; "Second Weddings," *Bride's*, December 1968/January 1969, pp. 84, 122–125; "Bride's Decorating Center," *Bride's*, June 1969, pp. 134–135.

33. "The Cost of a Wedding," *Bride's*, August 1969, p. 176; Cohen, *A Consumers' Republic*, p. 124. Income information for this period comes from Norman L. Rosenberg and Emily S. Rosenberg, *In Our Times: America since World War II*, 5th ed. (Englewood Cliffs, N.J.: Prentice Hall, 1995), p. 197.

34. Hanson, *For Richer, For Poorer*, p. 27.

35. For a more detailed statement of this argument, see, for instance, Beverly Jones, "The Dynamics of Marriage and Motherhood," in Robin Morgan, ed., *Sisterhood Is Powerful: An Anthology of Writings from the Women's Liberation Movement* (New York: Vintage, 1970), pp. 46–61. For discussion of some of the alternatives to patriarchal family life that radical feminists proposed, see Shulamith Firestone, *The Dialectic of Sex: The Case for Feminist Revolution* (New York: Bantam, 1972), pp. 226–242. For analysis of the popular media's dissemination of feminist ideas to the general public in the early 1970s, see Susan J. Douglas, *Where the Girls Are: Growing Up Female with the Mass Media* (New York: Times, 1995), pp. 163–191.

36. Glenda Riley, *Divorce: An American Tradition* (New York: Oxford University Press, 1991), pp. 156–157, 159, 163; Mariano, *The Veteran and His Marriage*, pp. 49, 207.

37. Riley, pp. 156, 185.

38. Cott, *Public Vows*, pp. 206–207; Karla B. Hackstaff, *Marriage in a Culture of Divorce* (Philadelphia: Temple University Press, 1999), pp. 28–31.

39. George Donelson Moss, *Moving On: The American People since 1945* (Englewood Cliffs, N.J.: Prentice Hall, 1994), pp. 298–299; Julia Kirk Blackwelder, *Now Hiring: The Feminization of Work in the United States, 1900–1995* (College Station: Texas A&M University Press, 1997), p. 196. Specifically, between 1970 and 1980 the proportion of wage earners rose from 30 percent to 45.1 percent of all married women who had children under six years of age and from 49.1 percent to 61.7 percent of all married women with children six to eighteen years old. See Blackwelder, p. 195.

40. Andrew J. Cherlin, *Marriage, Divorce, Remarriage* (Cambridge, Mass.: Harvard University Press, 1981), pp. 7, 18, 59, 66, 123; Joseph Veroff, Elizabeth Douvan, and Richard A. Kulka, *The Inner American: A Self-Portrait from 1957 to*

1976 (New York: Basic, 1981), p. 197. Women's increased marriage age was merely one of several factors that contributed to the steadily decreasing birthrate between the mid-1960s and the mid-1970s. For instance, introduction of an oral contraceptive in 1960 and legalized abortion in 1973 also played roles in this equation.

41. Cherlin, *Marriage, Divorce, Remarriage*, pp. 35, 122–123.

42. Veroff et al., *The Inner American*, pp. 147–149, 182, 191–192.

43. Cherlin, *Marriage, Divorce, Remarriage*, pp. 12–13.

44. Khoren Arisian, *The New Wedding: Creating Your Own Marriage Ceremony* (New York: Alfred A. Knopf, 1973), pp. 3, 12, 15, 97.

45. Seligson, *The Eternal Bliss Machine*, pp. 1–2, 16, 38. See also chapter 15 of Seligson's book for further discussion of the era's small-scale New Wedding movement.

46. Weiss, *To Have and To Hold*, p. 208.

47. Ibid., pp. 177–222. Among Weiss's sample of women who gave birth to the Baby Boom generation, one-fourth returned to school following their primary reproductive and child-rearing years. National statistics regarding housewives' plans for reemployment come from Veroff et al., *The Inner American*, pp. 260, 290.

48. Eisler, *Private Lives*, pp. 313–334, 349–371.

49. Rosanna Hertz, "Dual-Career Corporate Couples: Shaping Marriages through Work," in Barbara J. Risman and Pepper Schwartz, eds., *Gender in Intimate Relationships: A Microstructural Approach* (Belmont, Calif.: Wadsworth, 1989), pp. 194–195, 197. See also material throughout Hertz's book-length study, *More Equal Than Others: Women and Men in Dual-Career Marriages* (Berkeley: University of California Press, 1986).

50. Hertz, "Dual-Career Corporate Couples," pp. 195–196, 200–201.

51. Hackstaff, *Marriage in a Culture of Divorce*, pp. 18–19, 24–25, 37–38, 121–122, 124–125, 134, 142–144. For further discussion of studies showing that post-1970 brides and grooms believe that divorce "can't happen" to them, regardless of their knowledge of high divorce rates, see Margaret F. Brinig, *From Contract to Covenant: Beyond the Law and Economics of the Family* (Cambridge, Mass.: Harvard University Press, 2000), pp. 17–18, 39.

52. Hackstaff, *Marriage in a Culture of Divorce*, pp. 18–19.

53. Hertz, "Dual-Career Corporate Couples," pp. 194, 200–201; Hackstaff, *Marriage in a Culture of Divorce*, pp. 143–144, 163–179. Statistics on housework in dual-career marriages derives from Veroff et al., *The Inner American*, pp. 179–180.

54. Blackwelder, *Now Hiring*, pp. 186–188.

55. Ibid., p. 189.

56. Barbara Ehrenreich, *Fear of Falling: The Inner Life of the Middle Class* (New York: Pantheon, 1989), p. 216.

57. Hertz, *More Equal Than Others*, p. 2.

58. Ibid., pp. 216–219.

59. Jacqueline Jones, *Labor of Love, Labor of Sorrow: Black Women, Work, and the Family from Slavery to the Present* (New York: Basic, 1985), pp. 269–274.

60. Robert E. Weems Jr., "Consumerism and the Construction of Black Female Identity in Twentieth-Century America," in Jennifer Scanlon, ed., *The Gender and Consumer Reader* (New York: New York University Press, 2000), p. 166. See also Annie S. Barnes, *The Black Middle Class Family: A Study of Black Subsociety, Neighborhood, and Home in Interaction* (Bristol, Ind.: Wyndham Hall, 1985), pp. 137–138. For discussion of white weddings among members of the black elite in the nineteenth century, see Willard B. Gatewood, *Aristocrats of Color: The Black Elite, 1880–1920* (Bloomington: Indiana University Press, 1990), pp. 165, 203–206.

61. Cohen, *A Consumers' Republic*, p. 308; Seligson, *The Eternal Bliss Machine*, pp. 65–66; "*Essence* Designers of the Month: Renee and Larry Greer," *Essence*, April 1973, p. 32–33; Njoki McElroy, "Alternative to a Traditional Wedding," *Essence*, April 1974, pp. 58–59.

62. Seligson, *The Eternal Bliss Machine*, p. 65; Liz Gant, "The Lowdown on Costs," *Essence*, June 1978, p. 98. The lack of a 1970s "*Essence* alternative" to the wedding advice found in white-targeted magazines contrasts with the so-called *Ebony* alternative that historian Jacqueline Jones has documented within black periodicals of the 1950s. In her famous critique of magazines with a predominantly white female readership, Betty Friedan noted in *The Feminine Mystique* (1963) that such publications overwhelmingly portrayed women as happy full-time wives and mothers. In contrast, Jones found that during the same era, magazines with a black readership presented a greater diversity of roles for women, including the reality-based portrayal of African American women as wage earners. See Jones, *Labor of Love, Labor of Sorrow*, pp. 269–274.

63. Seligson, *The Eternal Bliss Machine*, pp. 282–287.

64. Ibid., p. 263.

65. Jerry Smale, sales representative for Bridal Originals, telephone interview with the author, 15 July 1995.

66. Maggie Jones, "Wedding Wars," *Working Woman*, May 1995, p. 64.

67. Ibid., p. 65.

68. Ibid., p. 64.

69. Dolnick interview; Marcelle S. Fischler, "White Is O.K. (Excess, Too) at Wedding No. 2," *New York Times*, 17 March 2002, Section 9, pp. 1–2.

70. Dolnick and Smale interviews; Jones, "Wedding Wars," p. 66.

71. Dolnick interview; McBride-Mellinger, *The Wedding Dress*, pp. 41–42. Marriage age statistics derive from John D'Emilio and Estelle B. Freedman, *Intimate Matters: A History of Sexuality in America*, 2nd ed. (Chicago: University of Chicago Press, 1997), p. 330, and Carroll Stoner, *Weddings for Grownups: Everything You Need to Know to Plan Your Wedding Your Way* (San Francisco: Chronicle, 1993), p. 50.

72. Elizabeth M. Sporkin and Veronica Burns, "Wedding Belle," *People Weekly*, 8 July 1991, p. 66; Jones, "Wedding Wars," p. 67; Cohen, *A Consumers' Republic*, p. 312.

73. Barbara Mayer, "Economy Cuts Spending on Weddings," *Commercial Appeal* (Memphis), 9 February 1992, p. F4.

74. "'Brides Today' Magazine Is First Tailored to Blacks," *Commercial Appeal* (Memphis), 9 February 1992, p. F8; Harriette Cole, *Jumping the Broom: The African-American Wedding Planner* (New York: Henry Holt, 1993), pp. 20–21, 69, 198–203. For discussion of how bridal magazines have historically neglected African American brides and other brides of color, see Chrys Ingraham, *White Weddings: Romancing Heterosexuality in Popular Culture* (New York: Routledge, 1999), pp. 92–95.

75. Judith Stacey, "Gay and Lesbian Families: Queer Like Us," in Mary Ann Mason, Arlene Skolnick, and Stephen D. Sugarman, eds., *All Our Families: New Policies for a New Century* (New York: Oxford University Press, 1998), p. 127. Advice books of the era include Becky Butler, *Ceremonies of the Heart: Celebrating Lesbian Unions* (Seattle: Seal, 1990); Suzanne Sherman, ed., *Lesbian and Gay Marriage: Private Commitments, Public Ceremonies* (Philadelphia: Temple University Press, 1992); and Tess Ayers and Paul Brown, *The Essential Guide to Lesbian and Gay Weddings* (San Francisco: Harper San Francisco, 1994). For further discussion of lesbian and gay ceremonies in the late twentieth century, see Pleck, *Celebrating the Family*, pp. 223–224.

76. Marisa Keller and Mike Mashon, *TV Weddings: An Illustrated Guide* (New York: TV Books, 1999), pp. 161–163; Stacey, "Gay and Lesbian Families," p. 125.

77. For further discussion of these issues, see material throughout Ingraham, *White Weddings*.

78. Robert Kerr, "Older Brides, Bridegrooms See the New Trends Trailing Along," *Commercial Appeal* (Memphis), 9 February 1992, p. F2; Dolnick interview; Jennifer Welner, "Oh, Romeo, Romeo, Why Marry Now?" *Columbus* (Ohio) *Dispatch*, 28 April 1996, p. 8K; Diane M. Niebuhr, interview with the author, Hope's Bridal Boutique, rural Atkins, Iowa, 26 August 1992.

79. See the essays in Dundes, ed., *Cinderella*—particularly Jane Yolen, "America's Cinderella," pp. 294–306.

80. Marshall Hood, "Say 'I Do' to Simplicity," *Columbus* (Ohio) *Dispatch*, 13 January 1998, p. 2F.

81. See, for instance, Stoner, *Weddings for Grownups*, p. 45.

82. Sara Rimer, "Searching for a Fairy Tale Wedding Gown, at a Bargain Price," *New York Times*, 20 May 1997, p. A8; Cohen, *A Consumers' Republic*, p. 313; Sharon Boden, *Consumerism, Romance, and the Wedding Experience* (New York: Palgrave Macmillan, 2003), pp. 93, 158.

83. Lois Smith Brady, "Vows," *New York Times*, 6 December 1998, Section 9, p. 13; Lois Smith Brady, "Vows," *New York Times*, 13 December 1998, Section 9, p. 11. For further discussion of "Vows" features of this period, see Ingraham, *White Weddings*, pp. 112–120.

84. Lois Smith Brady, "Vows," *New York Times*, 9 May 1999, Section 9, p. 7.

85. Ingraham, *White Weddings*, pp. 89–90; Andy Wickstrom, "Video Should Get Good Reception from Brides," *Cincinnati Enquirer*, 19 May 1991, p. E5; Amy Bernstein, "Eye on the '90s: Wedding March," *U.S. News & World Report*, 10 May 1993, p. 17; Melissa A. Weisman, "On the Web, See How the Bride Cut the Cake," *New York Times*, 14 April 1998, p. B9; Emily Cohen, "Going to the Chapel," *PC Magazine*, 30 June 1998, p. 40; Suein Hwang, "I Was an Internet Bride," *Wall Street Journal*, 24 September 1999, pp. W1, W4.

86. Blanche McCrary Boyd, "Both Sides Now," *Ms.*, June/July 2000, pp. 57–58; Lisa Miya-Jervis, "Who Wants to Marry a Feminist?" *Ms.*, June/July 2000, pp. 63–64.

87. Susan Weidman Schneider, "Isn't It Ironic . . . Retro Weddings in a Feminist Age," *Lilith*, Spring 2000, p. 16; Sarah Blustain, "A Counterproposal: One Young Woman Resists On-Bended-Knee Conventions," *Lilith*, Spring 2000, p. 19.

88. Jay Molishever, "Bridal Gowns That Draw Oohs a Second (or Fifth) Time Around," *New York Times*, 28 July 2002, Section 9, p. 11. Age at first marriage statistics derive from Ethan Watters, "In My Tribe," *New York Times Magazine*, 14 October 2001, p. 25.

89. Kamy Wicoff, *I Do but I Don't: Walking down the Aisle without Losing Your Mind* (Cambridge, Mass.: Da Capo, 2006), p. 159.

90. Molly Jong-Fast/Matthew Greenfield wedding announcement, *New York Times*, 2 November 2003, Section 9, p. 13.

CHAPTER 2. LOOK LIKE A PRINCESS: THE WEDDING GOWN

1. Jaclyn Geller, *Here Comes the Bride: Women, Weddings, and the Marriage Mystique* (New York: Four Walls Eight Windows, 2001), pp. 222–223.

2. Designers cited are Arnold Scaasi, whose comments appear in Charles L. Mo, *To Have and To Hold: 135 Years of Wedding Fashions* (Charlotte, N.C.: Mint

Museum of Art, 2000), p. 70, and Ron LoVece, who is quoted in Maria Mcbride-Mellinger, *The Wedding Dress* (New York: Random House, 1993), p. 53. For discussion of the sacralizing of the wedding dress, see Simon R. Charsley, *Rites of Marrying: The Wedding Industry in Scotland* (New York: Manchester University Press, 1991), pp. 66–72, 181–182, 194, and Tina M. Lowrey and Cele Otnes, "Construction of a Meaningful Wedding: Differences in the Priorities of Brides and Grooms," in Janeen Arnold Costa, ed., *Gender Issues and Consumer Behavior* (Thousand Oaks, Calif.: Sage, 1994), pp. 168–169.

3. Michelle R. Nelson and Sameer Deshpande, "Love without Borders: An Examination of Cross-Cultural Wedding Rituals," in Cele C. Otnes and Tina M. Lowrey, eds., *Contemporary Consumption Rituals: A Research Anthology* (Mahwah, N.J.: Lawrence Erlbaum, 2004), p. 136; Ann Monsarrat, *And the Bride Wore . . . : The Story of the White Wedding* (London: Gentry, 1973), pp. 1–2, 108, 158; Vicki Howard, *Brides, Inc.: American Weddings and the Business of Tradition* (Philadelphia: University of Pennsylvania Press, 2006), pp. 158–159.

4. McBride-Mellinger, *The Wedding Dress*, p. 120; Howard, *Brides, Inc.*, pp. 121–129.

5. For discussion of the Depression's impact on American marriage, see Stephanie Coontz, *Marriage, a History: From Obedience to Intimacy, or How Love Conquered Marriage* (New York: Viking, 2005), pp. 216–220.

6. McBride-Mellinger, *The Wedding Dress*, p. 99; Marcia Seligson, *The Eternal Bliss Machine: America's Way of Wedding* (New York: William Morrow, 1973), p. 132; Willie Dolnick, Bridal Originals sales representative since 1947, interview with the author, Chicago, 14 October 1995.

7. Jerry Smale, Bridal Originals sales representative, telephone interview with the author, 15 July 1995; McBride-Mellinger, *The Wedding Dress*, p. 123.

8. Kitty Hanson, *For Richer, For Poorer* (New York: Abelard-Schuman, 1967), p. 114.

9. Bridal and Bridesmaid's Apparel Association advertisement, *Bride's*, Spring 1959, p. 146. See Eric Hobsbawm, "Introduction: Inventing Traditions," in Eric Hobsbawm and Terence Ranger, eds., *The Invention of Tradition* (New York: Cambridge University Press, 1995), pp. 1–14. Although the Association of Bridal Manufacturers was ultimately successful in persuading the government to ease some fabric restrictions, silk in particular remained in short supply for civilian use, limiting the number of formal wedding gowns manufactured during the war. See McBride-Mellinger, *The Wedding Dress*, pp. 34, 37.

10. Karla B. Hackstaff, *Marriage in a Culture of Divorce* (Philadelphia: Temple University Press, 1999), p. 119; Beth L. Bailey, *From Front Porch to Back Seat:*

Courtship in Twentieth-Century America (Baltimore: Johns Hopkins University Press, 1988), p. 41.

11. Dolnick interview; Lizabeth Cohen, *A Consumers' Republic: The Politics of Mass Consumption in Postwar America* (New York: Vintage, 2004), p. 301.

12. "Spring Weddings and Our Bridal Service," *Strawbridge and Clothier Store Chat*, March 1949, p. 2; "The Curtain Lifts on Our New Bride's Shop: Glimpses of the Shop and Its Personalities," *Strawbridge and Clothier Store Chat*, April-May 1949, pp. 10–12. *Store Chat* was Strawbridge and Clothier's in-house publication for its employees. The magazine is available to researchers at the Imprints Department, Hagley Museum and Library, Wilmington, Delaware.

13. "The Curtain Lifts on Our New Bride's Shop," p. 12; "Wedding Gift Service," *Strawbridge and Clothier Store Chat*, February 1954, p. 8; "A Bride Is Worth $3,300 to a Department Store," *Strawbridge and Clothier Store Chat*, February 1956, p. 6.

14. "A Bride Is Worth $3,300 to a Department Store," p. 6. Cost of a new car in the mid-1950s derives from U.S. Bureau of the Census, *Statistical Abstract of the United States: 1970* (Washington, D.C.: Government Printing Office, 1970), p. 546.

15. "Bridal Shows Draw Big Crowds," *Strawbridge and Clothier Store Chat*, February 1958, p. 2; "Bridal Director on TV Show," *Strawbridge and Clothier Store Chat*, February-March 1955, p. 5.

16. "The Most Romantic Spot on Our Beautiful Fashion Floor Is the Bride's Shop," *Strawbridge and Clothier Store Chat*, August-September 1949, p. 4; "An Invitation to Brides-to-be," *Strawbridge and Clothier Store Chat*, February 1957, p. 6; "The Bride's Shop Staff Wishes Much Happiness to–," *Strawbridge and Clothier Store Chat*, August-September 1949, p. 5; "The Bride's Shop Wishes Much Happiness to These Registered Store Brides," *Strawbridge and Clothier Store Chat*, November 1949, inside front cover; "A Group of Lovely Store Brides of This Past Summer," *Strawbridge and Clothier Store Chat*, August-September 1950, pp. 6–7.

17. "Bride Bonanza: Annual Expenditure in Philadelphia Area Is Nearly $50,000,000," *Strawbridge and Clothier Store Chat*, January 1962, p. 6.

18. For further discussion of the role of department stores in wedding-oriented consumption, see chapter 4 of Howard, *Brides, Inc.*

19. Mo, *To Have and To Hold*, pp. 51, 55; McBride-Mellinger, *The Wedding Dress*, pp. 34, 37; Hanson, *For Richer, For Poorer*, p. 114; "The Wedding Business," *Life*, 9 June 1952, p. 124; Gaylyn Studlar, "'Chi-Chi Cinderella': Audrey Hepburn as Couture Countermodel," in David Desser and Garth S. Jowett, eds., *Hollywood Goes Shopping* (Minneapolis: University of Minnesota Press, 2000), p. 170.

20. "So to Speak . . . ," *Du Pont Magazine*, June-July 1946, p. 1. Copies of this in-house company publication are available to researchers at the Imprints Department, Hagley Museum and Library, Wilmington, Delaware. Du Pont nylon advertisement, *Life*, 14 June 1948, p. 16; Celanese acetate advertisement, *Life*, 9 June 1952, p. 135. For discussion of the popularity of synthetic-fabric wedding dresses in the postwar era, see McBride-Mellinger, *The Wedding Dress*, p. 37. For discussion specifically of the use of leftover parachute material for the manufacture of postwar wedding gowns, see Mo, *To Have and To Hold*, p. 55. For a dramatic first-person story of using parachute material to make a wedding dress—in this instance, a confiscated Japanese silk parachute—see Madeleine Poston's account of her wartime internment in the Philippines and her marriage to one of the American officers who liberated her in Poston, *My Upside-Down World* (Portland, Ore.: Benneta, 2002), pp. 284–289.

21. "'Dream Wedding' of Miss America 1960" brochure, included in Miss America 1960 Dream Wedding promotional campaign scrapbook, Joseph Bancroft and Sons Company Collection, Accession 72.430, Pictorial Collections, Hagley Museum and Library, Wilmington, Delaware. Hereafter cited as Bancroft Collection.

22. Page from "'Dream Wedding' for Miss America 1960" layout, *Modern Bride*, Holiday 1959; letter from Pat Zitomer, art director, Alfred Angelo, Inc., to Kathleen Walsh, Craig Advertising Agency, 12 April 1960; retailer's registration card for Miss America campaign. All materials included in Miss America 1960 Dream Wedding promotional campaign scrapbook, Bancroft Collection.

23. Page from "'Dream Wedding' for Miss America 1960" layout, *Modern Bride*, Holiday 1959, included in Miss America 1960 Dream Wedding promotional campaign scrapbook, Bancroft Collection.

24. John D'Emilio and Estelle B. Freedman, *Intimate Matters: A History of Sexuality in America*, 2nd ed. (Chicago: University of Chicago Press, 1997), p. 301.

25. Field report on San Francisco Macy's store from Holly M. Kraeuter, Everglaze marketing division, to JGW, 17 December 1959. Everglaze was the trade name of a cotton fabric finishing process licensed to Bancroft and Sons, and the company's Everglaze division was responsible for marketing both its Everglaze and Ban-Lon products. Note from Mr. Bartlett, Pollard's of Lowell, Mass., to Henry Smith, Promotion Merchandise Manager, *Modern Bride*, no date. Bartlett's note stated that his store had sold ten gowns on the evening of its bridal fashion show for a total of $1,350, indicating that retailers perhaps sold the dress for less than the suggested price of $175 in working-class communities like Lowell. Letter from Marianne Sinclair, Fashion Office, Kresge-Newark, Inc., to Henry Smith, Promotion Merchandise Manager, *Modern Bride*, 27 January 1960; letter from Henry Smith,

Promotion Merchandise Manager, *Modern Bride*, to Mr. Bartlett, Pollard's of Lowell, Mass., 26 January 1960; "Miss Patricia Mildred Lackey Weds Robert Eugene McCulloch," clipping from the Paducah, Kentucky, *Sun-Democrat*, 30 December 1959; "Honeymoon in Florida: Mr. and Mrs. George P. Tysz," clipping from Riverhead, New York, *News Review*, 2 June 1960; hanger tag for Miss America 1960 wedding gown. All materials cited are included in the Miss America 1960 Dream Wedding promotional campaign scrapbook, Bancroft Collection.

26. As scholar Karal Ann Marling has noted, "Color was an index of status and fashion in the 1950s. It signified a break with the sameness of the military uniform, an answer to the drabness of hard times, a visible sign of a car or a set of kitchen cabinets bought brand, spanking new. Color was an extra, a mark of futuristic technology at work, of miracle fabrics and plastics in a thousand unimaginable rainbow-tinted hues." See Marling, *As Seen on TV: The Visual Culture of Everyday Life in the 1950s* (Cambridge, Mass.: Harvard University Press, 1994), p. 220.

27. The dress's suggested retail price is listed in "'Dream Wedding' for Miss America 1961," *Modern Bride*, Holiday 1960, p. 79. Biographical information about Fleming taken from "Eight Decades of Miss Americas," *People Weekly*, 16 October 2000, p. 154.

28. Press release from Everglaze marketing division, 18 November 1960, Miss America 1961 Dream Wedding promotional campaign scrapbook, Bancroft Collection.

29. Woolf Brothers advertisement, *Kansas City Times*, 28 December 1960; J. P. Allen and Company fashion show photo and captions; Best's Apparel window display photo and captions. All materials included in Miss America 1961 Dream Wedding promotional campaign scrapbook, Bancroft Collection.

30. Letter from James N. Kidder, Priscilla of Boston, Inc., to Marie Flatly, Bridal Buyer, Lord and Taylor, 23 February 1961, Miss America 1961 Dream Wedding promotional campaign scrapbook, Bancroft Collection.

31. Letter from James N. Kidder, Priscilla of Boston, Inc., to Lola Martin, Everglaze marketing division, 23 February 1961, Miss America 1961 Dream Wedding promotional campaign scrapbook, Bancroft Collection.

32. Hanson, *For Richer, For Poorer*, pp. 28, 122.

33. "Eight Decades of Miss Americas," p. 159; Advertisements and promotional card included in folder labeled "1964—Pictures and Pamphlets—Miss America and 'Ban-Lon,'" Box 6, Bancroft Collection.

34. Howard, *Brides, Inc.*, pp. 123, 126–127.

35. Elizabeth Cleghorn Wall, interview with the author, Memphis, 24 June 1993; Rosalie Brody, *Emily Post Weddings* (New York: Simon & Schuster, 1963), p. 11.

36. Wall interview.

37. Ibid.

38. Hanson, *For Richer, For Poorer*, p. 113.

39. Martin King Whyte, *Dating, Mating, and Marriage* (New York: Aldine de Gruyter, 1990), pp. 201–203; Hanson, *For Richer, For Poorer*, p. 15; "January Bridal Show," *Strawbridge and Clothier Store Chat*, January-February 1967, p. 16.

40. "No More Miss America," in Alexander Bloom and Wini Breines, eds., *"Takin' It to the Streets": A Sixties Reader* (New York: Oxford University Press, 1995), pp. 482–483; Elizabeth H. Pleck, *Celebrating the Family: Ethnicity, Consumer Culture, and Family Rituals* (Cambridge, Mass.: Harvard University Press, 2000), pp. 222–223.

41. D'Emilio and Freedman, *Intimate Matters*, pp. 307–318, 333–334; Blanche Linden-Ward and Carol Hurd Green, *Changing the Future: American Women in the 1960s* (New York: Twayne, 1993), p. 68.

42. Glenda Riley, *Divorce: An American Tradition* (New York: Oxford University Press, 1991), pp. 156, 185; D'Emilio and Freedman, *Intimate Matters*, p. 331.

43. McBride-Mellinger, *The Wedding Dress*, p. 41; Seligson, *The Eternal Bliss Machine*, pp. 1, 126–127.

44. Seligson, *The Eternal Bliss Machine*, pp. 12, 38, 141–142.

45. "Bridal Fashions," *Strawbridge and Clothier Store Chat*, January-February 1974, p. 3; "'Thank Heaven for Little Girls', the Fabulous Bridal Show by S & C," *Strawbridge and Clothier Store Chat*, June-July 1974, p. 24.

46. Dolnick and Smale interviews; Cele Otnes, "'Friend of the Bride'—And Then Some: Roles of the Bridal Salon during Wedding Planning," in John F. Sherry Jr., ed., *ServiceScapes: The Concept of Place in Contemporary Markets* (Chicago: NTC Business, 1998), p. 244. For discussion of the "informalization" of American society in the 1960s and 1970s, see Kenneth Cmiel, "The Politics of Civility," in David Farber, ed., *The Sixties: From Memory to History* (Chapel Hill: University of North Carolina Press, 1994), pp. 275–278, 281–284.

47. Ann Hardy Vrana, interview with the author, Wahoo, Nebraska, 6 March 1993.

48. Wall and Vrana interviews.

49. Ibid.

50. Vrana interview; Lowrey and Otnes, "Construction of a Meaningful Wedding," p. 169.

51. Dolnick interview; Marcelle S. Fischler, "White Is O.K. (Excess, Too) at Wedding No. 2," *New York Times*, 17 March 2002, Section 9, pp. 1–2; Rebecca Mead, "You're Getting Married: The Wal-Martization of the Bridal Business," *New Yorker*, 21 and 28 April 2003, pp. 86–87.

52. Cover, *Ebony*, June 1947; "Modern Living: Gowns for June Brides," *Jet*, 4 June 1953, p. 39; "Fashion Fair," *Ebony*, June 1953, pp. 85–88, 90; Cohen, *A Consumers' Republic*, p. 326.

53. Daniel C. Thompson, *A Black Elite: A Profile of Graduates of UNCF Colleges* (Westport, Conn.: Greenwood, 1986), p. 128; "Our Best Clothes, Our Best Stores," *Essence*, July 1997, p. 84; "I Want to Buy from Black Designers . . . ," *Essence*, July 1997, p. 88; "The Book on Our Style," *Essence*, February 1998, p. 122; "And the Bride Wore . . . ," *Essence*, February 1998, p. 120; Julia Chance, "Wedded to Culture," *Essence*, February 1996, p. 30; "Bridal Gowns That Satisfy the Soul," *Essence*, February 1999, p. 124. For thoughtful analysis of various segments of the African American population in the late twentieth-century economy, see the essays in Robert Cherry and William M. Rodgers III, eds., *Prosperity for All?: The Economic Boom and African Americans* (New York: Russell Sage Foundation, 2000).

54. Dolnick and Smale interviews; "White House Wedding Consultant Conducts Clinic," *Strawbridge and Clothier Store Chat*, March 1972, p. 2; Maggie Jones, "Wedding Wars," *Working Woman*, May 1995, p. 66.

55. Otnes, "'Friend of the Bride'—And Then Some," pp. 248–249; Mead, "You're Getting Married," p. 79. For discussion of the decline of department store salons, see Howard, *Brides, Inc.*, pp. 98 and 260 n. 2.

56. Diane M. Niebuhr, interview with the author, rural Atkins, Iowa, 26 August 1992.

57. Lowrey and Otnes, "Construction of a Meaningful Wedding," p. 169; Smale interview; Mead, "You're Getting Married," pp. 77–78, 85–86; Otnes, "'Friend of the Bride'—And Then Some," p. 248.

58. Dolnick and Smale interviews; "Informal Phone Survey #2," "Invitation to Expand," Advertisement for *"Bridal Insight* Seminars," "Spotlight on Lyle Scifres, Abbington's Bridal, Owensboro, Kentucky," all in *Bridal Insight*, September/October 1995, pp. 3–5, 8.

59. Mead, "You're Getting Married," pp. 85–86.

60. Ibid.

61. Ibid., pp. 78, 84.

62. Julie Flaherty, "Freedom to Marry, and to Spend on It," *New York Times*, 16 May 2004, Section 9, p. 2. For detailed discussion of the Vermont civil union law and reaction to it, see chapter 5 of Martin Dupuis, *Same-Sex Marriage, Legal Mobilization, and the Politics of Rights* (New York: Peter Lang, 2002).

63. "Gay Weddings Go Prime Time," *Newsweek Web*, 22 August 2002, accessed at http://www.msnbc.com/news/797708.asp; Flaherty, "Freedom to Marry, and to Spend on It," Section 9, p. 2; Michael Colton, "Why Is This Wedding Different from All Other Weddings?" *New York Times*, 27 September 1999, p. B8.

64. "One Man, One Woman," Joy Padgett 2004 campaign flier, in possession of the author; Adam Liptak, "Caution in Court for Gay Rights Groups," *New York Times*, 12 November 2004, p. A16.

65. Elizabeth Austin, "Why Homer's My Hero: The All-American Family Shouldn't Have to Wear Gucci to Feel Good," *Washington Monthly*, October 2000, pp. 30–35; Gregory L. White and Shirley Leung, "Middle Market Shrinks as Americans Migrate toward the High End," *Wall Street Journal*, 29 March 2002, Section A, p. 1; cartoon, *New Yorker*, 8 May 2006, p. 32.

66. Jennifer Saranow, "To Have and to Hit Up," *Wall Street Journal*, 6 May 2005, p. W3; eBay items accessed on 4 November 2005 at http://cgi.ebay.com/AUTH -VERA-WANG-WEDDING-BRIDAL-GOWN-DRESS-size-10-12 and http://cgi .ebay.com/VERA-WANG-LUXE-WEDDING-DRESS-GOWN-CINDERELLA -2005. Thank you to Jane Lancaster for suggesting eBay as a research source.

67. Seligson, *The Eternal Bliss Machine*, p. 140.

68. Hanson, *For Richer, For Poorer*, p. 111.

CHAPTER 3. LIKE A ROYAL WEDDING: THE CELEBRITY WEDDING

1. Cover, *People Weekly*, 11 December 2000; Anne-Marie O'Neill, "Some Enchanted Evening!" *People Weekly*, 11 December 2000, pp. 64–74, 79–80, 82; B. J. Sigesmund, "Newsmakers," *Newsweek*, 4 December 2000, p. 71.

2. Sigesmund, "Newsmakers," p. 71; Martin King Whyte, *Dating, Mating, and Marriage* (New York: Aldine de Gruyter, 1990), pp. 61–63, 90; Lisa Miya-Jervis, "Who Wants to Marry a Feminist?" *Ms.*, June/July 2000, p. 65; Barbara Kantrowitz and Pat Wingert, "Unmarried with Children," *Newsweek*, 28 May 2001, p. 49; Sarah Lyall, "The Wedding Pictures: 2 Stars in Court Drama," *New York Times*, 11 February 2003, p. A4.

3. Alex Williams and Eric Dash, "Other Prenuptial Agreements Tie Stars to Blushing Vendors," *New York Times*, 13 January 2005, pp. A1, A25.

4. Neal Gabler, *Life the Movie: How Entertainment Conquered Reality* (New York: Vintage, 2000), p. 201; Leo Braudy, *The Frenzy of Renown: Fame and Its History* (New York: Oxford University Press, 1986), pp. 23, 578. Commentators note that celebrity watchers most keenly feel a shared sense of experience when the object of their attention meets a tragic fate—as happened to Princess Grace, Princess Diana, and Carolyn Bessette Kennedy. See, for instance, Wheeler Winston Dixon's discussion of reaction to Diana's death in *Disaster and Memory: Celebrity Culture and the Crisis of Hollywood Cinema* (New York: Columbia University Press, 1999), pp. 9–10. See also Richard Schickel's discussion of reaction to the John F. Kennedy assassination in *Intimate Strangers: The Culture of Celebrity* (Garden City, N.Y.: Doubleday, 1985), p. 181.

5. Schickel, *Intimate Strangers*, pp. 4, 15–16.

6. Wilbur Cross and Ann Novotny, *White House Weddings* (New York: David McKay, 1967), pp. 112–161; Letitia Baldrige, *Legendary Brides* (New York: Harper-Collins, 2000), pp. 37–41, 58–64.

7. Baldrige, *Legendary Brides*, p. 79; "A Royal Wedding Brings Joy to Britain," *Life*, 1 December 1947, pp. 31–32.

8. "Prince of Monaco to Wed Grace Kelly," *New York Times*, 6 January 1956, pp. 1, 4; "Kelly-Rainier Wedding Barred in Promotions," *New York Times*, 9 March 1956, p. 35; Steven Englund, *Grace of Monaco: An Interpretive Biography* (Garden City, N.Y.: Doubleday, 1984), pp. 152–153.

9. Jeffrey Robinson, *Rainier and Grace: An Intimate Portrait* (New York: Atlantic Monthly, 1989), pp. 85, 89; Englund, *Grace of Monaco*, pp. 149, 168; "All About Grace," *New York Times*, 15 April 1956, Section 4, p. 2E; "Some Day My Prince Will Come," *People Weekly*, 26 July 1993, p. 97; "Monaco's 375 Acres Jammed for Prince's Wedding to Star," *New York Times*, 18 April 1956, p. 28; Baldrige, *Legendary Brides*, p. 122.

10. "To Show Wedding Gown," *New York Times*, 13 March 1956, p. 22; Baldrige, *Legendary Brides*, p. 34; Maria McBride-Mellinger, *The Wedding Dress* (New York: Random House, 1993), p. 37; Charles L. Mo, *To Have and To Hold: 135 Years of Wedding Fashions* (Charlotte, N.C.: Mint Museum of Art, 2000), pp. 59–60; "Best and Worst Wedding Dresses of the Century," *People Weekly*, 26 July 1993, p. 94; H. Kristina Haugland, *Grace Kelly: Icon of Style to Royal Bride* (New Haven, Conn.: Yale University Press, 2006), p. 66.

11. "Some Day My Prince Will Come," p. 97. The report that Kelly's father provided a $2 million "dowry" that covered the wedding expenses remains in doubt. See Robinson, *Rainier and Grace*, p. 77; Englund, *Grace of Monaco*, p. 236.

12. "Some Day My Prince Will Come," p. 97; McBride-Mellinger, *The Wedding Dress*, pp. 37–38; Mo, *To Have and To Hold*, p. 60; Haugland, *Grace Kelly*, p. 61.

13. Robinson, *Rainier and Grace*, p. 79; Englund, *Grace of Monaco*, p. 140. For discussion of how the press typically characterized wealthy celebrities as having the same values and desires as middle-class media consumers, see Schickel, *Intimate Strangers*, pp. 75–76.

14. Englund, *Grace of Monaco*, pp. 141–142, 162–163.

15. Marcia Seligson, *The Eternal Bliss Machine: America's Way of Wedding* (New York: William Morrow, 1973), p. 175; "Lynda's Wedding Will Be Different," *New York Times*, 3 December 1967, Section 4, p. 4; Lady Bird Johnson, *A White House Diary* (New York: Holt, Rinehart, and Winston, 1970), pp. 396, 406–411; "Best and Worst Bridesmaids' Dresses," *People Weekly*, 24 July 1995, p. 108.

16. "Trousseau Started by Lynda Johnson, Trade Paper Says," *New York Times*, 27 September 1967, p. 35; "But What Will She Wear?" *New York Times*, 18

October 1967, p. 50; "Bridesmaids to Wear Red," *New York Times*, 22 November 1967, p. 52.

17. "Lynda Johnson Will Be Wed Dec. 9 in White House," *New York Times*, 26 September 1967, p. 37; "Lynda Johnson's Wedding Set for 4 p.m.; Guest List Held to 500," *New York Times*, 16 October 1967, p. 31; "White House 'Rush Day': A Rehearsal and a Party," *New York Times*, 9 December 1967, p. 58; Johnson, *White House Diary*, pp. 598–605.

18. "TV: Commercials Mar NBC Coverage of Bridal," *New York Times*, 11 December 1967, p. 95.

19. "Copy of Lynda's Wedding Dress to Be in Stores Thursday," *New York Times*, 12 December 1967, p. 54.

20. Nixon-Eisenhower engagement noted in caption accompanying photo illustrating "Lynda's Wedding Will Be Different," *New York Times*; Seligson, *The Eternal Bliss Machine*, pp. 138, 173.

21. Throughout *A White House Diary*, Lady Bird Johnson comments on various ways in which her daughters flouted convention or made missteps that the press widely reported. The only event that seemed to produce anything approaching a family crisis, however, was Luci's conversion to Catholicism. According to the former first lady, this was the only development that seriously caused her to "feel a sense of separation" from one of her daughters. See pp. 203, 285–286.

22. Julie Nixon Eisenhower, *Pat Nixon: The Untold Story* (New York: Simon & Schuster, 1986), pp. 257–258; Seligson, *The Eternal Bliss Machine*, p. 173.

23. "A Simple Spectacular at the White House," *Time*, 14 June 1971, pp. 13, 15.

24. "Notes on People" column, *New York Times*, 19 May 1971, p. 43; "The Wedding Cake: White House Chef Explains Mrs. Nixon's Recipe," *New York Times*, 2 June 1971, p. 36; "No Retest, White House Decides," *New York Times*, 3 June 1971, p. 45; "The Making (and Then Remaking) of a Recipe, Step by Step," *New York Times*, 4 June 1971, p. 17. The *Times*'s home economist also entered the debate—and perpetuated it—by reporting her continued difficulty in making a decent cake from a scaled-down version of the recipe that the White House released for use by the nation's housewives.

25. Eisenhower, *Pat Nixon*, p. 312; "A Simple Spectacular at the White House," p. 13.

26. Seligson, *The Eternal Bliss Machine*, pp. 173–174.

27. Conversation 477-14, President Nixon, William Rogers, Ronald Ziegler, 12 April 1971; Conversation 251-17, President and H. R. Haldeman, 27 April 1971; Conversation 491-5, President, Ziegler, Tricia Nixon, *Look* photographer Howell Conant, 28 April 1971; Conversation 491-11, President, Haldeman, Ziegler, 28 April

1971. All in Nixon Tapes, Richard M. Nixon Presidential materials, National Archives II, College Park, Maryland. See also Seligson, *The Eternal Bliss Machine*, p. 173, and Gil Troy, *Affairs of State: The Rise and Rejection of the Presidential Couple since World War II* (New York: Free Press, 1997), pp. 193–195.

28. Seligson, *The Eternal Bliss Machine*, p. 176; "A Simple Spectacular at the White House," p. 15; "Tricia's Gown Is Going Public," *New York Times*, 15 June 1971, p. 52; "No Stampede for That Gown," *New York Times*, 23 June 1971, p. 50.

29. Amy Blumenfeld and Richard Jerome, "When Dad Is President," *People Weekly*, 18 June 2001, p. 55.

30. Seligson, *The Eternal Bliss Machine*, p. 43.

31. R. W. Apple Jr., "Charles and Lady Diana Wed Today: Beacons Burn across a Joyful Britain," *New York Times*, 29 July 1981, p. A8; "Live TV Coverage Set for Wedding Today," *New York Times*, 29 July 1981, p. A8; David Emanuel and Elizabeth Emanuel, *A Dress for Diana* (New York: Collins Design, 2006), p. 148; Jay Cocks, "'Why Ever Not?'" *Time*, 10 August 1981, p. 30.

32. Cocks, "'Why Ever Not?'" p. 29.

33. R. W. Apple Jr., "Amid Splendor, Charles Weds Diana," *New York Times*, 30 July 1981, p. A1. For discussion of feminist criticism of the Charles-Diana marriage and the issue of her virginity, see chapter 8 of Beatrix Campbell, *Diana, Princess of Wales: How Sexual Politics Shook the Monarchy* (London: Women's Press, 1998).

34. Colette Dowling, *The Cinderella Complex: Women's Hidden Fear of Independence* (New York: Simon & Schuster, 1981), p. 21.

35. Emanuel and Emanuel, *A Dress for Diana*, p. 158.

36. George Donelson Moss, *Moving On: The American People since 1945* (Englewood Cliffs, N.J.: Prentice Hall, 1994), pp. 322, 326; Debora Silverman, *Selling Culture: Bloomingdale's, Diana Vreeland, and the New Aristocracy of Taste in Reagan's America* (New York: Pantheon, 1986), pp. 11, 43, 141, 152. Daniel Delis Hill uses the term "luxurious exhibitionism" to describe the fashions that Nancy Reagan and the female characters on *Dallas* and *Dynasty* popularized in the 1980s. See Hill, *Advertising to the American Woman, 1900–1999* (Columbus: Ohio State University Press, 2002), p. 152. Film scholar Rebecca L. Epstein coined the term "excessory chic" to denote "the profligate use of accessories but also the material excesses of fashion of the 1980s." See Epstein, "Sharon Stone in a Gap Turtleneck," in David Desser and Garth S. Jowett, eds., *Hollywood Goes Shopping* (Minneapolis: University of Minnesota Press, 2000), p. 204.

37. Silverman, *Selling Culture*, pp. 159–160.

38. Jay Mulvaney, *Kennedy Weddings: A Family Album* (New York: St. Martin's, 1999), pp. 98–125.

39. Campbell, *Diana, Princess of Wales*, pp. 4, 168, 202, 214–215, 251; Julie Burchill, *Diana* (London: Weidenfeld & Nicolson, 1998), pp. 152, 221–222; Andrew Morton, *Diana: Her True Story—In Her Own Words* (New York: Simon & Schuster, 1997), pp. 256–258; Rosalind Brunt, "Princess Diana: A Sign of the Times," in Jeffrey Richards, Scott Wilson, and Linda Woodhead, eds., *Diana: The Making of a Media Saint* (London: I. B. Tauris, 1999), p. 29; Paul Heelas, "Diana's Self and the Quest Within," in *Diana: The Making of a Media Saint*, p. 98.

40. "Princess Bride," *Bride's*, December/January 1997-1998, p. 40. For further discussion of Diana's impact on the wedding industry of the 1980s and 1990s, see Chrys Ingraham, *White Weddings: Romancing Heterosexuality in Popular Culture* (New York: Routledge, 1999), pp. 34–40, 105–108.

41. "The Most Eligible Bachelor and His Bride," *Time*, 26 July 1999, pp. 40–41; Mulvaney, *Kennedy Weddings*, pp. 170–173.

42. Barbara Mayer, "Queen Victoria Helped Popularize White Gowns," *Columbus* (Ohio) *Dispatch*, 13 January 1998, p. 2F; Cathy Horyn, "Narciso Rodriguez, Building on Stardom," *New York Times*, 6 May 2003, p. C18; Baldrige, *Legendary Brides*, p. 161; Marshall Hood, "Say 'I Do' to Simplicity," *Columbus* (Ohio) *Dispatch*, 13 January 1998, p. 1F; Stephen Henderson, "Get Me to the Gym on Time," quoted in Ingraham, *White Weddings*, p. 113.

43. "The Most Eligible Bachelor and His Bride," p. 40; anonymous bride, conversation with the author, Athens, Ohio, 27 October 2000; Kamy Wicoff, *I Do but I Don't: Walking down the Aisle without Losing Your Mind* (Cambridge, Mass.: Da Capo, 2006), p. 137.

44. Burchill, *Diana*, p. 210.

45. Ellen Goodstein, "Celebrity-style Wedding on Mere Mortal's Budget," accessed at http://www.bankrate.com/brm/news/cheap/20050404a1.asp.

46. Chrissy Balz, "Weddings: A Veil of Sadness," *Newsweek*, 7 August 2006, accessed at http://www.msnbc.msn.com/id/14096481/; "Celebrity Wedding Database," accessed at http://www.lovetripper.com/bridalstars/wedding-database/database-index.html; Alex Kuczynski, "The Curse of the *InStyle* Wedding," *New York Times*, 2 June 2002, Section 9, pp. 1, 10.

47. Kuczynski, "The Curse of the *InStyle* Wedding," pp. 1, 10.

48. Baldrige, *Legendary Brides*, p. 11. Among the individual weddings that Baldrige devotes an entire chapter to are those of Grace Kelly, Diana Spencer, and Carolyn Bessette.

CHAPTER 4. WATCHING *CINDERELLA* ON VIDEO: THE MOVIE WEDDING

1. Lori Leibovich, "The Fail-Safe Summer Wedding Film," *New York Times*, 11 May 2003, Section 2A, p. 11.

2. Joel Zwick, director, *My Big Fat Greek Wedding* (2002). Along with starring in the film, Nia Vardalos also wrote the screenplay.

3. Leibovich, "The Fail-Safe Summer Wedding Film," p. 11.

4. Michael Wood, *America in the Movies: Or "Santa Maria, It Had Slipped My Mind"* (New York: Columbia University Press, 1989), pp. 192–193.

5. Statistics derive from Loren Baritz, *The Good Life: The Meaning of Success for the American Middle Class* (New York: Harper & Row, 1990), p. 160; George Donelson Moss, *Moving On: The American People since 1945* (Englewood Cliffs, N.J.: Prentice Hall, 1994), p. 404; Chrys Ingraham, *White Weddings: Romancing Heterosexuality in Popular Culture* (New York: Routledge, 1999), pp. 177–178, 180–183.

6. Neal Gabler, *Life the Movie: How Entertainment Conquered Reality* (New York: Vintage, 2000), p. 57; James Rorty, *Our Master's Voice: Advertising* (New York: John Day, 1934), p. 256; Heather Addison, "Hollywood, Consumer Culture, and the Rise of 'Body Shaping,'" in David Desser and Garth S. Jowett, eds., *Hollywood Goes Shopping* (Minneapolis: University of Minnesota Press, 2000), p. 9.

7. Sue Hart, "Madison Avenue Goes to War: Patriotism in Advertising during World War II," in M. Paul Holsinger and Mary Anne Schofield, eds., *Visions of War: World War II in Popular Literature and Culture* (Bowling Green, Ohio: Bowling Green State University Popular Press, 1992), pp. 114, 120. See also material throughout Cynthia Lee Henthorn, *From Submarines to Suburbs: Selling a Better America, 1939–1959* (Athens: Ohio University Press, 2006).

8. Vincente Minnelli, director, *The Clock* (1945); Stephen Harvey, *Directed by Vincente Minnelli* (New York: Harper & Row, 1989), pp. 193–194.

9. Harvey, *Directed by Vincente Minnelli*, p. 191.

10. Francis Davis, "Storming the Home Front," *Atlantic Monthly*, March 2003, pp. 125–132. In addition to the Oscar for Best Picture, *The Best Years of Our Lives* won seven other Academy Awards, including one for director William Wyler, one for screenwriter Robert E. Sherwood, one for Best Actor Fredric March, and two for real-life veteran Harold Russell, who had lost both hands during the war. Russell, who was not a professional actor, won the award for Best Supporting Actor and also won a special Oscar "for bringing hope and courage to his fellow veterans through his appearance in *The Best Years of Our Lives*." See Richard Shale, *The Academy Awards Index: The Complete Categorical and Chronological Record* (Westport, Conn.: Greenwood, 1993), pp. 430–433.

11. William Wyler, director, *The Best Years of Our Lives* (1946). Thanks to Elaine Tyler May for suggesting I examine the wedding scene in this picture.

12. Henthorn, *From Submarines to Suburbs*, p. 168.

13. Wilfred Jackson, Hamilton Luske, and Clyde Geronimi, directors, *Cinder-*

ella (1950); Jane Yolen, "America's Cinderella," in Alan Dundes, ed., *Cinderella: A Casebook* (Madison: University of Wisconsin Press, 1988), pp. 302–303.

14. For discussion of the history and conventions of debutante balls, see Karal Ann Marling, *Debutante: Rites and Regalia of American Debdom* (Lawrence: University Press of Kansas, 2004).

15. "Top Grosses of 1950," *Variety*, 3 January 1951, p. 58; Yolen, "America's Cinderella," pp. 302–303.

16. Sharon Boden, *Consumerism, Romance, and the Wedding Experience* (New York: Palgrave, 2003), pp. 113, 176.

17. Bosley Crowther, *Father of the Bride* review, *New York Times*, 19 May 1950, p. 31; Elizabeth Freeman, *The Wedding Complex: Forms of Belonging in Modern American Culture* (Durham, N.C.: Duke University Press, 2002), p. 185; Shale, *The Academy Awards Index*, pp. 450–451; Jackie Byars, *All That Hollywood Allows: Re-reading Gender in 1950s Melodrama* (Chapel Hill: University of North Carolina Press, 1991), p. 306; Harvey, *Directed by Vincente Minnelli*, p. 160. The 1951 sequel, *Father's Little Dividend*, pokes gentle fun at the pronatalist philosophy of the 1950s by having the Elizabeth Taylor character give birth to a baby who provides Spencer Tracy with a new set of domestic frustrations.

18. Vincente Minnelli, director, *Father of the Bride* (1950). See "Wedding in Movieland: At 18, Beautiful and Starry-Eyed, Elizabeth Taylor Is Married to Nick Hilton, Son of the Hotel Owner," *Life*, 22 May 1950, pp. 46–47. The original 1949 novel was written by Edward Streeter and published by Simon & Schuster. For the story of a real-life California family whose experiences paralleled those of the fictional Banks clan, see "Father of the Bride: An Unsung Hero Is Finally Honored," *Life*, 25 July 1949, pp. 67–73.

19. Byars, *All That Hollywood Allows*, pp. 95–97. Scholar Martin King Whyte found this "all or nothing" pattern among the 459 wedding celebrations of the 1924–1984 period that he investigated in Detroit. Noting the interrelated nature of various wedding celebration commodities and services, Whyte reported that among the former brides he surveyed, "some had most or all of them, while others had few or none." See Whyte's *Dating, Mating, and Marriage* (New York: Aldine de Gruyter, 1990), p. 87.

20. Daniel Delis Hill, *Advertising to the American Woman, 1900–1999* (Columbus: Ohio State University Press, 2002), p. 109; Artcarved advertisement, *Life*, 5 June 1950, p. 62; James Naremore, *The Films of Vincente Minnelli* (New York: Cambridge University Press, 1993), pp. 108–109.

21. Richard Brooks, director, *The Catered Affair* (1956). "Bride in the Bronx: Chayefsky Builds His New Play on Wedding Plans," *Life*, 6 June 1955, pp. 117–118.

Writer Gore Vidal adapted Chayefsky's original teleplay for the big screen. For further discussion of Chayefsky's focus on working-class subject matter and analysis of the storyline of *The Catered Affair*, see John M. Clum, *Paddy Chayefsky* (Boston: G. K. Hall, 1976), pp. 30–31, 51, 54–57.

22. Among the extravagances at Reynolds's real-life wedding, held at Grossinger's resort in upstate New York, was an "elaborate six-layer wedding cake" that towered over the heads of the bridal couple. See "Debbie's Ring on at Last," *Life*, 10 October 1955, p. 61. The fact that Reynolds herself was a recent bride aided in publicizing *The Catered Affair* in 1956, just as Elizabeth Taylor's 1950 wedding to hotel heir Nicky Hilton helped promote *Father of the Bride* six years earlier. In fact, MGM studios even paid for and stage-managed Taylor's glamorous white wedding to Hilton as a means to publicize her celluloid celebration in *Father of the Bride*. In the late 1950s, the scandalous rivalry between Reynolds and Taylor for Eddie Fisher's affections merited even greater publicity than had either actress's earlier outing as a first-time bride.

23. For discussion of the earlier Davis film persona, see Jeanine Basinger, *A Woman's View: How Hollywood Spoke to Women, 1930–1960* (New York: Alfred A. Knopf, 1993), pp. 16–17, 97–99, 132–135, 438–444. For discussion of maternal archetypes in Hollywood films, see E. Ann Kaplan, "The Case of the Missing Mother: Maternal Issues in Vidor's *Stella Dallas*," in E. Ann Kaplan, ed., *Feminism and Film* (New York: Oxford University Press, 2000), p. 468.

24. Cele C. Otnes and Elizabeth H. Pleck, *Cinderella Dreams: The Allure of the Lavish Wedding* (Berkeley: University of California Press, 2003), p. 175.

25. Mike Nichols, director, *The Graduate* (1967). *The Graduate* became one of the highest grossing films in history up to that time and earned the Oscar for Best Director. It also received nominations for Best Picture and Best Adapted Screenplay. Katharine Ross received a nomination as Best Supporting Actress, and Dustin Hoffman and Anne Bancroft received acting nominations as well. Shale, *The Academy Awards Index*, pp. 546–547. For discussion of the significant impact *The Graduate* had on the motion picture industry and American culture in general, see Peter Biskind, *Easy Riders, Raging Bulls: How the Sex-Drugs-and-Rock 'n' Roll Generation Saved Hollywood* (New York: Simon & Schuster, 1998), pp. 15, 18, 34, 47–49, 81, 125.

26. Larry Peerce, director, *Goodbye, Columbus* (1969). *Goodbye, Columbus*, based on a novella by Philip Roth, received an Oscar nomination for Best Adapted Screenplay and was the eighth-highest-grossing film of 1969. See Shale, *The Academy Awards Index*, p. 557, and "Big Rental Films of 1969," *Variety*, 7 January 1970, p. 15. Information on Atlas and his customers is found in Marcia Seligson, *The*

Eternal Bliss Machine: America's Way of Wedding (New York: William Morrow, 1973), p. 82. For discussion of the ways in which both *The Graduate* and *Goodbye, Columbus* use the white wedding to comment on upper-middle-class vulgarity, see Parley Ann Boswell, "The Pleasure of Our Company: Hollywood Throws a Wedding Bash," in Paul Loukides and Linda K. Fuller, eds., *Beyond the Stars II: Plot Conventions in American Popular Film* (Bowling Green, Ohio: Bowling Green State University Popular Press, 1991), pp. 8–9.

27. I. C. Jarvie, *Movies as Social Criticism: Aspects of Their Social Psychology* (Metuchen, N.J.: Scarecrow, 1978), pp. 52–61, 122, 156, 160.

28. Cy Howard, director, *Lovers and Other Strangers* (1970); Robert Altman, director, *A Wedding* (1978). For further discussion of wedding scenes in the Coppola, Cimino, and Huston films, see Boswell, "The Pleasure of Our Company," pp. 12–16.

29. Robert Kerr, "Older Brides, Bridegrooms See the New Trends Trailing Along," *Commercial Appeal* (Memphis), 9 February 1992, p. F2; Barbara Mayer, "Economy Cuts Spending on Weddings," *Commercial Appeal* (Memphis), 9 February 1992, p. F4. The $16,144 figure was based on a survey of *Bride's* magazine readers.

30. Charles Shyer, director, *Father of the Bride* (1991).

31. Rosanna Hertz, *More Equal Than Others: Women and Men in Dual-Career Marriages* (Berkeley: University of California Press, 1986), p. 3.

32. Kerr, "Older Brides, Bridegrooms," p. F2.

33. Franck's supposed real-life model, Colin Cowie, had himself used the wedding industry to realize his version of the American dream. He arrived in Los Angeles from South Africa as a twenty-two-year-old immigrant, and eleven years later, *People* magazine referred to him as "Hollywood's wedding designer nonpareil." See "An Affair to Remember," *People Weekly*, 24 July 1995, pp. 131–134, 136, 138.

34. Naremore, *The Films of Vincente Minnelli*, pp. 93, 111.

35. The Hallmark company did not use these commercials to promote its wedding-related products exclusively but to endorse its entire line of greeting cards and party props.

36. Alan Alda, director, *Betsy's Wedding* (1990). Alda's film ranked sixtieth in box-office earnings for 1990. In contrast, *Father of the Bride*, released in the last month of 1991, still managed to rank as the thirtieth-top-grossing film of that year. Earnings for 1992 showed that it ranked thirty-first in that year. "Top Rental Films for 1990," *Variety*, 7 January 1991, p. 80; "Top Rental Films for 1991," *Variety*, 6 January 1992, p. 82; "Top Rental Films for 1992," *Variety*, 11 January 1993, p. 22.

37. Otnes and Pleck, *Cinderella Dreams*, pp. 164, 185–186, 192, 194.

38. Rebecca Mead, "You're Getting Married: The Wal-Martization of the Bridal Business," *New Yorker*, 21 and 28 April 2003, p. 84. Thanks to Robin Dearmon Jenkins for suggesting this interpretation.

39. Kitty Hanson, *For Richer, For Poorer* (New York: Abelard-Schuman, 1967), p. 27; Kamy Wicoff, *I Do but I Don't: Walking down the Aisle without Losing Your Mind* (Cambridge, Mass.: Da Capo, 2006), p. 217.

40. Robert DeNiro, director, *The Good Shepherd* (2006). I wish to thank Karal Ann Marling for bringing this scene to my attention.

CHAPTER 5. ADDICTED TO THE SHOW: THE REALITY WEDDING

1. *Who Wants to Marry a Multimillionaire?* Fox, originally broadcast 15 February 2000; Bill Carter, "Lights, Camera, Marriage, and Big Ratings," *New York Times*, 17 February 2000, pp. A1, C24; Kyle Smith, "TV's Reality Check," *People Weekly*, 6 March 2000, pp. 62–65; Michael A. Lipton, "Turned Off," *People Weekly*, 6 March 2000, p. 66. I'd like to thank Kimberly Little for sharing a video recording of the program with me.

2. Carter, "Lights, Camera, Marriage," pp. A1, C24; Lipton, "Turned Off," p. 66.

3. Smith, "TV's Reality Check," pp. 63–65.

4. "Wedded in Mockery," *Evening Independent* (Massillion, Ohio), 9 February 1894, p. 1; "Unique Marriage Service," *Kalamazoo* (Michigan) *Morning Gazette-News*, 10 May 1902, no page number; Marion Spalding's 1907 Scrapbook, A-1032, Cleo Hoyt Collection, and 1922–1924 Scrapbook, A-2334, Box 1, Ruth Scherer Collection, Western Michigan University Archives and Regional History Collections, Kalamazoo, Michigan; "Half Thousand Coeds Romp at Big Gym Party," *Western Herald* (Michigan Normal School), 29 November 1916, p. 1; 1931 "Tom Thumb" wedding photo, *Lincoln* (Iowa) *Centennial Book*, State Historical Society of Iowa Library, Iowa City; Theo Coffelt, letter to the "Can You Give Me a Hand?" feature, *Reminisce Magazine*, March/April 1994, p. 66; Betty Sweeney, interview with the author, Lenexa, Kansas, 20 March 1994; Katherine Jellison, "From the Farmhouse Parlor to the Pink Barn: The Commercialization of Weddings in the Rural Midwest," *Iowa Heritage Illustrated* 77 (Summer 1996): 54–55.

5. Luce purchased rights to the title *Life* from a humor magazine that appeared as a weekly periodical from 1883 to 1931 and then as a monthly publication from 1931 to 1936. Erika Doss, "Introduction—Looking at *Life*: Rethinking America's Favorite Magazine, 1936–1972," in Erika Doss, ed., *Looking at* Life *Magazine* (Washington, D.C.: Smithsonian Institution, 2001), pp. 2, 4, 11, and 19–20, n. 3. See also Terry Smith, "*Life*-Style Modernity: Making Modern America," in ibid., p.

27; James L. Baughman, "Who Read *Life?*: The Circulation of America's Favorite Magazine," in ibid., pp. 42, 48. Thanks to Noralee Frankel for long ago suggesting *Life* as a rich source of material for this project.

6. Baughman, "Who Read *Life?*" pp. 42, 44–45; Charles Peters, "The Greatest Convention," *Washington Monthly*, July/August 2004, p. 18. The magazine's publicity department put *Life*'s 1940 readership statistic in perspective by noting that it represented "the combined population of San Francisco, Chicago, Boston, Detroit, New York City, Baltimore, Philadelphia, Providence, Cleveland, St. Louis, Pittsburgh, Atlanta, Portland, Seattle, Minneapolis and Galveston, with not quite enough left over for Ypsilanti." See Loudon Wainwright, *The Great American Magazine: An Inside History of* Life (New York: Alfred A. Knopf, 1986), p. 114.

7. Wendy Kozol, Life*'s America: Family and Nation in Postwar Photojournalism* (Philadelphia: Temple University Press, 1994), pp. 158–167, 202–204; Rickie Solinger, "The Smutty Side of *Life*: Picturing Babes as Icons of Gender Difference in the Early 1950s," in Doss, *Looking at* Life *Magazine*, pp. 201–219. For further discussion of the male gaze, see Laura Mulvey's classic article "Visual Pleasure and Narrative Cinema," *Screen* 16 (Autumn 1975): 6–18. For discussion of the white gown and veil as the most widely recognized artifacts of a formal wedding, see Simon R. Charsley, *Rites of Marrying: The Wedding Industry in Scotland* (New York: Manchester University Press, 1991), p. 66, and Chrys Ingraham, *White Weddings: Romancing Heterosexuality in Popular Culture* (New York: Routledge, 1999), p. 34.

8. "Speaking of Pictures . . . This Is a Jewish Wedding," *Life*, 5 April 1937, pp. 4–5; "'The Third Mass Marriage at the Tientsen YMCA,'" *Life*, 8 March 1937, pp. 28–29; "Speaking of Pictures . . . This Is a Wedding in a Country Church," *Life*, 19 September 1938, pp. 6–8; "*Life* Goes to a Party," *Life*, 21 June 1937, pp. 88–89, 90, 92; "*Life* Goes to a Kentucky Mountain Wedding," *Life*, 28 July 1941, pp. 82–85. In this tabulation, images of nuptial celebrations were counted as white weddings if they featured a bride in veil and formal white dress or a dress that was intended to be "read" as white in black-and-white photos. For instance, in deference to the Chinese association of white with the color of mourning clothes, the Tientsen YMCA brides wore pale pink veils and dresses that nevertheless photographed as white for the pages of *Life*. Also for the purposes of this tabulation, only images of contemporary brides were counted, excluding, for instance, an archival photo of First Lady Eleanor Roosevelt on her wedding day in 1905 or a picture of actress Miriam Hopkins dressed in a Victorian bridal gown for a movie role.

9. Kozol, Life*'s America*, pp. 56–69; "Furlough Brides: They Marry in Haste but Manage to Have Pretty, Formal Weddings with Traditional Satin and Veil," *Life*, 22 June 1942, pp. 37–40; Jergens ad, *Life*, 20 November 1944, p. 18.

10. Doss, "Introduction," p. 13; Baughman, "Who Read *Life*?" p. 42; Kozol, *Life's America*, pp. 39, 53, 91, 94.

11. Solinger, "The Smutty Side of *Life*," pp. 206, 216; Neil Harris, "The *Life* of the Party," in Doss, *Looking at* Life *Magazine*, p. 252; Wendy Kozol, "Gazing at Race in the Pages of *Life*: Picturing Segregation through Theory and History," in Doss, *Looking at* Life *Magazine*, p. 161; Kozol, *Life's America*, pp. 163–164.

12. "A Royal Wedding Brings Joy to Britain," *Life*, 1 December 1947, pp. 31–43; "*Life* Goes to a Harlem Wedding," *Life*, 19 April 1948, pp. 146–148; "*Life* Goes to the Wedding of Senator Chavez' Daughter," *Life*, 4 March 1946, pp. 118–120. For discussion of *Life*'s position on the civil rights movement and its use of domestic imagery to promote the movement to readers, see Kozol, "Gazing at Race in the Pages of *Life*," pp. 159–161.

13. "Career Girl Marries: Gwyned Filling's Story Has a Happy Ending," *Life*, 29 November 1948, p. 135. The earlier account of Filling's experiences had appeared on pp. 103–114 of the 3 May 1948 issue.

14. W. B. Waldkirch, letter to the editor, *Life*, 21 May 1948, p. 13; "Career Girl Marries," p. 136.

15. "June Wedding: Kansas City Girl Marries with All the Fixings," *Life*, 14 July 1947, p. 89.

16. Ibid., pp. 89–91, 96.

17. Ibid., pp. 90–91, 94–95.

18. Ibid., pp. 92–93, 96.

19. "Father of the Bride: An Unsung American Hero Is Finally Honored," *Life*, 25 July 1949, pp. 67–68.

20. Ibid., pp. 67–69, 71.

21. For further discussion of *Life*'s portrayal of male breadwinners and their incompetence when taking on women's domestic tasks, see Kozol, *Life's America*, p. 71 and p. 207, n. 92.

22. Joyce Kanner, letter to the editor, *Life*, 15 August 1949, p. 6.

23. Wainwright, *The Great American Magazine*, pp. 174, 179–180; "The Wedding Business: It Profits from the U.S. Sentiment for Brides at the Unsentimental Rate of $3 Billion a Year," *Life*, 9 June 1952, p. 119.

24. Between 1950 and 1957, *Life* featured only a handful of formally clad brides of color, including a member of the cast of *Porgy and Bess* on tour in the Soviet Union ("A Social Note from Moscow: 'Porgy' Pair Has Russian Wedding," *Life*, 30 January 1956, p. 47) and features picturing Asian, African, and Jamaican brides in Western-style wedding dress. For further discussion of the lack of nonwhites in *Life* advertising of the period, see Kozol, *Life's America*, p. 146.

25. Julia Kirk Blackwelder, *Now Hiring: The Feminization of Work in the United States, 1900–1995* (College Station: Texas A&M University Press, 1997), pp. 195, 225.

26. "'My Wife Works and I Like It': Jim Magill Argues that Jennie's Full-Time Job Is Good for Her, Good for Him, Good for Their Children—and Good for the Budget," *Life*, 24 December 1956, pp. 140–141; Kozol, *Life's America*, pp. 163–166.

27. For further discussion of the 1950s and the complex relationship between women's prescribed domestic role and their increased workforce participation, see Blackwelder, *Now Hiring*, pp. 147–176.

28. Wainwright, *The Great American Magazine*, pp. 179–180.

29. Ibid., p. 180; Doss, "Introduction," pp. 2, 15; John Gennari, "Bridging the Two Americas: *Life* Looks at the 1960s," in Doss, *Looking at Life Magazine*, pp. 261–277.

30. Erik Barnouw, *Tube of Plenty: The Evolution of American Television*, 2nd rev. ed. (New York: Oxford University Press, 1990), p. 198; Carolyn Kitch, *The Girl on the Magazine Cover: The Origins of Visual Stereotypes in American Mass Media* (Chapel Hill: University of North Carolina Press, 2001), p. 186. For in-depth discussion of how television programs of the period portrayed white middle-class values and practices as the universal norm, see chapter 2 of Ella Taylor, *Prime-Time Families: Television Culture in Postwar America* (Berkeley: University of California Press, 1989), and material throughout Nina C. Leibman, *Living Room Lectures: The Fifties Family in Film and Television* (Austin: University of Texas Press, 1995).

31. Susan J. Douglas, *Where the Girls Are: Growing Up Female with the Mass Media* (New York: Times, 1995), pp. 32–33, 36–38; Howard Blake, "An Apologia from the Man Who Produced the Worst Program in TV History," in Lawrence W. Lichty and Malachi C. Topping, eds., *American Broadcasting: A Source Book on the History of Radio and Television* (New York: Hastings House, 1975), pp. 415–420; Carole Srole, "*Queen for a Day*: Whiteness, Consumerism, and the 'Worthy Poor' in the 1950s and 1960s," unpublished paper presented at the annual conference of the Western Association of Women Historians, Berkeley, California, 2003. (I would like to thank Professor Srole for granting permission to cite her paper.) See also Shawn Hanley, "Queen for a Day," accessed at http://history.acusd.edu/gen/projects/hanley/queen.html. Hanley's paper discusses his mother's experiences on the show in 1961. *Queen for a Day*, which was based in Southern California, originated on radio in 1945. The show moved to television in the mid-1950s (spending part of its run on NBC and another portion on ABC), and it remained on the air until 1964. Through much of its run, it was the most highly rated daytime program on U.S. television.

32. Earl and Claudine Stiles, interview with the author, Lee County, Arkansas, 21 July 1993; Dennis Roddy, "Picture This: A TV Wedding That Lasts," *Pittsburgh Post-Gazette*, 26 February 2000, accessed at http://www.post-gazette.com/columnists/20000226roddy.asp; Lisa Gutierrez, "As Wed on TV: Couple Will Celebrate 50-Year Anniversary after Marriage on TV Show," *Kansas City Star*, 3 August 2002, accessed at http://www.kansascity.com/mld/kansascity/living/3779887.htm?1c. CBS broadcast the program from 1951 to 1953; it then moved to NBC for the full 1953–1954 season and after that was broadcast only on a periodic basis until it left the air entirely in 1958.

33. Stiles interview.

34. Ibid.

35. *Bride and Groom*, NBC, originally broadcast 9 March 1954, Museum of Television and Radio collection, New York City.

36. For discussion of the increasing homogenization of wedding celebrations as a result of greater reliance on commercial services and the adoption of middle-class "American" standards, see Martin King Whyte, *Dating, Mating, and Marriage* (New York: Aldine de Gruyter, 1990), pp. 89–90, and Jellison, "From the Farmhouse Parlor to the Pink Barn," pp. 57–58. The location of a commercialized wedding celebration, however, could often help reinforce a couple's ethnic identity. Members of a particular ethnic neighborhood or house of worship might gravitate to a specific restaurant or public hall because of its convenient location or because a fellow member of their community ran the establishment. Thus, the locale became known as the place where "all the Poles" or "all the Italians" held their wedding receptions. But even at these reception locations, Hit Parade tunes and "American" banquet entrees increasingly joined or supplanted ethnic music and cuisine. See Vicki Howard, *Brides, Inc.: American Weddings and the Business of Tradition* (Philadelphia: University of Pennsylvania Press, 2006), pp. 207–208, and Elizabeth H. Pleck, *Celebrating the Family: Ethnicity, Consumer Culture, and Family Rituals* (Cambridge, Mass.: Harvard University Press, 2000), pp. 227–228.

37. Betty Norwood Chaney, "A Proper Kind of Wedding," *Redbook*, August 1973, p. 47.

38. Loren Baritz, *The Good Life: The Meaning of Success for the American Middle Class* (New York: Harper & Row, 1990), p. 184; Norman L. Rosenberg and Emily S. Rosenberg, *In Our Times: America since World War II*, 5th ed. (Englewood Cliffs, N.J.: Prentice Hall, 1995), p. 91; "The Wedding Business," p. 130.

39. Quoted in Ted Ownby, *American Dreams in Mississippi: Consumers, Poverty, and Culture, 1838–1998* (Chapel Hill: University of North Carolina Press, 1999), p. 149. For further discussion of the role of television advertising in raising black expectations and inciting activism, see Mary Ann Watson, *The Expanding*

Vista: American Television in the Kennedy Years (Durham, N.C.: Duke University Press, 1994), pp. 177–180.

40. Chaney, "A Proper Kind of Wedding," p. 47.

41. Ibid., p. 49.

42. Ibid., pp. 47, 49.

43. Erika Engstrom and Beth Semic, "Portrayal of Religion in Reality TV Programming: Hegemony and the Contemporary American Wedding," unpublished paper presented at the annual meeting of the Association for Education in Journalism and Mass Communication, Miami, 2002, pp. 9–10. I would like to thank the authors for allowing me to cite this paper. See also Erika Engstrom, "Hegemony in Reality-Based TV Programming: The World According to *A Wedding Story*," *Media Report to Women* 31 (Winter 2003): 10–11.

44. Engstrom, "Hegemony in Reality-Based TV Programming," p. 14; Erika Engstrom, "Gender and Cultural Hegemony in Reality-Based Television Programming: The World According to *A Wedding Story*," unpublished paper presented at the annual conference of the Association for Education in Journalism and Mass Communication, New Orleans, 1999, pp. 12–14, 16, 19–20. In her study of the fifty 1998 episodes, Engstrom found that 84 percent of the weddings took place on the East Coast, 88 percent of grooms were white, and 84 percent of brides were white. I would like to thank Professor Engstrom for granting permission to cite from her unpublished work.

45. Gregory L. White and Shirley Leung, "Middle Market Shrinks as Americans Migrate toward the High End," *Wall Street Journal*, 29 March 2002, Section A, p. 1. For further commentary on the upscaling of American tastes in the late 1990s and early 2000s, see Elizabeth Austin, "Why Homer's My Hero: The All-American Family Shouldn't Have to Wear Gucci to Feel Good," *Washington Monthly*, October 2000, pp. 30–35.

46. Engstrom, "Gender and Cultural Hegemony in Reality-Based Television Programming," pp. 13–15; Jennifer Maher, "What Do Women Watch?: Tuning In to the Compulsory Heterosexuality Channel," in Susan Murray and Laurie Ouellette, eds., *Reality TV: Remaking Television Culture* (New York: New York University Press, 2004), p. 202.

47. Marshall Hood, "Say 'I Do' to Simplicity," *Columbus* (Ohio) *Dispatch*, 13 January 1998, p. 2F; Douglas, *Where the Girls Are*, p. 246; Carroll Stoner, *Weddings for Grownups: Everything You Need to Know to Plan Your Wedding Your Way* (San Francisco: Chronicle, 1993), p. 45.

48. Employment and income data for the 1990s are taken from Blackwelder, *Now Hiring*, pp. 211, 221, 225.

49. Jennifer Bayot, "For Richer or Poorer, to Our Credit Limit," *New York Times*, 13 July 2003, pp. 1, 17.

50. Maher, "What Do Women Watch?" pp. 202, 209.

51. Ibid., pp. 210–211.

52. Chad Raphael, "The Political Economic Origins of Reali-TV," p. 122; Susan Murray, "'I Think We Need a New Name for It': The Meeting of Documentary and Reality TV," p. 46; Ted Magder, "The End of TV 101: Reality Programs, Formats, and the New Business of Television," p. 140, all in Murray and Ouellette, *Reality TV*; Sean Baker, "From *Dragnet* to *Survivor*: Historical and Cultural Perspectives on Reality Television," in Matthew J. Smith and Andrew F. Wood, eds., *Survivor Lessons: Essays on Communication and Reality Television* (Jefferson, N.C.: Mc-Farland, 2003), pp. 59, 67; Thomas Mallon, *Stolen Words* (New York: Harcourt, 2001), p. 194.

53. "On TV," *Columbus* (Ohio) *Dispatch*, 10 August 2003, p. H5. *The Bachelor*'s history was accessed at http://tv.yahoo.com/tvpdb?id=1808398728&d=tvi& cf=0.

54. Rehn's biography was accessed at http://abc.go.com/primetime/bachelorette/bios/trista.html. Excerpts from Rehn's January 2003 *Good Morning America* interview were accessed at http://abcnews.go.com/sections/GMA/GoodMorning America/GMA030107Bachelorette_pre .

55. *Trista and Ryan's Wedding*, ABC, originally broadcast 10 December 2003. I would like to thank Jacqueline Wolf for lending me a videocassette of the program. See also Dana Stevens, "The $3.77 Million Wedding: Trista and Ryan Tie Knot on ABC," *Slate*, 11 December 2003. Accessed at http://slate.msn.com/id/2092401.

56. *Trista and Ryan's Wedding*.

57. Ibid.; Stevens, "The $3.77 Million Wedding."

58. Stevens, "The $3.77 Million Wedding."

59. Frank Rich, "What's Love Got to Do with It? Not Much," *New York Times*, 1 February 2004, Section 2, p. 22. For further discussion of the upscaling of family celebrations since World War II, see material throughout Pleck, *Celebrating the Family*.

60. Nicole Saunders, quoted in "What, Me Marry? *Ms.* Staffers Tell All . . . ," *Ms.*, June/July 2000, pp. 65, 68.

EPILOGUE

1. Jaime Rehmann, e-mail to employees and students of the Ohio University College of Osteopathic Medicine, 19 September 2005. Thanks to Jacqueline Wolf for forwarding this e-mail to me.

2. Katharine Q. Seelye, "Weddings after a National Tragedy: Terror Attacks Bring a Finer Focus to a Life-Affirming Ritual," *New York Times*, 14 October 2001, p. A21.

3. Susan Shapiro Barash, *The New Wife: The Evolving Role of the American Wife* (Lenexa, Kans.: Nonetheless, 2004), pp. 41, 252; Sam Roberts, "It's Official: To Be Married Means to Be Outnumbered," *New York Times*, 15 October 2006, accessed at http://www.nytimes.com/2006/10/15/us/15census.html?_r=1&th=&em c=th&pagewanted.

4. Jennifer Bayot, "For Richer or Poorer, to Our Credit Limit," *New York Times*, 13 July 2003, p. 17; Dan Hurley, "Divorce Rate: It's Not as High as You Think," *New York Times*, 19 April 2005, p. F7; Barash, *The New Wife*, p. 41; Kamy Wicoff, *I Do but I Don't: Walking down the Aisle without Losing Your Mind* (Cambridge, Mass.: Da Capo, 2006), pp. 128–129.

5. Barash, *The New Wife*, p. 248.

6. Wicoff, *I Do but I Don't*, pp. xi–xii, 110; Ariel Hart, "City May Want Runaway Bride to Return Its 'Gift' of Itself," *New York Times*, 3 May 2005, p. A18; Jane Eisner, "The Era of Big Weddings Is upon Us," *Akron* (Ohio) *Beacon Journal*, 10 May 2005, p. B2.

7. See Francine Parnes, "A Big Wedding with a Smaller Bill," *New York Times*, 25 May 2002, p. A13; http://www.indiebride.com; and http://www.consciousweddings .com.

8. Although Samuel Johnson originally applied his well-known remark about the "triumph of hope over experience" to second marriages, the perceived fragility of all marriages in the twenty-first century now makes it an appropriate comment on marriage in general.

Bibliography

BOOKS

Arisian, Khoren. *The New Wedding: Creating Your Own Marriage Ceremony*. New York: Alfred A. Knopf, 1973.

Ayers, Tess, and Paul Brown. *The Essential Guide to Lesbian and Gay Weddings*. San Francisco: Harper San Francisco, 1994.

Bailey, Beth L. *From Front Porch to Back Seat: Courtship in Twentieth-Century America*. Baltimore: Johns Hopkins University Press, 1988.

Baldrige, Letitia. *Legendary Brides*. New York: HarperCollins, 2000.

Barash, Susan Shapiro. *The New Wife: The Evolving Role of the American Wife*. Lenexa, Kans.: Nonetheless, 2004.

Baritz, Loren. *The Good Life: The Meaning of Success for the American Middle Class*. New York: Harper & Row, 1990.

Barnes, Annie S. *The Black Middle Class Family: A Study of Black Subsociety, Neighborhood, and Home in Interaction*. Bristol, Ind.: Wyndham Hall, 1985.

Barnouw, Erik. *Tube of Plenty: The Evolution of American Television*. 2nd rev. ed. New York: Oxford University Press, 1990.

Basinger, Jeanine. *A Woman's View: How Hollywood Spoke to Women, 1930–1960*. New York: Alfred A. Knopf, 1993.

Biskind, Peter. *Easy Riders, Raging Bulls: How the Sex-Drugs-and-Rock 'n' Roll Generation Saved Hollywood*. New York: Simon & Schuster, 1998.

Blackwelder, Julia Kirk. *Now Hiring: The Feminization of Work in the United States, 1900–1995*. College Station: Texas A&M University Press, 1997.

Boden, Sharon. *Consumerism, Romance, and the Wedding Experience*. New York: Palgrave Macmillan, 2003.

Braudy, Leo. *The Frenzy of Renown: Fame and Its History*. New York: Oxford University Press, 1986.

Breines, Wini. *Young, White, and Miserable: Growing up Female in the Fifties*. Boston: Beacon, 1992.

Brinig, Margaret F. *From Contract to Covenant: Beyond the Law and Economics of the Family*. Cambridge, Mass.: Harvard University Press, 2000.

Brody, Rosalie. *Emily Post Weddings*. New York: Simon & Schuster, 1963.

Brumberg, Joan Jacobs. *The Body Project: An Intimate History of American Girls*. New York: Vintage, 1998.

Burchill, Julie. *Diana*. London: Weidenfeld & Nicolson, 1998.

Butler, Becky. *Ceremonies of the Heart: Celebrating Lesbian Unions*. Seattle: Seal, 1990.

Byars, Jackie. *All That Hollywood Allows: Re-reading Gender in 1950s Melodrama*. Chapel Hill: University of North Carolina Press, 1991.

Campbell, Beatrix. *Diana, Princess of Wales: How Sexual Politics Shook the Monarchy*. London: Women's Press, 1998.

Charsley, Simon R. *Rites of Marrying: The Wedding Industry in Scotland*. New York: Manchester University Press, 1991.

Cherlin, Andrew J. *Marriage, Divorce, Remarriage*. Cambridge, Mass.: Harvard University Press, 1981.

Cherry, Robert, and William M. Rodgers III, eds. *Prosperity for All?: The Economic Boom and African Americans*. New York: Russell Sage Foundation, 2000.

Clum, John M. *Paddy Chayefsky*. Boston: G. K. Hall, 1976.

Cohen, Lizabeth. *A Consumers' Republic: The Politics of Mass Consumption in Postwar America*. New York: Vintage, 2004.

Cole, Harriette. *Jumping the Broom: The African-American Wedding Planner*. New York: Henry Holt, 1993.

Coontz, Stephanie. *Marriage, A History: From Obedience to Intimacy, or How Love Conquered Marriage*. New York: Viking, 2005.

Cott, Nancy F. *Public Vows: A History of Marriage and the Nation*. Cambridge, Mass.: Harvard University Press, 2000.

Cross, Wilbur, and Ann Novotny. *White House Weddings*. New York: David McKay, 1967.

D'Emilio, John, and Estelle B. Freedman. *Intimate Matters: A History of Sexuality in America*. 2nd ed. Chicago: University of Chicago Press, 1997.

Dixon, Wheeler Winston. *Disaster and Memory: Celebrity Culture and the Crisis of Hollywood Cinema*. New York: Columbia University Press, 1999.

Douglas, Susan J. *Where the Girls Are: Growing up Female with the Mass Media*. New York: Times, 1995.

Dowling, Colette. *The Cinderella Complex: Women's Hidden Fear of Independence*. New York: Simon & Schuster, 1981.

Droke, Maxwell. *Good-by to G. I.: How to Be a Successful Civilian*. New York: Abingdon-Cokesbury, 1945.

Dundes, Alan, ed. *Cinderella: A Casebook*. Madison: University of Wisconsin Press, 1988.

Dupuis, Martin. *Same-Sex Marriage, Legal Mobilization, and the Politics of Rights*. New York: Peter Lang, 2002.

Ehrenreich, Barbara. *Fear of Falling: The Inner Life of the Middle Class*. New York: Pantheon, 1989.

Eisenhower, Julie Nixon. *Pat Nixon: The Untold Story*. New York: Simon & Schuster, 1986.

Eisler, Benita. *Private Lives: Men and Women of the Fifties*. New York: Franklin Watts, 1986.

Emanuel, David, and Elizabeth Emanuel. *A Dress for Diana*. New York: Collins Design, 2006.

Englund, Steven. *Grace of Monaco: An Interpretive Biography*. Garden City, N.Y.: Doubleday, 1984.

Firestone, Shulamith. *The Dialectic of Sex: The Case for Feminist Revolution*. New York: Bantam, 1972.

Frank, Thomas. *The Conquest of Cool: Business Culture, Counterculture, and the Rise of Hip Consumerism*. Chicago: University of Chicago Press, 1997.

Freeman, Elizabeth. *The Wedding Complex: Forms of Belonging in Modern American Culture*. Durham, N.C.: Duke University Press, 2002.

Gabler, Neal. *Life the Movie: How Entertainment Conquered Reality*. New York: Vintage, 2000.

Gatewood, Willard B. *Aristocrats of Color: The Black Elite, 1880–1920*. Bloomington: Indiana University Press, 1990.

Geller, Jaclyn. *Here Comes the Bride: Women, Weddings, and the Marriage Mystique*. New York: Four Walls Eight Windows, 2001.

Hackstaff, Karla B. *Marriage in a Culture of Divorce*. Philadelphia: Temple University Press, 1999.

Hanson, Kitty. *For Richer, For Poorer*. New York: Abelard-Schuman, 1967.

Hartmann, Susan M. *The Home Front and Beyond: American Women in the 1940s*. Boston: Twayne, 1982.

Harvey, Brett. *The Fifties: A Women's Oral History*. New York: Harper Perennial, 1994.

Harvey, Stephen. *Directed by Vincente Minnelli*. New York: Harper & Row, 1989.

Haugland, Kristina. *Grace Kelly: Icon of Style to Royal Bride*. New Haven, Conn.: Yale University Press, 2006.

Henthorn, Cynthia Lee. *From Submarines to Suburbs: Selling a Better America, 1939–1959*. Athens: Ohio University Press, 2006.

Hertz, Rosanna. *More Equal Than Others: Women and Men in Dual-Career Marriages*. Berkeley: University of California Press, 1986.

Hill, Daniel Delis. *Advertising to the American Woman, 1900–1999*. Columbus: Ohio State University Press, 2002.

Howard, Vicki. *Brides, Inc.: American Weddings and the Business of Tradition*. Philadelphia: University of Pennsylvania Press, 2006.

Ingraham, Chrys. *White Weddings: Romancing Heterosexuality in Popular Culture*. New York: Routledge, 1999.

Jarvie, I. C. *Movies as Social Criticism: Aspects of Their Social Psychology.* Metuchen, N.J.: Scarecrow, 1978.

Johnson, Lady Bird. *A White House Diary.* New York: Holt, Rinehart, and Winston, 1970.

Jones, Jacqueline. *Labor of Love, Labor of Sorrow: Black Women, Work, and the Family from Slavery to the Present.* New York: Basic, 1985.

Katz, Donald. *Home Fires: An Intimate Portrait of One Middle-Class Family in Postwar America.* New York: HarperCollins, 1992.

Keller, Marisa, and Mike Mashon. *TV Weddings: An Illustrated Guide.* New York: TV Books, 1999.

Kingston, Paul W. *The Classless Society.* Stanford, Calif.: Stanford University Press, 2000.

Kitch, Carolyn. *The Girl on the Magazine Cover: The Origins of Visual Stereotypes in American Mass Media.* Chapel Hill: University of North Carolina Press, 2001.

Kozol, Wendy. *Life's America: Family and Nation in Postwar Photojournalism.* Philadelphia: Temple University Press, 1994.

Leibman, Nina C. *Living Room Lectures: The Fifties Family in Film and Television.* Austin: University of Texas Press, 1995.

Lincoln (Iowa) *Centennial Book.* N. p., 1983.

Linden-Ward, Blanche, and Carol Hurd Green. *Changing the Future: American Women in the 1960s.* New York: Twayne, 1993.

Litoff, Judy Barrett, David C. Smith, Barbara Wooddall Taylor, and Charles E. Taylor. *Miss You: The World War II Letters of Barbara Wooddall Taylor and Charles E. Taylor.* Athens: University of Georgia Press, 1990.

McBride-Mellinger, Maria. *The Wedding Dress.* New York: Random House, 1993.

Mallon, Thomas. *Stolen Words.* New York: Harcourt, 2001.

Mariano, John H. *The Veteran and His Marriage.* New York: J. J. Little and Ives, 1945.

Marling, Karal Ann. *As Seen on TV: The Visual Culture of Everyday Life in the 1950s.* Cambridge, Mass.: Harvard University Press, 1994.

———. *Debutante: Rites and Regalia of American Debdom.* Lawrence: University Press of Kansas, 2004.

May, Elaine Tyler. *Homeward Bound: American Families in the Cold War Era.* New York: Basic, 1988.

Mo, Charles L. *To Have and To Hold: 135 Years of Wedding Fashions.* Charlotte, N.C.: Mint Museum of Art, 2000.

Monsarrat, Ann. *And the Bride Wore . . . : The Story of the White Wedding.* London: Gentry, 1973.

Morton, Andrew. *Diana: Her True Story—In Her Own Words*. New York: Simon & Schuster, 1997.

Moss, George Donelson. *Moving On: The American People since 1945*. Englewood Cliffs, N.J.: Prentice-Hall, 1994.

Mulvaney, Jay. *Kennedy Weddings: A Family Album*. New York: St. Martin's, 1999.

Naremore, James. *The Films of Vincente Minnelli*. New York: Cambridge University Press, 1993.

Otnes, Cele C., and Elizabeth H. Pleck. *Cinderella Dreams: The Allure of the Lavish Wedding*. Berkeley: University of California Press, 2003.

Ownby, Ted. *American Dreams in Mississippi: Consumers, Poverty, and Culture, 1838–1998*. Chapel Hill: University of North Carolina Press, 1999.

Pleck, Elizabeth H. *Celebrating the Family: Ethnicity, Consumer Culture, and Family Rituals*. Cambridge, Mass.: Harvard University Press, 2000.

Post, Emily. *Etiquette: The Blue Book of Social Usage*. New York: Funk and Wagnalls, 1937.

Poston, Madeleine. *My Upside-Down World*. Portland, Ore.: Benneta, 2002.

Riley, Glenda. *Divorce: An American Tradition*. New York: Oxford University Press, 1991.

Robinson, Jeffrey. *Rainier and Grace: An Intimate Portrait*. New York: Atlantic Monthly, 1989.

Rorty, James. *Our Master's Voice: Advertising*. New York: John Day, 1934.

Rosenberg, Norman L., and Emily S. Rosenberg. *In Our Times: America since World War II*. 5th ed. Englewood Cliffs, N.J.: Prentice-Hall, 1995.

Rothman, Ellen K. *Hands and Hearts: A History of Courtship in America*. Cambridge, Mass.: Harvard University Press, 1987.

St. Marie, Satenig, and Carolyn Flaherty. *Romantic Victorian Weddings: Then and Now*. New York: Dutton Studio, 1992.

Schickel, Richard. *Intimate Strangers: The Culture of Celebrity*. Garden City, N.Y.: Doubleday, 1985.

Seligson, Marcia. *The Eternal Bliss Machine: America's Way of Wedding*. New York: William Morrow, 1973.

Shale, Richard. *The Academy Awards Index: The Complete Categorical and Chronological Record*. Westport, Conn.: Greenwood, 1993.

Sherman, Suzanne, ed. *Lesbian and Gay Marriage: Private Commitments, Public Ceremonies*. Philadelphia: Temple University Press, 1992.

Silverman, Debora. *Selling Culture: Bloomingdale's, Diana Vreeland, and the New Aristocracy of Taste in Reagan's America*. New York: Pantheon, 1986.

Sivulka, Juliann. *Soap, Sex, and Cigarettes: A Cultural History of American Advertising.* Belmont, Calif.: Wadsworth, 1998.

Stoner, Carroll. *Weddings for Grownups: Everything You Need to Know to Plan Your Wedding Your Way.* San Francisco: Chronicle, 1993.

Taylor, Ella. *Prime-Time Families: Television Culture in Postwar America.* Berkeley: University of California Press, 1989.

Thompson, Daniel C. *A Black Elite: A Profile of Graduates of UNCF Colleges.* Westport, Conn.: Greenwood, 1986.

Troy, Gil. *Affairs of State: The Rise and Rejection of the Presidential Couple since World War II.* New York: Free Press, 1997.

Tuttle, William M., Jr. *"Daddy's Gone to War": The Second World War in the Lives of America's Children.* New York: Oxford University Press, 1993.

U.S. Bureau of the Census. *Statistical Abstracts of the United States: 1942.* Washington, D.C.: Government Printing Office, 1943.

———. *Statistical Abstracts of the United States: 1970.* Washington, D.C.: Government Printing Office, 1970.

Veroff, Joseph, Elizabeth Douvan, and Richard A. Kulka. *The Inner American: A Self-Portrait from 1957 to 1976.* New York: Basic, 1981.

Wainwright, Loudon. *The Great American Magazine: An Inside History of Life.* New York: Alfred A. Knopf, 1986.

Walker, Nancy A. *Shaping Our Mothers' World: American Women's Magazines.* Jackson: University Press of Mississippi, 2000.

Watson, Mary Ann. *The Expanding Vista: American Television in the Kennedy Years.* Durham, N.C.: Duke University Press, 1994.

Weiss, Jessica. *To Have and To Hold: Marriage, the Baby Boom, and Social Change.* Chicago: University of Chicago Press, 2000.

Whyte, Martin King. *Dating, Mating, and Marriage.* New York: Aldine de Gruyter, 1990.

Wicoff, Kamy. *I Do but I Don't: Walking down the Aisle without Losing Your Mind.* Cambridge, Mass.: Da Capo, 2006.

Wood, Michael. *America in the Movies: Or "Santa Maria, It Had Slipped My Mind."* New York: Columbia University Press, 1989.

ARTICLES AND ESSAYS

Addison, Heather. "Hollywood, Consumer Culture, and the Rise of 'Body Shaping.'" In *Hollywood Goes Shopping*, edited by David Desser and Garth S. Jowett. Minneapolis: University of Minnesota Press, 2000.

"An Affair to Remember." *People Weekly*, 24 July 1995, 131–134, 136, 138.

"Afro: A Beauty Happening." *Bride's*, November 1969, 138–139.

"All About Grace." *New York Times*, 15 April 1956, sec. 4, 2E.

"And the Bride Wore. . . ." *Essence*, February 1998, 120.

Apple, R. W., Jr. "Amid Splendor, Charles Weds Diana." *New York Times*, 30 July 1981, A1.

———. "Charles and Lady Diana Wed Today: Beacons Burn across a Joyful Britain." *New York Times*, 29 July 1981, A8.

Austin, Elizabeth. "Why Homer's My Hero: The All-American Family Shouldn't Have to Wear Gucci to Feel Good." *Washington Monthly*, October 2000, 30–35.

"*Bachelorette* in Love: Trista Turns Dating Tables and Finds True Love." ABCNews.com., 7 January 2003. http://abcnews.go.com/sections/GMA/GoodMorningAmerica/GMA030107Bachelorette_pre.

Baker, Sean. "From *Dragnet* to *Survivor*: Historical and Cultural Perspectives on Reality Television." In *Survivor Lessons: Essays on Communication and Reality Television*, edited by Matthew J. Smith and Andrew F. Wood. Jefferson, N.C.: McFarland, 2003.

Balz, Chrissy. "Weddings: A Veil of Sadness." *Newsweek*, 7 August 2006. http://www.msnbc.msn.com/id/14096481.

Baughman, James L. "Who Read *Life*?: The Circulation of America's Favorite Magazine." In *Looking at* Life *Magazine*, edited by Erika Doss. Washington, D.C.: Smithsonian Institution, 2001.

Bayot, Jennifer. "For Richer or Poorer, to Our Credit Limit." *New York Times*, 13 July 2003, 1, 17.

Bernstein, Amy. "Eye on the '90s: Wedding March." *U.S. News and World Report*, 10 May 1993, 17.

"Best and Worst Bridesmaids' Dresses." *People Weekly*, 24 July 1995, 108–116, 118, 120, 122.

"Best and Worst Wedding Dresses of the Century." *People Weekly*, 26 July 1993, 84–88, 90–94.

"Big Rental Films of 1969." *Variety*, 7 January 1970, 15.

Blake, Howard. "An Apologia from the Man Who Produced the Worst Program in TV History." In *American Broadcasting: A Source Book on the History of Radio and Television*, edited by Lawrence W. Lichty and Malachi C. Topping. New York: Hastings House, 1975.

Blumenfeld, Amy, and Richard Jerome. "When Dad Is President." *People Weekly*, 18 June 2001, 52–58.

Blustain, Sarah. "A Counterproposal: One Young Woman Resists On-Bended-Knee Conventions." *Lilith*, Spring 2000, 17–19.

"The Book on Our Style." *Essence*, February 1998, 122.

Boswell, Parley Ann. "The Pleasure of Our Company: Hollywood Throws a Wedding Bash." In *Beyond the Stars II: Plot Conventions in American Popular Film*, edited by Paul Loukides and Linda K. Fuller. Bowling Green, Ohio: Bowling Green State University Popular Press, 1991.

Boyd, Blanche McCrary. "Both Sides Now." *Ms.*, June/July 2000, 56–59.

Brady, Lois Smith. "Vows." *New York Times*, 6 December 1998, sec. 9, 13.

———. "Vows." *New York Times*, 13 December 1998, sec. 9, 11.

———. "Vows." *New York Times*, 9 May 1999, sec. 9, 7.

"Bridal Director on TV Show." *Strawbridge and Clothier Store Chat*, February-March 1955, 5.

"Bridal Fashions." *Strawbridge and Clothier Store Chat*, January-February 1974, 3.

"Bridal Gowns That Satisfy the Soul." *Essence*, February 1999, 124.

"Bridal Shows Draw Big Crowds." *Strawbridge and Clothier Store Chat*, February 1958, 2.

"Bride Bonanza: Annual Expenditure in Philadelphia Area Is Nearly $50,000,000." *Strawbridge and Clothier Store Chat*, January 1962, 6.

"Bride in the Bronx: Chayefsky Builds His New Play on Wedding Plans." *Life*, 6 June 1955, 117–118.

"A Bride Is Worth $3,300 to a Department Store." *Strawbridge and Clothier Store Chat*, February 1956, 6.

"*Bride's* Decorating Center." *Bride's*, June 1969, 134–135.

"The Bride's Shop Staff Wishes Much Happiness to–." *Strawbridge and Clothier Store Chat*, August-September 1949, 5.

"The Bride's Shop Wishes Much Happiness to These Registered Store Brides." *Strawbridge and Clothier Store Chat*, November 1949, inside front cover.

"'Brides Today' Magazine Is First Tailored to Blacks." *Commercial Appeal* (Memphis), 9 February 1992, F8.

"Bridesmaids to Wear Red." *New York Times*, 22 November 1967, 52.

Brunt, Rosalind. "Princess Diana: A Sign of the Times." In *Diana: The Making of a Media Saint*, edited by Jeffrey Richards, Scott Wilson, and Linda Woodhead. London: I. B. Tauris, 1999.

"But What Will She Wear?" *New York Times*, 18 October 1967, 50.

"Can You Give Me a Hand?" *Reminisce Magazine*, March/April 1994, 66.

Caplan, Jeremy. "Metrosexual Matrimony." *Time*, 3 October 2005, 67.

"Capture and Train Your Maid." *Bride's*, Winter 1936–1937, 62, 104, 106.

"Career Girl Marries: Gwyned Filling's Story Has a Happy Ending." *Life*, 29 November 1948, 135–136.

Carter, Bill. "Lights, Camera, Marriage, and Big Ratings." *New York Times*, 17
February 2000, A1, C24.

Chance, Julia. "Wedded to Culture." *Essence*, February 1996, 30.

Chaney, Betty Norwood. "A Proper Kind of Wedding." *Redbook*, August 1973, 47, 49.

Cmiel, Kenneth. "The Politics of Civility." In *The Sixties: From Memory to
History*, edited by David Farber. Chapel Hill: University of North Carolina
Press, 1994.

Cocks, Jay. "'Why Ever Not?'" *Time*, 10 August 1981, 29–31.

Cohen, Emily. "Going to the Chapel." *PC Magazine*, 30 June 1998, 40.

Colton, Michael. "Why Is This Wedding Different from All Other Weddings?"
New York Times, 27 September 1999, B8.

"Copy of Lynda's Wedding Dress to Be in Stores Thursday." *New York Times*, 12
December 1967, 54.

"The Cost of a Wedding." *Bride's*, August 1969, 176.

Crowther, Bosley. Review of *Father of the Bride* (movie). *New York Times*, 19 May
1950, 31.

"The Curtain Lifts on Our New Bride's Shop: Glimpses of the Shop and Its
Personalities." *Strawbridge and Clothier Store Chat*, April-May 1949, 10–12.

Davis, Francis. "Storming the Home Front." *Atlantic Monthly*, March 2003, 125–132.

"Debbie's Ring on at Last." *Life*, 10 October 1955, 59, 61–62.

Doss, Erika. "Introduction—Looking at *Life*: Rethinking America's Favorite
Magazine, 1936–1972." In *Looking at* Life *Magazine*, edited by Erika Doss.
Washington, D.C.: Smithsonian Institution, 2001.

Doty, Cate. "Along with 'I Do' Comes a Chance to Say 'We Care.'" *New York
Times*, 14 November 2005, E3.

"'Dream Wedding' for Miss America 1961." *Modern Bride*, Holiday 1960, 78–79.

"Eight Decades of Miss Americas." *People Weekly*, 16 October 2000, 143–144, 147–148,
151, 153–154, 157, 159–160, 163–164, 167–168, 171–172, 175–177, 179, 181–182, 184.

Eisner, Jane. "The Era of Big Weddings Is upon Us." *Akron* (Ohio) *Beacon
Journal*, 10 May 2005, B2.

Engstrom, Erika. "Hegemony in Reality-Based TV Programming: The World
According to *A Wedding Story*." *Media Report to Women* 31 (Winter 2003):
10–14.

Epstein, Rebecca L. "Sharon Stone in a Gap Turtleneck." In *Hollywood Goes
Shopping*, edited by David Desser and Garth S. Jowett. Minneapolis:
University of Minnesota Press, 2000.

"*Essence* Designers of the Month: Renee and Larry Greer." *Essence*, April 1973,
32–33.

"Fashion Fair." *Ebony*, June 1953, 85–88, 90.

"Father of the Bride: An Unsung Hero Is Finally Honored." *Life*, 25 July 1949, 67–73.

Fischler, Marcelle S. "White is O.K. (Excess, Too) at Wedding No. 2." *New York Times*, 17 March 2002, sec. 9, 1–2.

Flaherty, Julie. "Freedom to Marry and to Spend on It." *New York Times*, 16 May 2004, sec. 9, 2.

"Furlough Brides: They Marry in Haste but Manage to Have Pretty, Formal Weddings with Traditional Satin and Veil." *Life*, 22 June 1942, 37–40.

Gant, Liz. "The Lowdown on Costs." *Essence*, June 1978, 98–99, 132, 135, 137–138.

"Gay Weddings Go Prime Time." *Newsweek Web*, 22 August 2002. http://www.msnbc.com/news/797708.asp.

Gennari, John. "Bridging the Two Americas: *Life* Looks at the 1960s." In *Looking at* Life *Magazine*, edited by Erika Doss. Washington, D.C.: Smithsonian Institution, 2001.

Goodstein, Ellen. "Celebrity-Style Wedding on Mere Mortal's Budget." Bankrate.com. http://www.bankrate.com/brm/news/cheap/20050404a1.asp.

"A Group of Lovely Store Brides of this Past Summer." *Strawbridge and Clothier Store Chat*, August-September 1950, 6–7.

Gutierrez, Lisa. "As Wed on TV: Couple Will Celebrate 50-Year Anniversary after Marriage on TV Show." *Kansas City Star*, 3 August 2002. http://www.kansascity.com/mld/kansascity/living/3779887.htm?1c.

"Half Thousand Coeds Romp at Big Gym Party." *Western* (Michigan Normal School) *Herald*, 29 November 1916, 1.

Harris, Neil. "The *Life* of the Party." In *Looking at* Life *Magazine*, edited by Erika Doss. Washington, D.C.: Smithsonian Institution, 2001.

Hart, Ariel. "City May Want Runaway Bride to Return Its 'Gift' of Itself." *New York Times*, 3 May 2005, A18.

Hart, Sue. "Madison Avenue Goes to War: Patriotism in Advertising during World War II." In *Visions of War: World War II in Popular Literature and Culture*, edited by M. Paul Holsinger and Mary Anne Schofield. Bowling Green, Ohio: Bowling Green State University Popular Press, 1992.

Heelas, Paul. "Diana's Self and the Quest Within." In *Diana: The Making of a Media Saint*, edited by Jeffrey Richards, Scott Wilson, and Linda Woodhead. London: I.B. Tauris, 1999.

"Here Comes the Bride . . . Presenting Some S&C Brides of 1964." *Strawbridge and Clothier Store Chat*, March 1965, 8–9.

Hertz, Rosanna. "Dual-Career Corporate Couples: Shaping Marriages through Work." In *Gender in Intimate Relationships: A Microstructural Approach*, edited by Barbara J. Risman and Pepper Schwartz. Belmont, Calif.: Wadsworth, 1989.

Hobsbawm, Eric. "Introduction: Inventing Tradition." In *The Invention of Tradition*, edited by Eric Hobsbawm and Terence Ranger. New York: Cambridge University Press, 1995.

Hood, Marshall. "Say 'I Do' to Simplicity." *Columbus* (Ohio) *Dispatch*, 13 January 1998, 1F–2F.

Horyn, Cathy. "Narciso Rodriguez, Building on Stardom." *New York Times*, 6 May 2003, C18.

"How Much of a Wedding." *Bride's*, Winter 1946–1947, 108–109, 153–154.

Hurley, Dan. "Divorce Rate: It's not as High as You Think." *New York Times*, 19 April 2005, F7.

Hwang, Suein. "I Was an Internet Bride." *Wall Street Journal*, 24 September 1999, W1, W4.

"I Do! I Do?" *Ms.*, June/July 2000, 54–55.

"I Want to Buy from Black Designers. . . ." *Essence*, July 1997, 88.

"Informal Phone Survey #2." *Bridal Insight*, September/October 1995, 3.

"An Invitation to Brides-to-Be." *Strawbridge and Clothier Store Chat*, February 1957, 6.

"Invitation to Expand." *Bridal Insight*, September/October 1995, 4.

"January Bridal Show." *Strawbridge and Clothier Store Chat*, January-February 1967, 16.

Jellison, Katherine. "From the Farmhouse Parlor to the Pink Barn: The Commercialization of Weddings in the Rural Midwest." *Iowa Heritage Illustrated* 77 (Summer 1996): 50–65.

Jones, Beverly. "The Dynamics of Marriage and Motherhood." In *Sisterhood Is Powerful: An Anthology of Writings from the Women's Liberation Movement*, edited by Robin Morgan. New York: Vintage, 1970.

Jones, Maggie. "Wedding Wars." *Working Woman*, May 1995, 62–67, 103.

Jong, Erica. "From Fear of Flying to No Fear of Tying the Knot." *Sunday Times* (London), 9 November 2003, sec. 5, 7.

"June Wedding: Kansas City Girl Marries with All the Fixings." *Life*, 14 July 1947, 89–96.

Kanner, Joyce. "Letter to the Editor." *Life*, 15 August 1949, 6.

Kantrowitz, Barbara, and Pat Wingert. "Unmarried, with Children." *Newsweek*, 28 May 2001, 46–52, 54–55.

Kaplan, E. Ann. "The Case of the Missing Mother: Maternal Issues in Vidor's *Stella Dallas*." In *Feminism and Film*, edited by E. Ann Kaplan. New York: Oxford University Press, 2000.

"Kelly-Rainier Wedding Barred in Promotions." *New York Times*, 9 March 1956, 35.

Kerr, Robert. "Older Brides, Bridegrooms See the New Trends Trailing Along." *Commercial Appeal* (Memphis), 9 February 1992, F2.

Kolhatkar, Sheelah. "Gloria Steinem, Power Geezer." *New York Observer*, 11 January 2006. http://alternet.org/story/30494.

Kozol, Wendy. "Gazing at Race in the Pages of *Life*: Picturing Segregation through Theory and History." In *Looking at* Life *Magazine*, edited by Erika Doss. Washington, D.C.: Smithsonian Institution, 2001.

Kuczynski, Alex. "The Curse of the *InStyle* Wedding." *New York Times*, 2 June 2002, sec. 9, 1, 10.

Leibovich, Lori. "The Fail-Safe Summer Wedding Film." *New York Times*, 11 May 2003, sec. 2A, 11, 33.

"*Life* Goes to a Harlem Wedding." *Life*, 19 April 1948, 146–148.

"*Life* Goes to a Kentucky Mountain Wedding." *Life*, 28 July 1941, 82–85.

"*Life* Goes to a Party." *Life*, 21 June 1937, 88–89, 90, 92.

"*Life* Goes to the Wedding of Senator Chavez' Daughter." *Life*, 4 March 1946, 118–120.

"*Life* Visits Palumbo's: In Philadelphia Nearly Everybody Has His Wedding in an Italian Restaurant on Catherine Street." *Life*, 27 June 1949, 113–116.

Liptak, Adam. "Caution in Court for Gay Rights Groups." *New York Times*, 12 November 2004, A16.

Lipton, Michael A. "Turned Off." *People Weekly*, 6 March 2000, 66–69.

"Live TV Coverage Set for Wedding Today." *New York Times*, 29 July 1981, A8.

Lowrey, Tina M., and Cele Otnes. "Construction of a Meaningful Wedding: Differences in the Priorities of Brides and Grooms." In *Gender Issues and Consumer Behavior*, edited by Janeen Arnold Costa. Thousand Oaks, Calif.: Sage, 1994.

Lyall, Sarah. "The Wedding Pictures: 2 Stars in Court Drama." *New York Times*, 11 February 2003, A4.

"Lynda Johnson Will Be Wed Dec. 9 in White House." *New York Times*, 26 September 1967, 37.

"Lynda Johnson's Wedding Set for 4 p.m.: Guest List Held to 500." *New York Times*, 16 October 1967, 31.

"Lynda's Wedding Will Be Different." *New York Times*, 3 December 1967, sec. 4, 4.

McElroy, Njoki. "Alternative to a Traditional Wedding." *Essence*, April 1974, 58–59.

Magder, Ted. "The End of TV 101: Reality Programs, Formats, and the New Business of Television." In *Reality TV: Remaking Television Culture*, edited by Susan Murray and Laurie Ouellette. New York: New York University Press, 2004.

Maher, Jennifer. "What Do Women Watch?: Tuning in to the Compulsory Heterosexuality Channel." In *Reality TV: Remaking Television Culture*, edited by Susan Murray and Laurie Ouellette. New York: New York University Press, 2004.

Mainardi, Pat. "The Politics of Housework." In *"Takin' It to the Streets": A Sixties Reader*, edited by Alexander Bloom and Wini Breines. New York: Oxford University Press, 1995.

"The Making (and Then Remaking) of a Recipe, Step by Step." *New York Times*, 4 June 1971, 17.

Mann, Denise. "The Spectacularization of Everyday Life: Recycling Hollywood Stars and Fans in Early Television Variety Shows." In *Private Screenings: Television and the Female Consumer*, edited by Lynn Spigel and Denise Mann. Minneapolis: University of Minnesota Press, 1992.

Mayer, Barbara. "Economy Cuts Spending on Weddings." *Commercial Appeal* (Memphis), 9 February 1992, F4.

———. "Queen Victoria Helped Popularize White Gowns." *Columbus* (Ohio) *Dispatch*, 13 January 1998, 2F.

Mead, Rebecca. "You're Getting Married: The Wal-Martization of the Bridal Business." *New Yorker*, 21 and 28 April 2003, 76–78, 83–86, 91.

Miya-Jervis, Lisa. "Who Wants to Marry a Feminist?" *Ms.*, June/July 2000, 63–65.

"Modern Living: Gowns for June Brides." *Jet*, 4 June 1953, 39.

Molishever, Jay. "Bridal Gowns That Draw Oohs a Second (or Fifth) Time Around." *New York Times*, 28 July 2002, sec. 9, 11.

"Molly Jong-Fast, Matthew Greenfield." *New York Times*, 2 November 2003, sec. 9, 13.

"Monaco's 375 Acres Jammed for Prince's Wedding to Star." *New York Times*, 18 April 1956, 28.

"The Most Eligible Bachelor and His Bride." *Time*, 26 July 1999, 40–41.

"The Most Romantic Spot on Our Beautiful Fashion Floor Is the Bride's Shop." *Strawbridge and Clothier Store Chat*, August-September 1949, 4.

Mulvey, Laura. "Visual Pleasure and Narrative Cinema." *Screen* 16 (Autumn 1975): 6–18.

Murray, Susan. "'I Think We Need a New Name for It': The Meeting of Documentary and Reality TV." In *Reality TV: Remaking Television Culture*, edited by Susan Murray and Laurie Ouellette. New York: New York University Press, 2004.

"'My Wife Works and I Like It': Jim Magill Argues that Jennie's Full-Time Job Is Good for Her, Good for Him, Good for Their Children—and Good for the Budget." *Life*, 24 December 1956, 140–141.

Nelson, Michelle R., and Sameer Deshpande. "Love without Borders: An Examination of Cross-Cultural Wedding Rituals." In *Contemporary Consumption Rituals: A Research Anthology*, edited by Cele C. Otnes and Tina M. Lowrey. Mahwah, N.J.: Lawrence Erlbaum, 2004.

"No More Miss America." In *"Takin' It to the Streets": A Sixties Reader*, edited by Alexander Bloom and Wini Breines. New York: Oxford University Press, 1995.

"No Retest, White House Decides." *New York Times*, 3 June 1971, 45.

"No Stampede for That Gown." *New York Times*, 23 June 1971, 50.

"Notes on People." *New York Times*, 19 May 1971, 43.

O'Neill, Anne-Marie. "Some Enchanted Evening!" *People Weekly*, 11 December 2000, 64–74, 79–80, 82.

"On TV." *Columbus* (Ohio) *Dispatch*, 10 August 2003, H5.

Otnes, Cele. "'Friend of the Bride'—and Then Some: Roles of the Bridal Salon during Wedding Planning." In *ServiceScapes: The Concept of Place in Contemporary Markets*, edited by John F. Sherry Jr. Chicago: NTC Business, 1998.

"Our Best Clothes, Our Best Stores." *Essence*, July 1997, 83–87.

Parnes, Francine. "A Big Wedding with a Smaller Bill." *New York Times*, 25 May 2002, A13.

Peters, Charles. "The Greatest Convention." *Washington Monthly*, July/August 2004, 15–16.

"Prince of Monaco to Wed Grace Kelly." *New York Times*, 6 January 1956, 1, 4.

"Princess Bride." *Bride's*, December/January 1997–1998, 40.

Raphael, Chad. "The Political Economic Origins of Reali-TV." In *Reality TV: Remaking Television Culture*, edited by Susan Murray and Laurie Ouellette. New York: New York University Press, 2004.

"Redstockings Manifesto." In *"Takin' It to the Streets": A Sixties Reader*, edited by Alexander Bloom and Wini Breines. New York: Oxford University Press, 1995.

Rich, Frank. "What's Love Got to Do with It? Not Much." *New York Times*, 1 February 2004, sec. 2, 1, 22.

Rimer, Sara. "Searching for a Fairy Tale Wedding Gown, at a Bargain Price." *New York Times*, 20 May 1997, A8.

Roberts, Sam. "It's Official: To Be Married Means to Be Outnumbered." *New York Times*, 15 October 2006. http://www.nytimes.com/2006/10/15/us/15census.html.

Roddy, Dennis. "Picture This: A TV Wedding That Lasts." *Pittsburgh Post-Gazette*, 26 February 2000. http://www.post-gazette.com/columnists/20000226roddy.asp.

"A Royal Wedding Brings Joy to Britain." *Life*, 1 December 1947, 31–43.

Saranow, Jennifer. "To Have and to Hit Up." *Wall Street Journal*, 6 May 2005, W1, W3.

Schneider, Susan Weidman. "Isn't It Ironic . . . Retro Weddings in a Feminist Age." *Lilith*, Spring 2000, 16.

"Second Weddings." *Bride's*, December 1968/January 1969, 84, 122–125.

Seelye, Katharine Q. "Weddings after a National Tragedy: Terror Attacks Bring a Finer Focus to a Life-Affirming Ritual." *New York Times*, 14 October 2001, A21.

Sigesmund, B. J. "Newsmakers." *Newsweek*, 4 December 2000, 71.

"A Simple Spectacular at the White House." *Time*, 14 June 1971, 13–17.

Smith, Kyle. "TV's Reality Check." *People Weekly*, 6 March 2000, 62–65.

Smith, Terry. "*Life*-Style Modernity: Making Modern America." In *Looking at* Life *Magazine*, edited by Erika Doss. Washington, D.C.: Smithsonian Institution, 2001.

Smith-Rosenberg, Carroll. "The Female World of Love and Ritual: Relations between Women in Nineteenth-Century America." *Signs* 1 (Autumn 1975): 1–29.

"So to Speak. . . ." *Du Pont Magazine*, June–July 1946, 1.

"A Social Note from Moscow: 'Porgy' Pair Has Russian Wedding." *Life*, 30 January 1956, 47.

Solinger, Rickie. "The Smutty Side of *Life*: Picturing Babes as Icons of Gender Difference in the Early 1950s." In *Looking at* Life *Magazine*, edited by Erika Doss. Washington, D.C.: Smithsonian Institution, 2001.

"Some Day My Prince Will Come." *People Weekly*, 26 July 1993, 96–98.

"Speaking of Pictures: Master Baker Builds Cake 'Spectaculars.'" *Life*, 24 June 1946, 12–13.

"Speaking of Pictures . . . This Is a Jewish Wedding." *Life*, 5 April 1937, 4–5.

"Speaking of Pictures . . . This Is a Wedding in a Country Church." *Life*, 19 September 1938, 6–8.

Sporkin, Elizabeth M., and Veronica Burns. "Wedding Belle." *People Weekly*, 8 July 1991, 65–66.

"Spotlight on Lyle Scifres, Abbington's Bridal, Owensboro, Kentucky." *Bridal Insight*, September/October 1995, 8.

"Spring Weddings and Our Bridal Service." *Strawbridge and Clothier Store Chat*, March 1949, 2.

Stacey, Judith. "Gay and Lesbian Families: Queer Like Us." In *All Our Families: New Policies for a New Century*, edited by Mary Ann Mason, Arlene Skolnick, and Stephen D. Sugarman. New York: Oxford University Press, 1998.

Stevens, Dana. "The $3.77 Million Wedding: Trista and Ryan Tie Knot on ABC." *Slate*, 11 December 2003. http://slate.msn.com/id/2092401.

Studlar, Gaylyn. "'Chi-Chi Cinderella': Audrey Hepburn as Couture Countermodel." In *Hollywood Goes Shopping*, edited by David Desser and Garth S. Jowett. Minneapolis: University of Minnesota Press, 2000.

"'Thank Heaven for Little Girls,' the Fabulous Bridal Show by S&C." *Strawbridge and Clothier Store Chat*, June-July 1974, 24.

"'The Third Mass Marriage at the Tientsen YMCA.'" *Life*, 8 March 1937, 28–29.

"To Show Wedding Gown." *New York Times*, 13 March 1956, 22.

"Top Grosses of 1950." *Variety*, 3 January 1951, 58.

"Top Rental Films for 1990." *Variety*, 7 January 1991, 80.

"Top Rental Films for 1991." *Variety*, 6 January 1992, 82, 84.

"Top Rental Films for 1992." *Variety*, 11 January 1993, 22, 24.

"Tricia's Gown Is Going Public." *New York Times*, 15 June 1971, 52.

"Trousseau Started by Lynda Johnson, Trade Paper Says." *New York Times*, 27 September 1967, 35.

"TV: Commercials Mar NBC Coverage of Bridal." *New York Times*, 11 December 1967, 95.

"Unique Marriage Service." *Kalamazoo* (Michigan) *Morning Gazette-News*, 10 May 1902, n.p.

Waldkirch, W. B. "Letter to the Editor." *Life*, 21 May 1948, 13.

Walker, Nancy A. "Introduction: Women's Magazines and Women's Roles." In *Women's Magazines 1940–1960: Gender Roles and the Popular Press*, edited by Nancy A. Walker. Boston: Bedford/St. Martin's, 1998.

Watters, Ethan. "In My Tribe." *New York Times Magazine*, 14 October 2001, 25–26.

"Wedded in Mockery." *Evening Independent* (Massillion, Ohio), 9 February 1894, 1.

"The Wedding Business: It Profits from the U.S. Sentiment for Brides at the Unsentimental Rate of $3 Billion a Year." *Life*, 9 June 1952, 118–124, 127–128, 130.

"The Wedding Cake: White House Chef Explains Mrs. Nixon's Recipe." *New York Times*, 2 June 1971, 36.

"Wedding Gift Service." *Strawbridge and Clothier Store Chat*, February 1954, 8.

"Wedding in Movieland: At 18, Beautiful and Starry-Eyed, Elizabeth Taylor Is Married to Nick Hilton, Son of the Hotel Owner." *Life*, 22 May 1950, 46–47.

Weems, Robert E., Jr. "Consumerism and the Construction of Black Female Identity in Twentieth-Century America." In *The Gender and Consumer*

Reader, edited by Jennifer Scanlon. New York: New York University Press, 2000.

Weisman, Melissa A. "On the Web, See How the Bride Cut the Cake." *New York Times*, 14 April 1998, B9.

Welner, Jennifer. "Oh, Romeo, Romeo, Why Marry Now?" *Columbus* (Ohio) *Dispatch*, 28 April 1996, 8K.

"What, Me Marry?: *Ms.* Staffers Tell All." *Ms.*, June/July 2000, 59, 64–65, 68–70.

"What Shall I Wear?" *Bride's*, Autumn 1940, 53.

White, Gregory L., and Shirley Leung. "Middle Market Shrinks as Americans Migrate toward the High End." *Wall Street Journal*, 29 March 2002, sec. A, 1, 8.

"White House 'Rush Day': A Rehearsal and a Party." *New York Times*, 9 December 1967, 58.

"White House Wedding Consultant Conducts Clinic." *Strawbridge and Clothier Store Chat*, March 1972, 2.

Wickstrom, Andy. "Video Should Get Good Reception from Brides." *Cincinnati Enquirer*, 19 May 1991, E5.

Williams, Alex, and Eric Dash. "Other Prenuptial Agreements Tie Stars to Blushing Vendors." *New York Times*, 13 January 2005, A1, A25.

Yolen, Jane. "America's Cinderella." In *Cinderella: A Casebook*, edited by Alan Dundes. Madison: University of Wisconsin Press, 1988.

UNPUBLISHED PAPERS

Engstrom, Erika. "Gender and Cultural Hegemony in Reality-Based Television Programming: The World According to *A Wedding Story*." Paper presented at the annual meeting of the Association for Education in Journalism and Mass Communication, New Orleans, 1999.

———, and Beth Semic. "Portrayal of Religion in Reality TV Programming: Hegemony and the Contemporary American Wedding." Paper presented at the annual meeting of the Association for Education in Journalism and Mass Communication, Miami, 2002.

Srole, Carole. "*Queen for a Day*: Whiteness, Consumerism, and the 'Worthy Poor' in the 1950s and 1960s." Paper presented at the annual meeting of the Western Association of Women Historians, University of California, Berkeley, 2003.

ADVERTISEMENTS

Bridal Insight, 1995.

Bride's, 1959.

Life, 1944–1957.

MANUSCRIPT COLLECTIONS

Hoyt, Cleo. Papers. Western Michigan University Archives and Regional History Collections, Kalamazoo.

Joseph Bancroft and Sons Company. Papers. Pictorial Collections, Hagley Museum and Library, Wilmington, Del.

McConnell, Edith N. Papers. Manuscripts and Archives Department, Hagley Museum and Library, Wilmington, Del.

Nixon, Richard M. Presidential materials. National Archives II, College Park, Maryland.

Scherer, Ruth. Papers. Western Michigan University Archives and Regional History Collections, Kalamazoo.

INTERVIEWS

Anonymous bride. Conversation with author. Athens, Ohio, 27 October 2000.

Dolnick, Willie. Interview with author. Chicago, 14 October 1995.

Niebuhr, Diane M. Interview with author. Atkins, Iowa, 26 August 1992.

Smale, Jerry. Telephone interview with author. 15 July 1995.

Stiles, Claudine and Earl. Interview with author. Lee County, Ark., 21 July 1993.

Sweeney, Betty. Interview with author. Lenexa, Kans., 20 March 1994.

Vrana, Ann Hardy. Interview with author. Wahoo, Neb., 6 March 1993.

Wall, Elizabeth Cleghorn. Interview with author. Memphis, 24 June 1993.

MOTION PICTURES

The Best Years of Our Lives. 1946. Directed by William Wyler.

Betsy's Wedding. 1990. Directed by Alan Alda.

The Catered Affair. 1956. Directed by Richard Brooks.

Cinderella. 1950. Directed by Wilfred Jackson, Hamilton Luske, and Clyde Geronimi.

The Clock. 1945. Directed by Vincente Minnelli.

Father of the Bride. 1950. Directed by Vincente Minnelli.

Father of the Bride. 1991. Directed by Charles Shyer.

The Good Shepherd. 2006. Directed by Robert DeNiro.

Goodbye, Columbus. 1969. Directed by Larry Peerce.

The Graduate. 1967. Directed by Mike Nichols.

Lovers and Other Strangers. 1970. Directed by Cy Howard.

My Big Fat Greek Wedding. 2002. Directed by Joel Zwick.

A Wedding. 1978. Directed by Robert Altman.

Bibliography

TELEVISION PROGRAMS

Bride and Groom. NBC. Originally aired 9 March 1954. Kinescope in possession
of Museum of Television and Radio, New York City.

Trista and Ryan's Wedding. ABC. Originally aired 10 December 2003.
Videocassette in possession of Jacqueline Wolf, Athens, Ohio.

Who Wants to Marry a Multimillionaire? Fox. Originally aired 15 February 2000.
Videocassette in possession of Kimberly Little, Athens, Ohio.

WEB SITES

http://abc.go.com/primetime/bachelorette/bios/trista.html.

http://cgi.ebay.com.

http://history.acusd.edu/gen/projects/hanley/queen.html.

http://tv.yahoo.com.

http://www.aier.org/research/col.php.

http://www.consciousweddings.com.

http://www.indiebride.com.

http://www.lovetripper.com/bridalstars/wedding-database/database-index.html.

OTHER SOURCES

Johnson, Carolita. Cartoon. *New Yorker*, 8 May 2006, 32.

"One Man, One Woman." Joy Padgett campaign flier, 2004. In the author's
possession.

Rehmann, Jaime. E-mail to Ohio University College of Osteopathic Medicine
employees and students, 19 September 2005. In the author's possession.

Index

ABC (American Broadcasting Company), 123, 133, 218–221, 266n31

Academy Award (Oscar), 115, 152, 158, 168, 259n10, 261n25, 261n26

Adams, Edie, 121

African American weddings, 28, 45–47, 52, 71–72, 97–99, 111, 145, 190–191, 207–210

Alda, Alan, 176, 262n36

Alfred Angelo, 66–67, 79–82, 84, 85, 117, 123, 127, 129

Allen, Fred, 218

Altman, Robert, 170

American Idol, 218

Anderson, Terry, 106–107

Andrew, Prince, 135, 211

Andrews, Dana, 152, 154

Aniston, Jennifer, 145, 146

Arisian, Khoren, 35

Arsenic and Old Lace, 151

Artcarved rings, 17, 162–163

Association of Bridal Manufacturers, 67, 73, 248n9

Astaire, Fred, 115

Atlas, Mel, 169–170

Baby Boomers
  attitudes toward marriage and weddings, 26, 36, 41–42, 45, 59, 232–233
  consumer attitudes and behavior, 27, 107, 169–170
  divorce and, 59–61, 233

Baby Story, A, 211

Bachelor, The, 218–219

Bachelorette, The, 219

Baldrige, Letitia, 117, 138, 147, 258n48

Bancroft, Anne, 261n25

Bancroft and Sons, 76, 82–84, 250n25

Ban-Lon, 76, 79–83, 85, 250n25

Becker, Susan, 117, 172

Beene, Geoffrey, 122

Bennett, Joan, 160, 167

Bessette, Carolyn. *See* Kennedy, Carolyn Bessette

Best Years of Our Lives, The, 152–155, 259n10

Betsy's Wedding, 176–177, 262n36

Beulah, 202

Borgnine, Ernest, 164

Boss, Martha, 198

Bourke-White, Margaret, 187

Brady, Lois Smith, 56–58

Bravo, 219

Bridal and Bridesmaids Apparel Association, 87–88

Bridal Guide, 58

Bridal Originals, 67, 69, 102

Bride Again, 95

Bride and Groom, 203–210, 222, 267n32

Bride Game, The, 65

Bride's, 14, 16, 21, 28–29, 47, 58, 85, 89, 137, 198
  reader surveys, 36, 51, 130, 262n29

Brides Today, 52

Bridezillas, 211

Bromfield, Cassandra, 98
Burchill, Julie, 142
Bush, George W., 106

Carroll, Leo G., 160, 173
Carson Pirie Scott, 65, 199
Cassini, Oleg, 63, 120
Catered Affair, The, 162, 164–168,
    177, 261n22
CBS (Columbia Broadcasting System),
    123, 203, 267n32
Celanese Corporation, 76, 78
Chaplin, Geraldine, 170
Charles, Prince of Wales, 131–137,
    144, 220
Chavez, Maria Gloria, 191
Chayefsky, Paddy, 162, 165,
    260–261n21
Christian Right, 42, 53
Churchill, Sarah, 115
Churchill, Winston, 115
Cimino, Michael, 170
Cinderella (Disney character), 125,
    155–157, 178
Cinderella (Disney movie), 149,
    155–158
Cinderella Complex, The, 132–133
Cinderella myth, 6, 16–17, 29, 35,
    44, 54–58, 62, 71, 94, 96, 104,
    108–109, 233–234, 240n13
    celebrity weddings and, 115, 129,
        132–133, 135, 137, 144
    magazines and, 47, 58, 191–192
    movies and, 148–149, 153–157, 165
    reality television and, 183, 216–218,
        222, 225
Civil Rights Act (1964), 41, 109
Clarke, Harold, 98

Cleghorn, Elizabeth, 85–88, 93–94
Cleghorn, Rosa, 85–88
Clinton, Bill, 54
Clock, The, 151–152
Cold War, 21, 153, 190
Cole, Harriette, 52
Cole, Nat "King," 191
Colson, Charles, 127
Conant, Howell, 127
Conger, Darva, 181–183, 217–218,
    223, 225
Coppola, Francis Ford, 170
Corbett, John, 148
counterculture, 4, 27–28, 35–38,
    47–48, 90–91, 168–169
Cowie, Colin, 262n33
Cox, Edward, 125, 130
Cox, Tricia Nixon. *See* Nixon, Tricia
Crowther, Bosley, 157
Cruise, Tom, 114

Dallas, 134, 257n36
Dating Game, The, 218
Dating Story, A, 211
David's Bridal, 99, 102–103
Davis, Bette, 162, 164–167
Deer Hunter, The, 170
Defense of Marriage Act, 54
DeNiro, Robert, 179
Dialectic of Sex, The, 29
Diana, Princess of Wales. *See* Spencer,
    Diana
Dior, Christian, 73
Disney. *See* Walt Disney Pictures
divorce
    Baby Boomers and, 59–61, 233
    celebrity couples and, 121, 133,
        135, 144, 146

choice of wedding attire and, 88, 95
feminization of poverty and, 32
heterosexual privilege and, 53
laws, 30–31, 90
rates, 6, 30–31, 33–34, 36, 39, 41,
    90–91, 170, 217, 222
Roman Catholic Church and, 31
Dolnick, Willie, 69, 102
Douglas, Susan J., 214
Dowling, Colette, 132–133
Du Pont, 76–77
Dynasty, 134, 257n36

Ebony, 97, 245n62
Eisenhower, David, 124
Elegant Bride, 58
Elizabeth II (queen), 115, 132, 144, 191
Emanuel, David, 131, 133
Emanuel, Elizabeth, 131, 133
Engstrom, Erika, 212–213, 268n44
Essence, 47, 52, 97–98, 245n62
Eternal Bliss Machine, The, 35
Evers, Myrlie, 208

Father Knows Best, 203
Father of the Bride (1950 movie),
    157–163, 164, 165, 167, 261n22
Father of the Bride (1991 movie),
    171–177, 262n36
Father of the Bride (novel), 158, 194,
    260n18
Father's Little Dividend, 260n17
Fear Factor, 218
Female Eunuch, The, 29
Feminine Mystique, The, 28, 245n62
Ferguson, Sarah, 135, 211
Filene's Basement, 56, 99
Filling, Gwyned, 191–193

Finley, William, 188
Firestone, Shulamith, 29
Fisher, Eddie, 165, 261n22
Fleetwood, Therez, 98
Folsom, Frances, 114
Fortune, 186
Four Weddings and a Funeral, 177
Fox Network, 181–183, 225
Friedan, Betty, 28, 245n62
Friends, 53–54

Garfunkel, Art, 112
Garland, Judy, 151
Gay Weddings, 219
Geller, Jaclyn, 63
General Hospital, 133
GI Bill, 153
Gingold, Chuck, 211
Gingrich, Candace, 54
Gingrich, Newt, 54
Godfather, The, 170
Goldbergs, The, 202
Gone with the Wind, 152, 178, 179
Goodbye, Columbus, 169, 261n26
Good Morning America, 219, 220, 222
Good Shepherd, The, 179
Grace, Princess. *See* Kelly, Grace
Graduate, The, 168–169, 176, 261n25
Gray, Ellen, 181
Greer, Germaine, 29

Haldeman, H. R., 127
Hallmark, 262n35
Hamilton, George, 124
Hanson, Kitty, 26, 109
Hardy, Ann, 93–96
Hardy, Jean, 93
Hepburn, Audrey, 73, 75

Here Comes the Bride, 63
Hertz, Rosanna, 43–44, 171
Hilton, Nicky, 162, 261n22
Hispanic weddings, 190–191
Hoffman, Abbie, 28
Hoffman, Dustin, 168, 261n25
Holmes, Katie, 114
Honeymooners, The, 202
Hope's Bridal Boutique, 54–55,
    100–101
Hurricane Brides, 231–232
Huston, John, 170

InStyle, 146
InStyle Weddings, 146
Internet, 6, 58, 108, 145–146, 216,
    221, 222, 234, 235
invented tradition, 68
Ireland, Patricia, 181
It Happened One Night, 150

Jet, 97, 223, 225
Jewish weddings, 7, 17–18, 28, 188, 206
Johnson, Lady Bird, 256n21
Johnson, Luci Baines, 121, 123, 124,
    125, 127
Johnson, Lynda Bird, 121–124, 125,
    126, 127
Johnson, Lyndon, 121
Jones, Star, 145
Jong, Erica, 7–8
Jong-Fast, Molly, 7–8, 59, 61–62
Jumping the Broom, 52

Katrina Brides, 232
Keaton, Diane, 171
Kelly, Grace
    death of, 140, 143, 254n4

as role-model bride, 114, 120–121,
    124–125, 129–130, 138,
    142–144, 146, 147, 197
wedding of, 115–118, 120–121,
    147, 258n48
wedding gown of, 116–120, 123,
    172
Kennedy, Caroline, 135
Kennedy, Carolyn Bessette, 114,
    137–145, 147, 254n4, 258n48
Kennedy, Jacqueline Bouvier, 108,
    197
Kennedy, John F., Jr., 137–142,
    182–183
Kennedy, Rory, 140
Kidder, James, 83–84
Kidder, Priscilla. *See* Priscilla of
    Boston (person)
Kitch, Carolyn, 203
Klein, Calvin, 137, 140, 145

Lacroix, Christian, 112
Lane hope chests, 17, 19
Leave It to Beaver, 203
Leen, Nina, 187, 193–194
Leibovich, Lori, 149
Life, 208, 263n5, 264n6
    advertisements in, 17–18
    coverage of weddings and wedding
        industry, 115, 184, 187–202,
        222–223
    middle-class orientation of,
        186–187, 189–190
Lifestyles of the Rich and Famous, 134
Lopez, Jennifer, 178
Lord and Taylor, 65, 83
Lovers and Other Strangers, 170
Loy, Myrna, 152, 154

Luce, Henry R., 184, 186, 189–190, 202, 263n5
Lux soap, 162

MacGraw, Ali, 89, 169
Magill, Jennie, 199–201
Makeover Story, A, 211
March, Fredric, 152, 154, 259n10
March of Time, 184
Margaret, Princess, 123
Martin, Steve, 171–172, 174–175
McConnell, Edith, 14–15
MGM (Metro-Goldwyn-Mayer), 64, 116, 151, 157, 162–163, 164, 168, 179, 261n22
Millett, Kate, 29
Minnelli, Vincente, 151, 157–158
Miss America, 19
   Dream Wedding campaign and, 75–77, 79–85
   feminist protest of, 88, 90, 182
mock weddings, 184–186
Modern Bride, 14, 47, 55, 58, 72, 76, 79, 81–84, 91, 168
Morgan, Robin, 29
Mountbatten, Philip. *See* Philip, Prince
Ms., 1–2, 59–60, 222–223
My Best Friend's Wedding, 177
My Big Fat Greek Wedding, 148–149
My Big, Wild, You're-Not-Going-to-Believe-This Wedding, 219

National Organization for Women (NOW), 181
NBC (National Broadcasting Company), 122–123, 162, 203, 204, 219, 266n31, 267n32

Neiman-Marcus, 116
New Look, 73, 79
Newlywed Game, The, 169
New Wedding, The (book), 35
New Wedding (ceremony), 35–36
New Yorker, 107, 109
New York Times, 56, 121, 122, 123, 132, 149, 157
Niebuhr, Diane, 55, 100–101
Nixon, Julie, 123–125
Nixon, Richard, 125, 127, 143
Nixon, Tricia, 114, 123, 125–131, 138, 140, 142–144, 147
Northern Exposure, 53
Norwood, Betty, 207–210
Nugent, Patrick, 121

O'Donnell, Cathy, 152, 154
Onassis, Jacqueline Kennedy. *See* Kennedy, Jacqueline Bouvier
Our Master's Voice, 150

Padgett, Joy, 106–107
Parker-Bowles, Camilla, 133
People, 112, 114, 138
Peters, Charles, 187
Philadelphia Story, The, 150
Philip, Prince, 115, 132, 191
Piccione, Alfred, 66–67, 127
Post, Elizabeth L., 95
Post, Emily, 8, 87, 95
Postum, 23–24
Powell, Adam Clayton, 191
Priscilla of Boston (company), 14, 82–84, 121, 124, 127–128, 130
Priscilla of Boston (person), 14, 67, 83, 98
Prizzi's Honor, 170

Queen for a Day, 203–204, 266n31

Race to the Altar, 219
Rainier, Prince, 114–118, 120, 146
Reagan, Nancy, 133–135, 257n36
Rehn, Trista, 219–222
Reynolds, Debbie, 164–166, 168, 177,
    178, 261n22
Rivers, Joan, 57
Robb, Charles, 122
Roberts, Julia, 177, 178
Rockwell, Rick, 181–183, 217–218,
    225
Rodriguez, Narciso, 138–139
Roman Catholicism, 31, 121, 256n21
Roosevelt, Alice, 114, 127
Roosevelt, Eleanor, 10, 264n8
Rorty, James, 150
Rose, Helen, 116
Rosenberg, Howard, 182
Ross, Katharine, 168, 261n25
Roth, Philip, 261n26
Rougier, Michael, 194
Runaway Bride (movie), 177
Runaway Bride (person), 234
Russell, Harold, 152, 154, 259n10

same-sex marriage, 1–4, 6, 47–48, 52–54,
    59, 104–107, 111, 145, 219
Saracco, Peter, 194–196
Sawyer, Andrew, 52
Sawyer, Diane, 222
Schwarzenegger, Arnold, 135
Schwedock, Harry, 206, 209
Schwedock, Shirlee Peck, 206, 209
Science Illustrated, 76
SDS (Students for a Democratic
    Society), 1

Seligson, Marcia, 35–36, 46
Seventeen, 43, 168
Sexual Politics, 29
Sherwood, Robert E., 153, 259n10
Short, Martin, 173
Shriver, Maria, 135
Simpson, Wallis, 114–115
Sisterhood is Powerful, 29
60 Minutes, 126
Smale, Jerry, 102
Smith-Rosenberg, Carroll, 2
Spears, Britney, 145
Spencer, Diana
    death of, 133, 137, 140, 254n4
    as role-model bride, 114, 134–135,
        137, 138, 140, 142–144, 146,
        147, 258n48
    wedding of, 131–133, 135, 220
    wedding gown of, 131, 133, 136,
        138, 232
Steinem, Gloria, 2
Stevens, Dana, 221
Stiles, Claudine Smith, 204–206, 209
Stiles, Earl, 204–206, 209
Strawbridge and Clothier, 14, 69–72
Streeter, Edward, 194, 260n18
Survivor, 218
Sutter, Ryan, 219–222

Taylor, Don, 158, 162
Taylor, Elizabeth, 157–159, 162–163,
    178, 260n17, 261n22
Time, 125, 126, 131, 140, 152, 184,
    186, 187
Tiny Tim, 114
Title IX, 41
TLC (The Learning Channel), 211,
    215–216

Tonight Show, The, 114

Tracy, Spencer, 158–159, 161, 164, 171, 174–175, 260n17

Travolta, John, 134–135

Trista and Ryan's Wedding, 219–222

Truman, Harry, 191

Truman, Margaret, 191, 197

Vanderbilt, Consuelo, 114

Vardalos, Nia, 148, 259n2

Victoria, Queen, 3, 64

Vidal, Gore, 261n21

Vietnam War, 27, 122

Villet, Grey, 199

"Vows," 56–58

Wainwright, Loudon, 200

Walker, Robert, 151

Walt Disney Pictures, 125, 149, 155–157, 158, 176, 178, 179

Wang, Vera, 51, 54, 108, 117, 138, 232, 234

War Production Board, 67

Web sites. *See* Internet

Wedding, A, 170

Wedding in Monaco, The, 116

Wedding Planner, The, 177, 178

Wedding Singer, The, 177

Weddings of a Lifetime, 211

Wedding Story, A, 211–218, 220, 268n44

West, Rebecca, 115

Who Wants to Marry a Multimillionaire?, 181–183, 218–219, 222–223

Who Wants to Marry My Dad?, 219

Wicoff, Kamy, 140, 142, 234

Williams, Kimberly, 171–172, 178

Will You Marry Me?, 211

Wilson, Eleanor, 122

Wilson, Woodrow, 122

Winn, Barbara, 193–194

WITCH (Women's International Terrorist Conspiracy from Hell), 1

Women's Wear Daily, 116, 122

Woodbury soap, 11–12, 18

World War II

  bridal industry and, 66–68, 73

  marriage and weddings during, 8, 10–13, 26–27, 30, 86, 188–189

  movies about, 150–155

  rationing, 67–68, 115

  synthetic fiber industry and, 76

Wright, Teresa, 153, 154

Wyler, William, 153, 259n10

Ziegler, Ron, 127